Fortress Introduction to

The History of Christianity in the United States

Fortress Introduction to

The History of Christianity in the United States

Nancy Koester

Fortress Press ◆ Minneapolis

FORTRESS INTRODUCTION TO THE HISTORY OF CHRSTIANITY IN THE UNITED STATES

Cover images: George Whitefield, reprinted from *The Life of Rev. George Whitefield*, New York: D. Newell, 1846; Illustration of African American slave, photo © Snark/Art Resource, NY; Bisbee Lutheran Church, Bisbee, North Dakota, photo courtesy of Region 3 Archives of the ELCA, Saint Paul, Minnesota; *Crucifix*, 1971, Jose Mondragon, photo © Smithsonian American Art Museum, Washington, D.C., Hemphill/Art Resource, NY.

Library of Congress Cataloging-in-Publication Data

Koester, Nancy, 1954–

Fortress introduction to the history of Christianity in the United States / Nancy Koester.

p. cm.

Includes bibliographical references and index.

ISBN-13: 978-0-8006-3277-9 (alk. paper)

1. United States—Church history. I. Title. II. Title: Introduction to the history of Christianity in the United States.

BR515.K64 2007

277.3—dc22

2006026179

The paper used in this publication meets the minimum requirements of American National Standard for Information Sciences—Permanence of Paper for Printed Library Materials, ANSI Z329.48-1984.

Manufactured in the U.S.A.

11 10 09 08 07 1 2 3 4 5 6 7 8 9 10

CONTENTS

PREFACE

This book introduces the history of Christianity in America, particularly the United States. It is written for college and seminary students, book clubs, and individual readers—anyone taking a first step into this rich and rewarding field.

Exploring the history of Christianity in America is like visiting a national park. For the first-time visitor, it helps to have a map that shows the principal sites, roads, and hiking trails. Each of these trails leads to a different part of the park, and no single trail can traverse the whole. Even those who return again and again will have new things to discover each time.

The difference, of course, is that this history is not a place set apart. It is a story, or many stories, woven into the fabric of everyday life and into beliefs about the meaning of American history. Christianity has been a powerful influence shaping American history and culture. For example, social reforms such as the abolition of slavery and civil rights drew inspiration from Christianity. And the Puritan vision of New England as a "City on a Hill"—the beacon to all the world of a fully reformed church and society—over time morphed into the belief that the United States has a special role to play in the world. One need not agree with this idea to see its importance for U.S. and world history, even today.

Back in the 1960s some experts predicted that the world would become more secular and religion would fade away. Just the opposite has happened. For better or worse, politicians are more alert than ever to religious concerns of voters. And even though the United States is religiously diverse, Christianity is still by any measure the dominant faith tradition. Some sectors of American Christianity are growing rapidly, especially evangelicalism and Pentecostalism. Yet many Americans know little of the story of Christianity in the United States.

The history of Christianity in America is complex; no two historians would introduce it in quite the same way. New perspectives are always emerging. In recent decades, some scholars have even questioned whether or not there *is* a central story to be told. Who decides what the story line will be? Much depends on the historian's training and point of view. But in history just as in a national park, there are certain land forms—mountains and valleys—that command attention, even though they can be explored in many ways. A short list of such "land forms" includes Puritanism, slavery, the growth of Catholicism, and the rise of Pentecostalism.

The history of Christianity in the U.S. intertwines with broad themes in American history, but it also has its own specialized areas of study. Among the subfields informing this book are the stories of specific denominations (Baptist, Methodist, etc.), studies of revivalism and social reform, and biographies of individuals. Another angle of vision comes from sociological studies that explore the dynamics of democratization, voluntarism, and competition among religious groups. The relatively new field of women's history has helped the author to integrate the contributions of women into this text. Last but not least of the subfields is the history of theology, the doctrines or teachings that seek to express religious truth. Attempts to define, defend, or revise theology—or push it to the sidelines—are a very significant part of the history of Christianity in America.

Together with specialized works, broad and synthetic studies have contributed to the *Fortress Introduction to the History of Christianity in the United States*. Secular histories of the United States have been a constant aid, as well as a few classic surveys of Christianity in America. Of these, the magisterial work of Sidney Ahlstrom, *A Religious History of the American People*, deserves special mention. That volume, published in 1972, ran to more than one thousand pages of first-rate historiography. But several decades later the fragmentation of the historical fields and the changing approaches to college and seminary education call for shorter, leaner texts to introduce fields of study.

The present volume intentionally uses a much shorter format than older surveys. When the *Fortress Introduction to the History of Christianity in the United States* is used as a textbook, the instructor may wish to combine it with a more specialized work on American religion, giving students both an introduction and a focus area of the instructor's or students' choice. Used in this way, the *Fortress Introduction* is both an overview and a springboard for further study. Each chapter includes discussion questions for group or individual use.

This book owes a great deal to the work of other scholars. The author has made every attempt to credit her sources, both for the sake of academic honesty and to give interested readers specific leads on how to pursue their interests in the history of Christianity in America. Suggested readings (in book form and on websites) are also provided as additional helps for the reader, along with a glossary and an index.

The author is grateful to all the scholars whose books and articles inform this work. Thanks are due to Dr. Erling Jorstad, who taught history and American Studies for many years at St. Olaf College, for reviewing the manuscript and suggesting ways to improve it. The author thanks the editors at Fortress Press for their patience when this book took longer to write than expected, and for their encouragement and expertise in seeing the work through its final stages. Last but not least, thanks are due to Craig Koester for his never-failing encouragement and support.

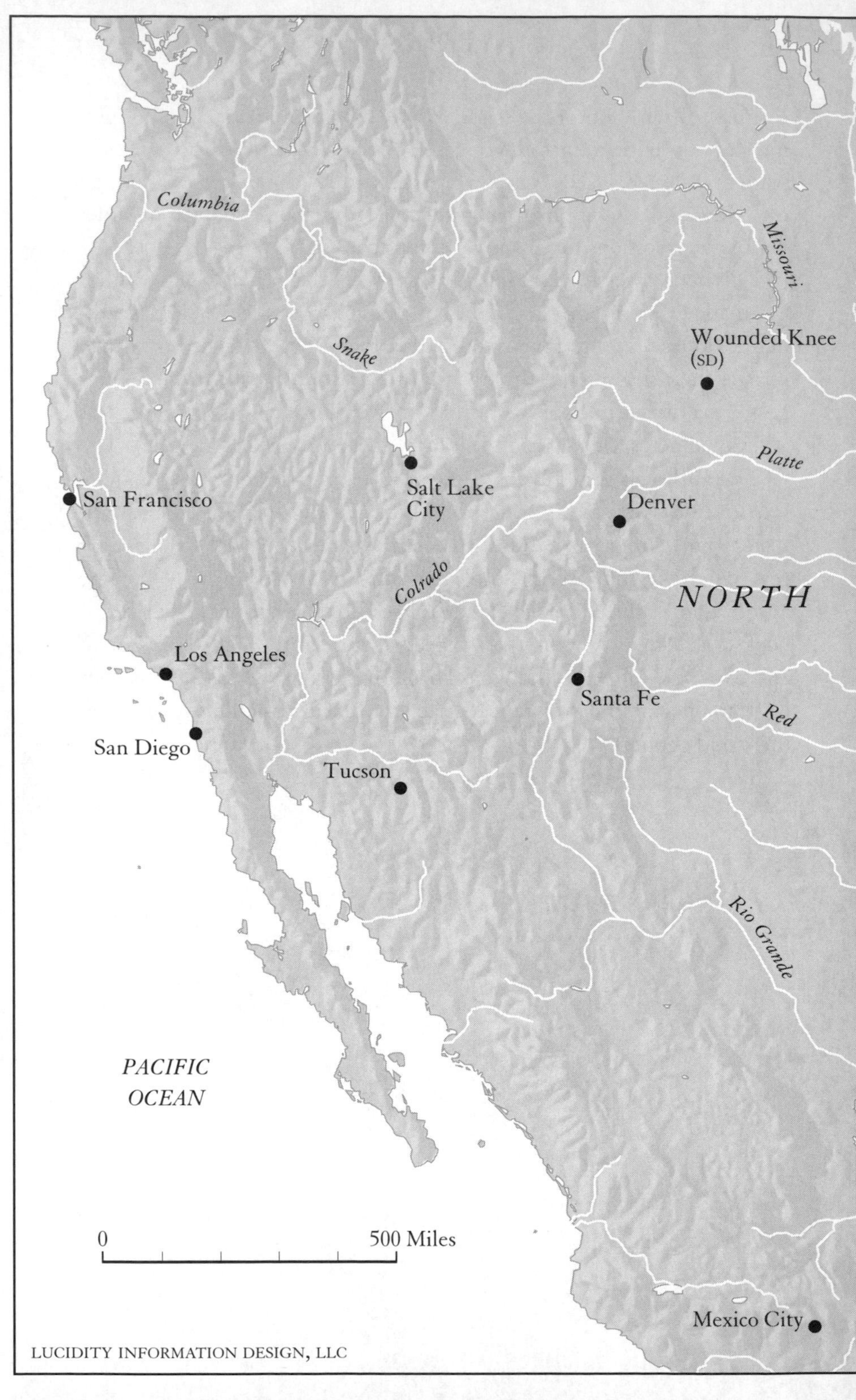
Columbia
Missouri
Snake
Wounded Knee
(SD)
Platte
Salt Lake
City
San Francisco
Denver
Colrado
NORTH
Los Angeles
Santa Fe
Red
San Diego
Tucson
Rio Grande
PACIFIC
OCEAN
0
500 Miles
Mexico City
LUCIDITY INFORMATION DESIGN, LLC

Quebec
St. Lawrence
Montreal
Lake Superior
Lake Huron
Lake Ontario
Lake Michigan
Lake Erie
Boston
Plymouth (MA)
Northampton (MA)
New York
Providence (RI)
Detroit
Gettysburg (PA)
Princeton (NJ)
Chicago
Oberlin (OH)
Philadelphia
Harper's Ferry (WV)
Baltimore
Nauvoo (IL)
Ohio
St. Louis
Cane Ridge (KY)
Jamestown (VA)
AMERICA
Mississippi
Dayton (TN)
ATLANTIC OCEAN
Charlestown
Savannah
Montgomery
San Salvador (BAHAMAS)
GULF of MEXICO
CARIBBEAN SEA

TIMELINE

1492	Columbus lands in the Caribbean
1517	Martin Luther begins Reformation in Europe
1531	"Our Lady of Guadalupe" tradition begins in Mexico
1534	England breaks with Rome
1536	John Calvin's *Institutes of the Christian Religion*
1545	Council of Trent begins
1607	Virginia Colony is founded in Jamestown
1619	African slaves arrive in Jamestown
1620	First Puritan colony is founded at Plymouth, Massachusetts
1639	Harvard College is founded
1640	The *Bay Psalm Book* is published in Massachusetts
1648	Peace of Westphalia ends Thirty Years' War, closing Reformation era in Europe
1662	Halfway Covenant of the Puritans
1680	Pueblo revolt
1681	Eusibio Kino, Jesuit Missionary, begins work in Mexico, Arizona
1692	Salem witch trials
1706	First American Presbytery is organized in Philadelphia
1732	Georgia, the last of the original thirteen colonies, is founded
1734	Revival at Northampton, Massachusetts, begins the Great Awakening
1738	George Whitefield's first preaching tour of the American colonies
1742	Henry Muhlenberg, German Lutheran missionary, arrives in America
1763	Peace of Paris ends Seven Years' War in Europe and French and Indian War in North America
1769	Junipero Serra founds San Diego Mission
1773	Jesuit Order is abolished (restored in 1801)
1776	Declaration of Independence
1784	Methodist Episcopal Church is founded in Baltimore
1789	French Revolution begins
1789	John Carroll becomes the first American Catholic bishop
1791	Bill of Rights (first amendment to the Constitution)
1801	Revival at Cane Ridge, Kentucky
1807	Slave trade ends in British Empire
1810	American Missions Board is founded
1816	African Methodist Episcopal Church (denomination) is organized
1821	Mexico achieves independence

1830 *Book of Mormon* is published; Indian Removal Act
1831 Nat Turner rebellion (slave revolt)
1833 American Anti-slavery Society founded
1835 Charles Finney publishes *Lectures on Revivals of Religion*
1844 YMCA is founded in London
1844 Methodist Church splits over slavery
1844 University of Notre Dame is founded
1844 Millerites expect Christ's return
1846 Mexican American War begins (–48)
1846 Mormon migration to Utah begins
1848 Seneca Falls Convention for women's rights
1848 Karl Marx publishes *The Communist Manifesto*
1852 *Uncle Tom's Cabin*, anti-slavery novel, is published
1853 Antionette Brown becomes the first American woman to be ordained
1859 John Brown's raid on Harper's Ferry, Virginia
1859 Charles Darwin publishes *Origin of Species*
1860 Abraham Lincoln is elected president
1861 Civil War begins
1863 Emancipation Proclamation takes effect
1865 Lincoln is assassinated; Civil War ends
1866 Ku Klux Klan is founded
1869 First Vatican Council affirms papal infallibility
1876 Dwight L. Moody achieves national fame as a revivalist
1877 Reconstruction ends
1890 Frontier closes; Battle of Wounded Knee
1891 Papal encyclical defends workers' rights
1893 World Parliament of Religions at Columbian Exposition in Chicago
1896 Supreme Court (*Plessy v. Ferguson)* approves "separate but equal"
1906 Azusa street revival begins (birth of modern Pentecostalism)
1908 Federal Council of Churches is founded (predecessor of National Council of Churches, 1950)
1909 National Association for the Advancement of Colored People is founded
1910 Edinburgh Missionary Conference (begins modern ecumenical movement)
1910 *The Fundamentals* begins publication
1914 World War I starts in Europe
1917 U.S. enters World War I; Russian Revolution

1920	Prohibition goes into effect; women achieve voting rights
1921	National Religious Broadcasters is founded
1925	Scopes "Monkey Trial"
1929	Stock market crash begins the Great Depression
1933	Prohibition is repealed
1939	Hitler invades Poland
1941	Bombing of Pearl Harbor; U.S. enters World War II
1942	National Association of Evangelicals is founded
1949	Billy Graham's revivals in Los Angeles boost him to national fame
1945	World War II ends
1954	Civil rights movement begins
1962	Second Vatican Council begins in Rome
1963	John F. Kennedy is assassinated
1963	Martin Luther King Jr. delivers "I have a dream" speech in Washington, D.C.
1965	U.S. combat troops sent to Vietnam
1965	Immigration Act abolishes quotas based on nationality
1968	Martin Luther King Jr. is assassinated
1973	American troops withdraw from Vietnam
	Supreme Court legalizes abortion
1976	Jimmy Carter, a Democrat and born-again Christian, is elected president
1976	Habitat for Humanity is founded
1978	American Indian Religious Freedom Act is passed
1979	Moral Majority is founded, signaling rise of "Religious Right"
1980	Archbishop Oscar Romero is assassinated in El Salvador
1991	Collapse of Soviet Union ends the Cold War
2001	Terrorist attack on the U.S. on September 11

CHAPTER ONE

Colonial Beginnings

Reformation and European Expansion

Medieval Europe dreamed of Christendom—one civilization united by one faith. This ideal of Christendom was shattered in the sixteenth century when Protestant reformers broke with papal authority in Rome. Europe became a patchwork in which each territory was its own little Christendom with its ruler determining the religion of the people. Meanwhile, several European powers laid claim to huge tracts of land across the Atlantic Ocean. These territories were named New Spain, New France, New Netherlands, New Sweden, and New England.

Thus, two great dramas overlap in time: the Reformation and European expansion in the Americas. For example, Luther began the Reformation in 1517, at about the same time Córdoba explored the Yucatan peninsula. William Tyndale prepared his English translation of the New Testament in 1524, the year that Verrazano probed the Atlantic coastline. In France, a young lawyer named John Calvin embraced the Reformation in 1534, the year Jacques Cartier first sailed into the St. Lawrence Gulf. By the close of the Reformation era in 1648, European settlements in North America included Jamestown, Quebec, Santa Fe, Boston, and New Amsterdam (New York).

The Reformation affected European exploration and settlement of America. Not only did Protestant and Catholic nations compete for territory; they also brought to America several assumptions and strategies forged in the Reformation. These concepts were the basis for colonial Christianity, at least in the early stages. One such concept was *territorialism.*

Territorialism was a strategy for dealing with the religious differences set loose by the Protestant Reformation. By 1648, religious and political wars had failed to establish either Catholicism or any type of Protestantism as Europe's sole faith. War could not settle the matter. The slogan *cuius regio, eius religio* ("whose the region, his the religion") expressed the strategy by means of which rulers tried to assert religious unity within their own realms. The ruler decided the religion.

European rulers expected their religious authority to extend to their American territories as well. To this day, the religious footprint of territorialism can still be seen in French-Catholic Canada, in the heritage of Spanish Catholicism in Mexico and the Southwest, and in the Anglo-Protestantism in much of the United States.

Another theme from the Reformation era was *freedom of conscience* to "obey God rather than men" (Acts 5:29). Here the individual is accountable to God alone in matters of faith. No human authority, not even a king or a bishop, has the right to gainsay God's claim on an individual. And if this does happen, the individual is bound by conscience to resist. These two views of religious authority—territorialism and individual conscience—clashed repeatedly in colonial America until religious freedom at last became the norm.

American Lutherans have sometimes been tempted to draw a straight line between Martin Luther and the rise of religious freedom in America. A crooked line would be better for two reasons. First, Calvinism (not Lutheranism) was the dominant influence in American Protestantism for generations. Second, Luther did not think that one person's beliefs were as good as any other person's, nor did he say that individuals should simply believe whatever appeals to them. Luther (and other reformers) did say that when *human* authority conflicts with the Word of God, then *God* must be obeyed. Martin Luther criticized the church of his day not because he was a free spirit but because his conscience was "captive to the Word of God." This and similar appeals to the Word of God continued to inspire dissent against religious territorialism in the colonies. With the Enlightenment came new forms of dissent. For those influenced by the Enlightenment, the conscience of the individual (rather than the Word of God) became the final court of appeal. In the story of Christianity in colonial America, territorial religion (in which the ruler sets religious policy) clashed with appeals to a higher authority—whether Scripture, conscience, or reason. These conflicts began in Europe during the Reformation and took on a life of their own in America.

Native American Religions

The Reformation was still in the future when Columbus landed on the island he called San Salvador in 1492. There he saw no temples or robed priests, heard no prayers or liturgies. Columbus wrote that "Los indios...will easily be made Christians, for they appear to me to have no religion."[1] Columbus was an explorer, not a sociologist of religion. Even if he had been able to see and describe the religion of the Taino people, this would have been one among hundreds of religions in North America at the time of European contact.

There is no separate word for "religion" in many Native American languages. Instead, there is a "whole complex of beliefs and actions that give meaning" to everyday life.[2] In Native American religion, spiritual forces helped people to carry out the central tasks of hunting, courtship, and warfare. Healing was especially important; shamans or holy people would use spiritual powers to remove the evils that caused pain and sickness, or to restore the good things that had been stolen by bad spirits.

Native American beliefs passed by word of mouth to each new generation. Stories told the people who they were in relation to the land and to other tribes and marked the rites of passage in life. In contrast to European Christians with their written scriptures and creeds, Native cultures relied on oral tradition.

Land was central to Native American religions. Land was not "private property" or "real estate." It was sacred, the mother of all living things. Land was revered not for its monetary value but for its beauty, for its abundance of game and fish, and as a reminder of great events and spirits of ancestors. But even before the Europeans came, native peoples could be displaced from their ancestral lands by tribal warfare or by changing patterns of climate, hunting, and trade. When the Europeans came with their relentless appetite for land, the conflicts had religious dimensions, not least because land was sacred to Native peoples.

From colonial times until well into the twentieth century, missionaries to Native American peoples seldom differentiated the Christian gospel from their own cultures. A common assumption was that Native converts must forsake all tribal ways in order to become Christian. Even so, missionaries tended to treat Native peoples more humanely than did most of their fellow Europeans. Missionaries were more likely to see Native people as human beings, with souls to be saved, than to see them as enemies to be killed or obstacles to be removed from the path to progress. Many missionaries learned the languages and customs of Native peoples. A few missionaries lived with Indian peoples and adapted to tribal ways. Missionaries sometimes became advocates for Native peoples, condemning white encroachment on Indian land or trying to stop the alcohol trade that all too soon blighted Native cultures. Some missionaries paid the ultimate price of martyrdom in their attempts to bring Christianity to Native peoples.

Even the best-intentioned Europeans, however, could unwittingly carry smallpox, measles, and other diseases against which tribal peoples had no immunities. The death toll from European diseases may never be fully known, but estimates run to the tens of millions of Native people. Hardest hit were those peoples who lived in larger, more settled communities. For example, the Pueblos of New Mexico had roughly forty-eight thousand people in the sixteenth century. But by 1800 they were down to about eight thousand people.[3] The loss of entire peoples, with their cultures and religions, can scarcely be measured.

Catholic Missions in North America: Spain and France

The first Catholic missionaries to America arrived with Columbus's second voyage in 1493, making their landing on the island of Hispaniola (now Haiti and the Dominican Republic). By the early 1500s, Spanish priests were active in Mexico, a large area whose northern lands later became part of the United States. This area, in turn, was part of a much larger Spanish empire extending through Central and much of South America.

Conquistadors (explorer-soldiers) advanced Spain's empire by crushing Native resistance. Spanish settlers carried on trade and provided a permanent European presence, while missionaries converted the Native peoples to Catholicism and taught them European ways. Thus, "conquest, settlement and evangelization" brought about a new rule whose purpose "was to create Christian peoples out of those regarded by their conquerors as members of barbarous and pagan races."[4] The Spaniards had many internal conflicts between military, church, and trading interests; but there was general agreement that Native peoples who became Christian had to abandon tribal ways.

Spain could send very few European settlers to the far edges of its empire. It therefore sought to keep other European powers away by converting Native peoples and making them into loyal Spanish subjects and devout Catholics. Consequently, Spain established missions in Florida and along the northern rim of the Gulf of Mexico. In New Mexico, twenty-five missions were established by 1630. Another stage of mission planting was led by the Jesuit missionary Eusebio Kino (1645–1711), who was active in what we now know as the southwestern United States and northwestern Mexico. Later on, Spain built a string of missions in California between San Diego and San Francisco, with the dual purpose of converting Indians and securing Spain's claims against Russian and English interests along the Pacific coast. The Franciscan missionary Junipero Serra (1713–1784) led in creating these California missions. Serra gathered Native peoples into the missions, where they were taught Christianity, European customs, and agriculture. He is said to have baptized six thousand persons and confirmed five thousand. In keeping with attitudes of his day, "Serra held that missionaries could and should treat their converts like small children. He instructed that baptized Indians who attempted to leave the missions should be forcibly returned, and he believed that corporal punishment—including the whip and the stocks—also had a place."[5]

Spanish missions often resembled medieval European villages. Inside the protective walls lay the church, school, and hospital as well as a dormitory and work areas for various trades. Outside the walls, the people grew crops and tended livestock; in some places, they worked in mines or quarries. Some of the most successful missions were located near

Old Mission Church, Zuni Pueblo, New Mexico
Photo: Timothy O'Sullivan (1840–1882), New York Public Library/Art Resource, NY

Native villages that already had a settled, stable population. But Spanish success was short-lived. Native peoples commonly deserted the missions as soon as they had opportunity, taking elements of Christian belief and ritual to blend with their own traditions. From the Spanish side, the mission compounds were costly to maintain and difficult to staff. After Texas (and then the United States) gained control of these territories, many of the old missions crumbled into ruins.

Native responses to Spanish missions ranged from violent resistance to adaptation and cooperation. Take, for example, the Pueblo peoples of what is now New Mexico. Early on, the Spaniards exacted hard labor from the Pueblos and punished them for practicing Native religions. In 1680 Pueblos organized a revolt involving many villages. Four hundred Spaniards, including twenty-one missionaries, were killed. Crops, churches, and other buildings were destroyed. The Pueblos drove the Spanish out, but later the Spanish returned and regained control. The two peoples learned to coexist; they intermarried and became allies against mutual enemies such as the Apaches.[6] Over many generations, the Spanish and Native cultures blended, producing a form of Catholicism distinctive to that region.

Far to the north and east of Mexico, French Catholic missionaries had similar goals: to convert Native peoples to Christianity and strengthen France's claims in the New World. But the territory called New France was a different world from that of New Spain. Colder climates meant that Native peoples depended much more on hunting and fishing than on agriculture and were less likely to form large permanent settlements. Conditions in Canada were not favorable to the mission-compound strategy that the Spanish had tried in the Southwest.

In addition to dealing with a cold climate, France also had to contend with Protestant rivals along the Atlantic coast. In this age of territorial religion, conflicts between Protestants and Catholics were common. For example, in Acadia (present-day Maine and the Canadian Maritimes), English and Dutch Protestants and their Iroquois allies expelled the French Catholics. France had better luck establishing mission stations in areas now known as Northern Ontario, Wisconsin, Michigan, and Illinois—along the rivers and lakes where the French were the only Europeans. French priests were great explorers of North America, mapping waterways of a vast region while searching for the fabled Northwest Passage to the Pacific Ocean. They also founded settlements as far south as Mobile and New Orleans.

Early French missionaries learned Native ways and adapted to a lifestyle of extreme hardship and danger. Several religious orders and "secular priests" (those not attached to an order) evangelized in New France, but none surpassed the Jesuit order. The Jesuits (also known as the Society of Jesus) were founded by Ignatius of Loyola (1491–1556), one of the most important Catholic leaders in the Reformation era. An ex-soldier, Loyola combined military ideals with a life of holiness. Pope Paul III approved the new order in 1540. Like "special ops" troops, Jesuit priests were trained to go anywhere, endure anything, and adapt to local conditions.

An early Jesuit missionary to New France was Jean de Brébeuf (1593–1649), who worked among the Huron peoples. In 1636 he wrote to would-be missionaries back in France, warning them to expect extreme heat and cold, dangerous travel through rapids and around waterfalls, and nights of torment from mosquitoes, fleas, and sand flies. Food was scanty; there was no medical care and little or no shelter. Hardest of all was learning the Huron language, a task to humble even the most learned priest. Brébeuf advised his colleagues to stay home unless they were prepared to die. Some thirteen years later, the Iroquois—sworn foes of the Huron—tortured and killed Brébeuf. In 1930 Brébeuf and several other Jesuit martyrs were elevated to sainthood by the Roman Catholic Church.

After the martyrs, another generation built more lasting Catholic settlements. A great leader in this effort was Francois Xavier de Montmorençy Laval (1623–1708), a Jesuit who became the first Catholic bishop in Canada. Laval established a seminary in Quebec in 1663, supported the work of women's orders in New France, and secured land grants for the church. He strove to protect Native peoples from exploitation at the hands of white trappers and rum traders. After Laval's time, the Jesuit mission was cut off—not only in New France but throughout the world. For largely political reasons, France suppressed the Jesuit order in 1763, and the pope abolished it completely in 1773. Jesuit missionaries were recalled to Europe, reassigned to other orders, or pensioned off. Although the Society of Jesus was restored in 1801, Catholic mission suffered a major setback. This is but one example of how decisions made far away in Europe affected Christianity in the Americas.

Around the time the Jesuits were suppressed, French and English hostilities came to a head in North America. When the British captured Montreal in 1760, the Governor of Canada surrendered to the British. In 1763 the Peace of Paris ended both the Seven Years' War in Europe and the French and Indian War in North America. England now formally controlled Canada, together with all its territories east of the Mississippi. But French Catholic heritage was laid deep in the foundations of Canada. French Catholicism had a lesser, though significant, impact in the United States, first through settlements such as Duluth and New Orleans, and later through the French priests imported to serve American Catholic parishes.

Map of the colony of Virginia, seventeenth century
From an expedition to the colony of Virginia by William Strachey as Secretary of State
Photo © HIP/Art Resource, NY

Protestant Settlements in North America

Many types of Protestants were active in early colonial America. The so-called magisterial groups, Reformed, Lutheran, and Anglican, represented state or "established" churches back in Europe. These groups were soon joined by radical Protestants such as Baptists and Quakers, which had known persecution in Europe. One may also describe the various Protestants in terms of nationality. There were Dutch and Swedish and German settlements as well as English; but because the English colonies had the greatest long-term influence on North American Christianity, they will receive greater attention.

England's thirteen colonies in North America differed sharply from each other in matters of religion. Though founded by England, the colonies did not all adhere to the Church of England. Indeed, New Englanders tried to keep the Church of England out. In an era of territorialism, one may ask how England ended up with more than one "established" church in its colonies, and with some colonies that openly welcomed dissent. At a practical level, this happened because England needed settlers and could not afford to be too selective. But a deeper reason for the religious patchwork in its colonies lies with England's own history.

During the Reformation and its aftermath—which overlapped with the early European settlements in America—England careened through several religious and political upheavals. It began in 1554 when King Henry VIII declared himself (and not the pope) to be the supreme head of the church. After Henry died, each of his successors became the head of the church, and they had authority over England's religion. What was legal under one monarch could bring exile or death under the next. Therefore, dissenters left England or returned, depending on who was in power. At last, the third monarch after Henry—Elizabeth I—achieved some religious stability for her country. The "Elizabethan Settlement" provided a moderate Protestant theology, set forth in *The Thirty-Nine Articles*, and a revised *Book of Common Prayer* as the basis for worship. The Church of England continued a "threefold ministry of bishops, priests and deacons and claimed to have kept the apostolic succession."[7] The church was firmly tied to the state because the Crown retained control over bishops.

Not everyone was satisfied with the Elizabethan Settlement. A coalition of zealous reformers wanted to free the Church of England from royal control and "purify" it from all remnants of Catholicism. These reformers were called Puritans. After enduring suppression and persecution, the Puritans executed King Charles in 1649 and briefly ruled England through the Lord Protector Oliver Cromwell. But after Cromwell died in 1658, the Puritans lost political power. The monarchy was restored, renewing the prospect for a Catholic king. But when Protestant monarchs William and Mary were crowned in 1688, England's Protestant identity seemed secure.

Because this period of turmoil overlapped with England's early claims and settlements in America, England could not secure a firm establishment of the Church of England in all of its American colonies. The Church of England was established in Virginia and other southern colonies and in some parts of New York. But Puritans had already set up their own establishment in New England, while Protestant dissenters and Catholics were settling in several other colonies. Thus, England's history played a large role in shaping colonial Christianity (as did African slavery, immigration from continental Europe, religious awakenings, and the Enlightenment, which are described in due course). With this background in mind, the balance of this chapter will survey the story of Christianity in the early colonial period by region—from the southern colonies to New England to the middle colonies.

The Southern Colonies

The first permanent English settlement on the Atlantic seaboard was Jamestown, Virginia. It was founded in 1607 by the Virginia Company, a group of private investors who sought profits through trade. Jamestown had a Church of England minister to hold worship services for the colonists and to evangelize Native peoples. But the Jamestown venture won few converts, lost money, and cost hundreds of lives.[8] Few of these early settlers knew how to raise crops; some may have refused to do menial labor, regarding it as below their class as gentlemen of trade. Soon starvation and disease took a heavy toll. The colony was saved by new recruits from England and by a regimen of strict rules for work, worship, and community discipline. In 1619, as Jamestown was beginning to stabilize, a Dutch trading ship arrived with captured Africans who were put to work in the tobacco fields.

The Virginia colony came under royal control in 1624, with the Church of England as its established church. Laws and punishments were devised to keep out dissenters—Congregationalists, Baptists, Puritans, and Quakers.[9] But the Anglican Church in Virginia still faced daunting challenges. Clergy had to serve large, sparsely settled parishes, where roads were poor or nonexistent. In Virginia and other areas in the south, well-to-do laypersons organized "vestries" that ran parish affairs and resisted clergy control.

Similar conditions prevailed in North and South Carolina. Except for towns like Charleston (founded in 1670), the colonists were spread so far apart that gathering for regular worship seemed nearly impossible. Anglican clergy reported a very low interest in religion among these colonists. Despite its status as the official religion, the Church of England was relatively weak in much of the South during the early colonial period. With a sparse population and so much backcountry, religious nonconformists could often avoid the reach of the established church. Religious diversity in the southern colonies increased when certain groups from continental Europe—such as French Huguenots and German Lutherans—received permission to settle in the Carolinas. This religious toleration was a privilege, however, not a right.

Maryland was a brief exception to the Anglican establishment. In 1634 a powerful English Catholic family, the Calverts, began the settlement of Maryland. The new colony was both a successful business venture and a place of refuge for English Catholics (the first settlers were a mix of Catholics and Protestants). Maryland's early Catholic colonists had large land grants and were active in colonial government. Their future looked bright in 1649, when the Maryland Assembly passed an Act of Toleration. This meant that the Church of England tolerated the presence of Catholics in the colony. But if toleration can be given, it can also be taken away. The Act of Toleration was repealed when Puritans briefly took power in Maryland. Years later and an ocean away, England's "Glorious Revolution" of 1688–89 rejected James II (a Catholic) as king and instead crowned William and Mary (Protestants). After that, Maryland Catholics could not vote, hold public office, or worship freely in Maryland until the American Revolution.

The last British colony, Georgia, was chartered in 1732. Some of Georgia's colonists came from overcrowded debtors' prisons in England. Others were religious exiles, like the Lutherans who were expelled from their home in Salzburg, Austria, by order of a Catholic ruler. Protestants across Europe raised money to pay for ships' passage to America for these exiles. Arriving in Georgia, the Salzburger Lutherans founded a community that they called Ebenezer, a biblical word meaning "rock of hope." By 1741 the Ebenezer settlement had twelve hundred people. Historian Abdel Ross Wentz describes these Lutherans, in the prime of their settlement, as living in peace with their neighbors, rejecting slavery, and evangelizing Indians. The Salzburger Lutherans grew cash crops and built churches, schools, and an orphanage. Their pastors had great authority and required no outside help to keep order in the Lutheran settlements. Wentz further notes that "the famed evangelist George Whitefield and the founders of Methodism, John and Charles Wesley, who visited Ebenezer, were deeply impressed with the faith and piety of these Lutherans."[10]

The Beginnings of Slavery

There were many forms of labor in England's American colonies. Indentured servants sailed to America on credit, working off their debt over a period of several years. There were also free laborers and debtors transported from English prisons. African slaves soon became the bottom layer of this diverse labor system.

When the first Africans and Creoles (persons of mixed descent) arrived in Virginia as captives, their long-term future was unclear. Perhaps, like the white indentured servants, they could be released after several years. Indeed, some Africans were able to negotiate their freedom and become landowners.[11] But loopholes began to close as the slave labor system developed. Historian Ira Berlin notes the essential characteristics of slavery: Africans became legally "chattel" (property) until they died; their children were born into a system that bound them for life to white masters, who could use irresistible force to back up their demands. In contrast to indentured servitude, which was based on economic status, slavery was based on race. This was the most important characteristic of all in the American context. To be sure, the circumstances of slavery could vary greatly from one generation to another, from one part of the country to another, and even from one plantation to another. But beneath all this variety, slavery had the same basis everywhere: race, chattel property, and the use (or threat) of force.

African slavery was present in all of the colonies, even in the North; but the slave system struck deepest root in the South, where labor-intensive crops—tobacco, rice, and finally cotton—made it profitable. Ambitious colonists, aspiring to be like the landed, titled nobility of Europe, found that slave labor increased the wealth and enhanced the social status of slave owners. Slavery quickly became embedded in colonial economies and social structures, so that everyone was affected by slavery, even those who did not own slaves.

Slavery had deeply religious dimensions. The Africans brought with them many tribal religions and probably some forms of Islam. But the slave trade disrupted African religions; it tore families apart, destroyed entire villages, and removed people from sacred places. Slave trade patterns often threw together Africans of diverse languages and beliefs. And slave owners suppressed African religions, fearing, above all else, a slave revolt. Any religious practice that might subvert the slave owner's power was forbidden. This meant, for example, that blacks were seldom if ever allowed to meet together without white supervision, even for religious ceremonies. Drumming was integral to African worship, but drums were banned lest they be used to send messages or inspire rebellion.

Nevertheless, many African beliefs and customs persisted. The spirit world remained vivid to most Africans. Spirits of ancestors might give help or do harm, and therefore needed tending. People wore amulets or charms to ward off evil spirits or attract good ones. Courtship rituals, tribal lore, and burial customs were carried to North America and adapted to new situations.

At first the English showed little interest in Christianizing the Africans; it seemed more prudent to withhold Christianity from the slaves. Baptism was problematic, since it declared people to be children of God rather than the property of this or that owner. To address this problem, several local laws were passed, such as the 1667 Virginia statute declaring that "Baptisme doth not alter the condition of the person as to his bondage or freedom."[12] Early in the eighteenth century, Anglican missionaries sought to evangelize the African slaves. To gain access to slaves on plantations, missionaries had to convince slave owners that Christianity would not subvert slavery. The bishop of London helped their cause by declaring in 1727 that baptism in no way changed a slave's status as property.

Armed with guarantees that Christianity would not harm slavery, Anglican missionaries could often obtain permission to preach to slaves on a plantation. Gaining access to plantation slaves was only the first hurdle; next came the problem of language. In the early years, there might be several African languages on any plantation, all in various stages of blending with English. Even if the language barriers could be breached, the message problem remained. The doctrinal instruction offered by early missionaries did not connect with the experience of slaves. Moreover, Africans had little reason to trust what a white person said to them. It is not surprising, then, that relatively few African Americans embraced Christianity in early colonial times.

New England: The Puritan Society of Visible Saints

The first Puritan colony in New England was Plymouth, Massachusetts (1620); it was followed by the colonies of Massachusetts Bay (1628) and Boston (1630). Between 1630 and 1640, the "Great Migration" brought some twenty thousand English Puritans to the New England colonies. Puritans also settled in the middle colonies, mingling with other types of Protestants. The Puritan movement did much to shape Christianity not only in the New England colonies but in the United States more broadly. So before continuing with the story of the Puritan colonies, we must sketch the broad range and reach of Puritanism.

As we have seen, Puritanism was a late-born child of the Reformation, dedicated to purifying the Church of England. Theologically, the Puritans drew from the Reformed wing of the Reformation, as articulated by John Calvin and his heirs. The challenge was how to put Calvinist theology into practice in an English context. Not all Puritans agreed on how this was to be done. Their various reform strategies gave rise to several groups: Congregationalists, Presbyterians, Baptists, the Society of Friends (Quakers), and many small radical sects. Later on, in the United States, Unitarianism split off from Congregationalism to become a sort of freethinking grandchild of Puritanism. Many nineteenth-century reforms, including abolitionism, had deep roots in the Puritan tradition.

Puritans saw themselves as God's chosen people, delivered from bondage and given a divine mission in a promised land. As David Gelernter points out, this set of beliefs arose from the Old Testament story of Israel as God's chosen people, which animated Puritanism and lives on today as the essence of "Americanism."[13] This belief (in a divinely chosen people with a special role to play in the world) runs like a red thread from the first Puritan settlements down to politics and foreign policy in the early twenty-first century. To be sure, there are also discontinuities between then and now. The remnant in the wilderness has become a superpower, and the old Puritan sense of accountability to divine judgment has all but vanished. Yet the chosen nation idea lives on. One need not accept this worldview to recognize its power in history.

The original Puritans wanted a godly society—a fully reformed church and nation. When they lost their political power in old England, New England became their last chance to complete the Reformation. This "holy experiment" was guided by religious convictions.[14] For example, people become Christians through an experience of *regeneration* (rebirth), which confirms them as God's chosen saints. A *covenant* (solemn promise) binds each saint to live out this new birth with God and in a faith community. Living in these covenanted relationships, the faithful become *visible saints*—their faith can be seen by all. (This was both a positive program and a critique of the national or territorial church, to which individuals belonged by birth, not by personal commitment). Puritans looked to the Bible as God's final authority. The minister's sermons interpreted the Bible for the community by applying Scripture to every facet of life, from prayer to politics to planting crops. Since Puritans revered Scripture, they also prized literacy for all their members. Determined to cultivate an educated ministry in New England, Puritans founded Harvard College in 1636; the Puritan tradition contributed much to the cause of literacy and education in the colonies. Thus, spiritual rebirth, covenant, and the Bible were pillars of Puritanism.

Those pillars, the Puritans believed, were set deep in the foundation of divine purpose. John Winthrop (1588–1649), governor of Massachusetts Bay Colony, expressed this faith in God's purpose. As a group of Puritans crossed the Atlantic aboard the ship *Arbella*, Winthrop spoke to them of a "special overruling providence" that would make their colony "a city upon a hill," with "the eyes of all people upon us." Winthrop exhorted his fellow Puritans to "choose life" by keeping all God's laws, so that "God may bless us in the land we go to possess." But he warned that if the people failed to serve God, they would bring down a curse and provoke God to remove them from the promised land.

Arriving in New England, Puritans created closely knit communities that were very different from the scattered and sparse settlements in the South. At the center of each Puritan settlement was the meeting

John Winthrop, Puritan governor of Massachusetts Bay Colony

house, where the Word of God was preached and community concerns addressed. Houses and other buildings clustered near the meeting house; animals grazed on common pasture. This arrangement gave early colonists maximum protection and mutual help. But the layout of the early Puritan village also reflected the centrality of the preached Word for the Puritan community. What Puritans lacked in privacy and personal freedom was more than compensated for by their sense of conducting a holy experiment with a divine purpose.

A society made up of dissenters and reformers, however, was bound to have conflicts. The first big controversy within New England Puritanism began when Anne Hutchinson (1591–1643) held meetings in her Boston home to discuss the sermons being preached in the colony. At first the meetings were for women only, but soon men began to attend as well. Hutchinson charged certain ministers with preaching a "covenant of works" (in which people save themselves) rather than a "covenant of grace" (in which God saves sinners). Hutchinson saw a strong bent toward legalism among the Puritans, and she called for a larger role for grace. She began to question certain ministers' interpretation of Scripture, and this was taken by some as a threat to ministerial authority. In 1637 Hutchinson's teachings were formally condemned as "antinomian" (against the law or promoting lawlessness). Appalled when Hutchinson claimed to receive private revelations of the Holy Spirit, Puritan leaders expelled her from the colony; some years later she was killed in a violent confrontation with Native Americans on Long Island. But Hutchinson's critique of Puritan legalism lived on, as did the Puritan dread of antinomianism.

Another insider critique came from Roger Williams (1603–1683), a minister who charged that the Puritans were not pure *enough*. Some of the Puritan congregations did not separate from the Church of England; Williams demanded complete separation from what he saw as a corrupt church. Williams also objected to the Puritans' settling on Native lands without negotiation or payment. Williams became such an irritant that the General Court of Massachusetts ordered him to return to England. Instead, Williams made his way through the wilderness to the tiny settlement of Rhode Island. Without the help of Native American friends, he may not have survived this winter exile.

Later on Williams did return to England, but for his own reasons. He sought an official charter for a new colony south of Massachusetts. In 1644 Parliament authorized Williams to organize Rhode Island as a new colony. Included in the charter was a guarantee of religious liberty, because Williams insisted that religious belief cannot be coerced by any government. Land for the new colony was purchased from the local Narragansett people. Since Rhode Island attracted people of many religious persuasions, including several who were expelled from Puritan colonies, the Puritans called Rhode Island the sewer of New England.

Meanwhile, Williams continued his spiritual quest. He came to believe that baptism is for adult believers and that Puritans were wrong to practice infant baptism. Williams helped to begin North America's first Baptist congregation in 1639, but soon he rejected the idea that this group was the one true church. Calling himself a seeker, Williams finally did not belong to any particular church. Williams's refusal to accept any form of religious coercion (whether from government or church) marks him as a pioneer of religious liberty.

Ablaze with intellect and zeal, both Hutchinson and Williams challenged Puritan authority in New England. But Puritans faced an even harder challenge from those who lacked zeal. Like lava flowing from a volcano, the Puritan movement eventually began to cool and harden. Those Puritan churches that required an experience of regeneration for full membership noted with dismay that fewer young adults could join the church. This raised some practical questions: Could unconverted churchgoers receive Holy Communion? Could their children be baptized? The deeper question was whether the Puritan ideal—a community of visible saints—could be sustained over time. Of several attempts to deal with this issue, the most important was the Halfway Covenant of 1662. The Halfway Covenant allowed unconverted children of members to have their children baptized, attend worship, and hear the preaching of the Word (there was always the hope that a halfway member might be converted and become a full member). Halfway members, however, could not receive Holy Communion or vote on church matters. The Halfway Covenant was not adopted by all of the New England churches, but it was a clear sign that the Puritan experiment was not producing the hoped-for results.

Back in England, there was little sympathy with the Puritans. The mother country wanted Massachusetts to be a profit-making venture, not a holy experiment. In 1691 the old charter of the Massachusetts Bay Colony was revoked. The new charter loosened the grip of the Puritan establishment on commerce, religion, and politics. The charter also declared religious toleration, clearing the way for an Anglican church to open in Boston. Henceforth, the British Crown would appoint the colonial governor, and property (rather than church membership) would be the basis for participation in politics.

Shortly after the new charter was imposed, witchcraft hysteria erupted in Salem, Massachusetts. Even though most Puritan ministers opposed the witch trials and sought to bring them to an end, the imprisonment of 150 people, 19 of whom were put to death, discredited the religious leadership of the colony. Historian Harry Stout notes that "Salem stands as a symbol of all people's vulnerability to mass suggestion and scapegoating."[15] The Puritans themselves explained their troubles as "God's controversy with New England," brought on by their own failure to live up to their holy covenant with God. In spite of these controversies and failures, however, Puritanism retained a strong hold on New England. In the 1730s a great religious revival began in New England under the Puritan preacher Jonathan Edwards, as we shall see in the next chapter.

The Middle Colonies: Ventures in Pluralism

The southern colonies had an Anglican religious establishment, not as strong as the Puritan stronghold in New England. In between lay the middle colonies, which, by the standards of those times, enjoyed some religious pluralism. The middle colonies (also called the mid-Atlantic colonies) included New York, New Jersey, Pennsylvania, and Delaware. Religious diversity in this region was partly by necessity and partly by design. The mid-Atlantic colonies were "the only part of British North America initially settled by non-English Europeans."[16] By the time the English gained control, Dutch Reformed and Lutheran communities were already planted. By today's standards, the religious pluralism of the middle colonies was limited and uneven, consisting of several Christian groups and a small number of Jews. Nevertheless, the middle colonies set a direction that pointed toward greater religious freedom for a new nation.

New Netherlands

Henry Hudson's explorations helped the Dutch to claim the Hudson River Valley, where the colony called New Netherlands was founded in 1624. At the tip of Manhattan Island, the Dutch trading town of New Amsterdam was home to the first Dutch Reformed congregation, which in turn was a forerunner of an extended family of Reformed churches in America.

The term "Reformed" refers to a cluster of Protestant movements arising from the Reformation. The chief theological mentor of this tradition was John Calvin (1509–1564), reformer of Geneva. (In some strains of the Reformed tradition, Ulrich Zwingli [1484–1531] of Zurich was also significant.) Reformed theology proclaims the sovereignty of God over all things—including the salvation of human beings—which Christ accomplishes apart from human choice or merit. Human beings, for their part, are "totally depraved" by sin. Religious authority rests in the Holy Scriptures, interpreted by theological statements such as the Canons of the Synod of Dort (1618). In Reformed polity (church structure), congregations are accountable to a presbytery (a ruling body made up of ministers and representative elders from congregations within a district). Church organization was important, and so was society; the Reformed tradition has shown a lively interest in ordering society according to God's will. The Reformed tradition was suppressed in France but strong in Switzerland, Holland, Scotland, and parts of Germany; it provided the theological backbone of the Puritan movement in England and New England, although most New England Puritans believed that the congregation, not the presbytery, was the true form of the church.

Despite the rigors of Dutch Reformed faith, religion in the colony of New Netherlands was weak. Relatively few Dutch settlers came to the colony, which was, after all, a trading venture and not a holy experiment. Peter Stuyvesant, who became governor in 1647, tried to achieve religious conformity by expelling a Dutch Lutheran pastor. But in the long run, it proved wiser to encourage trade than to enforce religious uniformity—a farsighted approach for the town that became New York City. By the time the English seized the colony in 1664, its inhabitants included not only Dutch Reformed but Lutherans, Anglicans, Congregationalists, Quakers, Huguenots, Roman Catholics, and a few Jews. About three hundred African slaves made up roughly one-fifth of the population at the time, giving New Amsterdam "the largest urban slave population in mainland North America."[17]

Religious freedom had a checkered career in the colony the English renamed New York. For example, a Catholic, Thomas Dongan, was the colonial governor from 1683–88. Under his leadership the colony adopted a "Charter of Liberties" that granted toleration to Protestants and Catholics and gave some civil liberties to Jews. These policies ended after William and Mary took the English throne. By 1691 New York had an anti-Roman Test Act, which required "all public officials . . . to deny transubstantiation as well as to declare the Mass and adoration of Mary or 'any other saint' to be 'superstitious and idolatrous.'"[18] As already noted in the story of Maryland's Catholics, windows of opportunity for religious freedom could open or close depending on the political and religious weather back in England. By 1694 the Anglicans established the Church of England in the four southernmost counties of New York, but the colony already housed so many religious groups that a larger establishment was impractical. Since trading partners, settlers, and laborers were needed—regardless of their religious belief—territorial religion took a backseat to practical needs.

New Sweden and Pennsylvania

New Sweden was the only colony founded by Lutherans. This Reformation tradition was called *evangelisch* ("evangelical") in Germany, but in America it became known as "Lutheran" in honor of its theological mentor, Martin Luther (1483–1546), who started the Protestant Reformation. Central to Lutheran theology is the doctrine of justification. According to Article IV of the Augsburg Confession (1530), justification means that people cannot make themselves right before God by their own works. Instead, they are "freely justified for Christ's sake through faith, when they believe that they are received into favor and that their sins are forgiven on account of Christ, who by his death made satisfaction for our sins. This faith God imputes for righteousness in his sight." In matters of polity, Lutherans have claimed gospel freedom to use different forms and strategies, ranging all the way from a state church to independent ("free church") congregations and many shades in between.

In 1638 Lutherans from Sweden founded Fort Christina (now Wilmington, Delaware). The colony branched out into several settlements along the Delaware River, with several congregations. Finnish and German Lutherans were present in these settlements, but the colonial churches of New Sweden were an extension of the Church of Sweden. The pastors were instructed by the Swedish Crown to teach and preach according to the Augsburg Confession and to conduct worship just as they had in the Church of Sweden. They were told to treat the Indians "with all humanity and respect, that no violence or wrong be done to them," and to instruct them "in the Christian religion . . . civilization and good government."[19] Toward that end, Pastor John Campanius translated Luther's *Small Catechism* into a local Native language, perhaps the earliest such translation.

The Swedish settlement was short-lived. The Dutch captured it in 1655 and, following a policy of territorialism, made the Dutch Reformed Church the only legal form of Christianity. Lutheran pastors were sent back to Europe, and their congregations languished. Then in 1664 the English seized the Dutch settlements and gave the Lutherans permission to worship freely. But the Swedish Lutherans never fully recovered from their setbacks at the hands of the Dutch.

Pennsylvania was another story. This colony began with a policy of religious openness. Its roots were in an English sect called the Society of Friends, also known as "Quakers" because they trembled under the power of God in worship. The Friends began as a radical wing of the Puritan movement, so extreme in their reforms that they alienated more conventional Puritans. For example, the Society of Friends saw no need for sacraments. They encouraged any believer moved by the Spirit to speak out in worship, rather than rely on professionally trained clergy. Inspired by their founder, George Fox (1624–91), the Friends proclaimed the "inner light" of Christ shining within each believer. Friends refused to take legal oaths, serve in an army, worship in a traditional church, or acknowledge social rank. This noncompliant behavior offended not only the Puritans but those loyal to the Crown and the Church of England. In England and some of its colonies, Friends could be forced to pay fines, put in jail, or even be put to death for their beliefs.

The founder of Pennsylvania was William Penn (1644–1718). Born into a high-ranking family in England, Penn attended the best schools. To his parents' dismay, he converted to the Society of Friends. He was jailed at least twice for leading Quakers in worship. Yet because Penn was connected to powerful and wealthy people, he was uniquely positioned to become an organizer and founder of colonies in America. Penn helped to set up East and West Jersey (later New Jersey) with policies of religious toleration. In the early 1680s, the Crown gave the Penn family a huge tract of land in North America to pay off an old debt. A new colony was chartered and named Pennsylvania. William Penn encouraged not only English and Dutch Quakers to settle there but also Mennonites,

William Penn's treaty with the Indians
Photo © Giraudon/Art Resource, NY

Amish, and others who had known persecution in Europe. Pennsylvania farmland also attracted a great many German Lutherans, while in Philadelphia a Catholic community gathered. A small and persecuted sect, the Quakers did much to set the stage for religious freedom in America.

No introduction to colonial Christianity would be complete, however, without the Presbyterians. They did not found a colony and were not an "established" church. But by 1776 they were second only to the Congregationalists in number. Presbyterians were most numerous in the middle colonies, but were also present in New England and some parts of the South. In early colonial times, the key Presbyterian leader was Francis Makemie (1658–1707). Born in Ireland and educated in Scotland, Makemie came to America in 1683 and traveled widely to preach and gather Presbyterian churches. He is remembered for defending religious liberty and for organizing the first American presbytery.

Presbyterians may be viewed as arising from the Puritan movement in England, with strong roots in Scotland as well. Like the Puritan Congregationalists, they subscribed to the Westminster Confession of

1646, which famously declares that "the chief end of man is to glorify God and enjoy him forever." The Presbyterians loved the Bible and therefore prized literacy and an educated ministry. In the colonies they quickly established an apprenticeship system for training ministers. In 1746 they founded the College of New Jersey (later renamed Princeton University).

At least two things distinguished the Presbyterians from their Congregationalist cousins. First was their polity, or mode of church organization. The Presbyterians, instead of defining the church as the local congregation, had a larger and more complex view of the church. They had clusters of congregations, "whose presbyters (or elders), clerical and lay, governed the church's affairs through the local session, the larger presbytery, the regional synod, and in America by the time of Independence, the national General Assembly."[20] A second distinguishing mark was the Scottish influence. In the early 1700s, a large migration of Scots-Irish Presbyterians gave a distinctive character to colonial Presbyterianism. The Scottish immigrants carried with them the legacy of John Knox (1513–1572), the reformer who used Calvin's theology to bring revolution to Scotland. Knox was a principal writer of the Scots Confession of 1640, which affirmed God's sovereignty in all things. This confession declared that "civil power is not absolute" and reserved for Christians "the right of just rebellion."[21] Scottish Presbyterians brought this militant faith to America, where they soon found new reasons to resist English control.

Suggestions for Further Reading

Books

Berlin, Ira. *Many Thousands Gone: The First Two Centuries of Slavery in America* (Belknap Press, 2000). This book explores the origins and development of slavery in America from 1619 up through the American Revolution. The lives and experiences of African American slaves varied greatly according to time and place, but as a system based on race, slavery was set apart from other forms of servitude in the colonies.

Gill, Sam. *Native American Religions: An Introduction* (2d ed., Wadsworth, 2004). Gill introduces Native American religions with an appreciation for their variety and complexity, drawing from a broad range of Native peoples and religious experiences.

Miller, Perry. *The New England Mind: The Seventeenth Century* (reprint ed., Belknap Press, 1983). First written in 1939, this is one of the landmark books in the study of American religion. Miller gives a penetrating analysis of Puritan theology and explores how the Puritan vision shaped their society.

Websites

Primary documents for the study of United States History, East Tennessee State University Department of History. See especially the "Colonial Period" section: www.etsu.edu/cas/history/americadocs.htm

"America as Refuge." Part 1 of an online exhibit by the Library of Congress entitled "Religion and the Founding of the American Republic." The site includes narrative descriptions and graphics on persecution in Europe, the Puritans, and Bible commonwealths: www.loc.gov/exhibits/religion/rel01.html

Discussion Questions

1. What was "territorialism"? How did it shape religion and society in North America in the early colonial period? What long-term effects of territorialism can still be seen in North America today?
2. Who were the Puritans? What is their continuing legacy in America?
3. What challenges did the Church of England face in Virginia and other southern colonies?
4. In the colonial period, Europeans used several different approaches to evangelize Native Americans. What insights may be drawn from these early encounters between European missionaries and Native peoples?
5. To gain access to slaves on plantations, missionaries often had to convince slave owners that Christianity would not subvert slavery. How do you respond to the claim that Christianity posed no threat to slavery?
6. Name several types of religious authority in England's North American colonies; then note at least one instance when rival claims to religious authority came into conflict.

CHAPTER TWO

Awakening, Enlightenment, and Revolution

Our first chapter surveyed the early history of Christianity in the colonies, region by region. Turning now to the later colonial period through the Revolution, we will look at larger movements and events that shaped American Christianity.

America as Mission Field

Around the turn of the century (from the seventeenth to the eighteenth), England experienced what Sidney Ahlstrom called "imperial awakening." From an English perspective, if the colonies were to grow into something more than "a meaningless string of feeble outposts,"[1] they would need closer management. One sign of this new management was the Society for the Propagation of the Gospel in Foreign Parts (SPG), founded in London in 1701. This new missionary arm of the Church of England sought to convert Native Americans and African slaves to Christianity, but it was more effective in expanding Anglicanism among white colonists. The SPG made a concerted effort to establish new Anglican parishes and strengthen existing ones. Anglicans also planted schools that were closely connected to the Church of England: these include King's College (later Columbia University) in 1754 and Philadelphia College (later the University of Pennsylvania) in 1755.

The Church of England stepped up its challenge to the Congregational establishment in New England and sought to infiltrate that bastion of Puritanism. Things took a dramatic turn in favor of the Anglicans when, in 1722, a few Congregational ministers sailed to England to obtain ordination in the Anglican Church. Then these newly minted Anglican priests sailed back to New England to serve existing Anglican parishes or gather new ones. Staunch Congregationalists dubbed this event the "Great Apostasy" (betrayal of the faith); after all, the first Puritans strove to reform the Church of England, if not to get away from in entirely—and now the Church of old England was being planted in New England by former Puritan ministers!

The English were not the only ones to see America as a mission field; German Lutherans sent missionaries to the colonies as well. These Lutherans were part of a movement called Pietism, which arose after the Reformation era to promote a warmhearted, active faith. The University of Halle in Germany was a training center for Pietists, and it sent missionaries around the world. North America was of special concern to the Halle Pietists, because German immigrants there were "like sheep without a shepherd." Therefore, the Halle Pietists sent one of their best and brightest, Henry Melchior Muhlenberg (1711–1787), to serve the German immigrants in America. Muhlenberg arrived in Philadelphia in 1742 at the height of the Great Awakening. Of his own ministry, Muhlenberg said, "By God's grace I laid the emphasis on true repentance, living faith, and godliness . . . these three points, together with the two sacraments, were the chief content of Evangelical Lutheran doctrine."[2] He spent a lifetime gathering congregations, recruiting Lutheran pastors, and providing pastoral care to immigrants.

Another noteworthy figure was Count Nikolaus von Zinzendorf (1700–1760). In Europe he became the patron and protector of the Moravians, a persecuted Protestant group that found refuge on Zinzendorf's estate in Saxony. The Moravians were known for their fervent hymn-singing, mystical piety, and communal lifestyle. Their community was called "Herrnhut," and it became, like the University of Halle, a sending agency for missionaries. Moravians who came to America sought to bring the gospel to Native Americans; their persistence and integrity won respect among the Cherokee nation. Zinzendorf himself visited America in 1741–43 to gather Moravian Christians into communities. He aroused the suspicion of Lutherans when he tried, unsuccessfully, to unite Moravians and Lutherans in Pennsylvania.

European missionary ventures unfolded against a backdrop of warfare. As the French and the English vied for power, their colonies suffered brutal attacks on settlements, saw pitched battles between armies, and sometimes had forts under siege. Both France and England had allies among the Native tribes. The French were more successful than the English at making and keeping allies, just as the French were more effective at converting Native Americans to Christianity. According to historian George Marsden, Native Americans were less likely to trust the English because "the English were almost always trying to settle the territories where they evangelized."[3] The French missions, in contrast, posed a lesser immediate threat to Native ways of life.

Of the many colonial wars involving Europeans and Native peoples, the most important was called the French and Indian War. This was an extension of a European conflict known as the Seven Years' War. British victories at Quebec (1759) and Montreal (1760) compelled France to surrender Canada and abandon other claims east of the Mississippi. At roughly the same time, Spain gave up its claims to Florida. Thus, Protestant England became the sole European power from the Atlantic to the Mississippi.

These conflicts had religious dimensions. In this age of territorialism, French Catholics in Canada abhorred the Protestant presence to their south, and the English Protestants felt the same about the Catholics to their north. The English felt pressure from the west as well, for the French built forts in the Ohio Valley and raided frontier settlements of English colonists. France's final defeat was hailed as a victory not only for England but for Protestantism. But colonial wars undermined missionary efforts among Native Americans. Several Christian missions were disrupted or destroyed in frontier raids. Worse, the conflict between the English and the French probably discredited Christianity in the eyes of Native peoples. France's defeat left its former Native allies with no buffer against English expansion.

The Great Awakening

In the 1730s, New England experienced a surge of revival preaching and adult conversions to Christianity. The revival spread to the middle colonies and penetrated parts of the South; it also traveled as far north as Nova Scotia. These revivals are remembered collectively as the Great Awakening. Central to the revivals was the experience of new birth—

also called conversion, regeneration, or salvation. The Awakening made new Christians and renewed the faith of existing ones. And the Awakening was controversial. It challenged old forms of religious authority. Christians in many places divided into pro- and anti-revival camps. Just as a forest fire burns down old trees and makes way for new growth, the Awakening reshaped American religion.

Like many fires, this one began on parched ground. In the early 1700s in New England and parts of the middle colonies, ministers complained of a discouraging dryness and dullness in religion. Compared to the original zeal of the Puritan founders, their congregations seemed cold and dead. A few ministers preached for conversion and reported some success,[4] but Jonathan Edwards (1703–1758), a Puritan (Congregational) minister in Northampton, Massachusetts, usually is credited with igniting the Great Awakening.

A man of luminous spirit and brilliant mind, Edwards could not accept dullness in religion. In 1734 several young adults known for loose living were convicted under Edwards' ministry. Lamenting their sins, these young adults experienced a breakthrough into new birth (conversion). Edwards stepped up his preaching for each person in his congregation to repent and be saved from the wrath of God. Edwards's congregation had a season of awakening, and soon a revival swept the town. Nearby churches invited Edwards to preach, and religious fervor spread in the villages along the Connecticut River valley. Supporters saw this as a fulfillment of the old Puritan vision: reborn souls testify to God's saving work in their lives and join a congregation of "visible saints." Indeed, Edwards's preaching brought many people over the threshold from "halfway" (unconverted) members to full members. But rather than extending an old era of religion, the Awakening opened up a new one.

In 1737 Edwards published his *Faithful Narrative of the Surprising Work of God in the Conversion of Many Hundred Souls in Northampton.* This work inspired revival preachers on both sides of the Atlantic, including John Wesley, the English Methodist. But by the time people were reading about Northhampton, that congregation had returned to business as usual—including petty infighting and spiritual dullness. Most distressing was the suicide of Edwards's own uncle, who may have despaired because, while others were rejoicing, he did not experience conversion.

Jonathan Edwards
Reprinted from *The Works of Jonathan Edwards* (London: Henry G. Bohn, 1865)

Edwards rekindled the revival, striving to lead the people more deeply into faith. But when Edwards, following an older Puritan practice, insisted that only converted persons could receive Communion, the congregation responded by asking Edwards to leave. He spent several years at an Indian mission school in Stockbridge, a western settlement vulnerable to French and Indian attack. During his exile, Edwards wrote some of the most profound theological works ever produced in America. He used Enlightenment philosophy and Puritan theology to address original sin, divine redemption, and the purpose for which God created the world. Edwards' ministerial colleagues recognized his brilliance. They called him to serve as president of the College of New Jersey (later Princeton). But shortly after assuming this prestigious post, Edwards died from a faulty smallpox inoculation.

The Awakening had its great theologian in Edwards, but its star preacher was George Whitefield (1715–1770). Based in London, Whitefield made several extended preaching tours in America, stopping at the major towns along the Atlantic seaboard. Whitefield was a minister of the Church of England, but he did not behave like one. Instead of staying in a settled parish, Whitefield "itinerated" (traveled) widely. Instead of preaching from a pulpit as any conventional minister would do, Whitefield often preached outside where he could gather huge crowds. Instead of using a prepared manuscript, Whitefield worked without notes, like an actor on stage.

Whitefield is aptly described as the "Divine Dramatist."[5] Whitefield dramatized Bible stories to drive home the message, "Ye must be born again!" Whitefield's expressive power was legendary; it was said that he could make people weep merely by pronouncing the word "Mesopotamia." In an age before microphones, Whitefield's voice could be heard by thousands at a time, and huge crowds of people flocked to hear him and to play their part in the story of salvation. Caught up in the drama, many people experienced a spiritual crisis that resulted in conversion.

Whitefield made enemies as well as converts. He was lampooned in the press and made fun of in cartoons. Ministers who disliked the Awakening snubbed him, but this only increased his popularity with the common people. Whitefield's flamboyance offended those who preferred a more reserved form of religion. Most obnoxious to the religious establishment (in old or New England) was Whitefield's charge that ministers who were not born again had no business preaching. For Whitefield, a minister's own conversion and the ability to win souls meant more than ordination, education, or other credentials. In other words, Whitefield subverted conventional religious authority. He pioneered a form of Christianity that was based on mass evangelism for personal conversion. A host of imitators copied Whitefield's style and traveled far and wide, preaching the new birth.

In contrast to the fanfare surrounding Whitefield, a quiet phase of the Awakening took place in the southern backcountry. Gathering congregations along the frontier was hardscrabble work. A leader who dedicated his life to this cause was Samuel Davies (1723–1761). A Presbyterian, Davies prepared for the ministry in Pennsylvania, where his denomination was strong and where the religious situation was relatively diverse and open. But in 1746 Davies went to Virginia, where the Church of England was established. To obtain a license for preaching and gathering congregations, Davies argued that England's Act of Toleration of 1689 applied also to England's colonies.[6] Davies'

George Whitefield
Reprinted from *The Life of Rev. George Whitefield* (New York: D. Newell, 1846)

appeal succeeded and helped to link the Awakening with the cause of religious freedom.

Armed with official permission, Davies traveled Virginia's backcountry. He preached a message of repentance and new birth among Scots-Irish and German immigrants. He worked among African slaves, writing hymns especially for them and teaching them to read. Davies was "eager to invite blacks to share in regular church services, including those which offered the Lord's Supper."[7] Davies valued an educated ministry and traveled to England to raise funds for the College of New Jersey (Princeton), where he later served as president. The Awakening spread, adapting to local conditions throughout the colonies. Its ministers ranged from the scholarly Edwards to the flamboyant Whitefield to the diligent Davies. A host of lesser known preachers followed in their train.

The preachers we have described thus far were leaders of integrity. But the revival also had a few crackpots, the most notorious of whom was James Davenport (1716–1757), a New England preacher. Davenport was a wild-eyed zealot who claimed to know, on sight, which people were God's chosen saints and which were hell-bound. His meetings incited some to religious frenzy, while spectators mocked and jeered. After much provocation, Davenport was jailed for disturbing the peace and for slandering religious leaders. He was judged to be not guilty on the grounds of insanity. A writer for the *Boston Evening Post* commented, "Were you to see him [Davenport] in his most violent agitations, you would be apt to think that he was a Madman just broke from his Chains."[8] Davenport made it necessary for Edwards and others to do damage control to show that the Awakening was not religious madness.

The older colonial churches were deeply shaken by the Awakening. The Anglicans lost a great many "ordinary people and became the church of the educated and wealthier classes."[9] The Presbyterians divided into pro- and anti-revival factions. The Congregationalists, once the strongest religious establishment in the colonies, fractured into several distinct parties, each one claiming to be the rightful heir to "the English dissenting tradition."[10] Congregationalism continued to grow after the Awakening but never recovered its former prestige and unity.

Meanwhile, the Awakening created an opening for new groups to grow and thrive, especially the Methodists and the Baptists. These groups were very small in colonial times, but by using the revival techniques of the Awakening, they became, as we shall see in another chapter, the largest Protestant groups in America.

Relatively few African Americans embraced Christianity before the Awakening. But in these eighteenth-century revivals, more blacks converted than ever before. African Americans responded to the Awakening for several reasons. The religious intensity of the revivals appealed to peoples who did not fear a vivid spiritual life. Some scholars think that the Christian rite of baptism may have evoked memories of African water rituals surrounding birth, death, and cleansing.[11] Most important was the Awakening's message: *Christ died for you. You can be born again as a child of God. Christ will set you free.* Slaves and free blacks took this message to heart in ways that white people did not anticipate. And as

African American converts began to preach this message, their black hearers had good reasons to listen.

Women also began preaching in the Great Awakening, in unofficial but powerful ways. Strong taboos forbade women to speak in public, but in the eighteenth-century revivals, some women could not keep silent. Historian Catherine Brekus documents many accounts of women sharing their conversion stories with congregations. There were also female "exhorters" who, like midwives, encouraged those who strove for new birth. Critics of the Awakening saw the public speaking of women as proof that revivals threatened the social order. Even pro-revival ministers saw female speaking as a public relations problem. All too soon the few venues for public religious expression for women, opened by the Awakening, were closed. By the time of the Revolutionary era, female preaching occurred only on the extreme fringes of Christianity.[12] The few women who became religious leaders did so by starting their own movements. A prime example is "Mother" Ann Lee (1736–1784), founder of the Shakers, a communitarian movement that recruited its members from among revival converts.

The Awakening inspired new converts—including slaves and women—to speak in public of the power of God. In a society based on hierarchy, this was something new. Colonial society was like a ladder with many rungs, according to historian Gordon Wood. Those higher up on the ladder gave their patronage to those below them, and inferiors or those of middling ranks gave deference to those above. But the Awakening "became in one way or another a massive defiance against traditional authority." It challenged clerical unity, shattered many churches, and cut people "loose from ancient religious bonds."[13] No longer would access to religion be controlled by people with the proper social rank. American Christianity was becoming the people's religion.

The Enlightenment

Overlapping with the Awakening was the Enlightenment, an intellectual movement that sought to understand the present and shape the future by means of human reason. The Awakening and the Enlightenment stand in sharp contrast to each other. The Awakening reached the

Benjamin Franklin
Engraving by R. W. Dodson. Photo © Art Resource, NY

common people; the Enlightenment began as a movement for the elite few. The Awakening raised "religious affections"; the Enlightenment exalted the mind. The Awakening proclaimed that God, by grace, saves sinful human beings; the Enlightenment proclaimed that people make progress on their own. The Awakening defined human beings by sin and grace; the Enlightenment defined human beings by reason. The Awakening promised eternal life with God; the Enlightenment promoted the pursuit of happiness in this life.

Of course, "Enlightenment" refers not just to one movement but to a cluster of movements that ushered in the modern era in Europe and America. Historian Henry May has described several types of Enlightenment, which we shall discuss here. First, the moderate or rational

Enlightenment stressed reason, order, and balance. Second, the skeptical Enlightenment questioned everything, including reason. Third, the revolutionary Enlightenment violently overturned old institutions. Finally, the didactic (teaching) Enlightenment sought to salvage the best of the Enlightenment while rejecting violence and radical skepticism.[14] Americans borrowed selectively from these various phases of the Enlightenment, choosing what was useful in creating a new nation and discarding what was not useful. Of these four types of Enlightenment, the "moderate" and the "didactic" were the most useful to Americans.

The Enlightenment (in its various phases) had much to say about religion. As early as the mid-1600s, thinkers of the moderate Enlightenment, called "Deists," believed in God but not in Christian creeds. The Deists reacted against the wars of religion that ravaged Europe after the Reformation; they also embraced a new scientific worldview guided by reason (not revelation). Deists rejected miracles, creeds, and sacraments. They wanted to strip away old relics of "dogma and priestcraft" in favor of a simple religion of virtue. Over a century after Deism began in England, Benjamin Franklin offered his own statement of its principles:

> Here is my Creed. I believe in one God, Creator of the Universe. That he governs it by his Providence. That he ought to be worshipped. That the most acceptable Service we render to him is doing good to his other Children. That the soul of Man is immortal, and will be treated with Justice in another Life respecting its Conduct in this. These I take to be the fundamental Principles of all sound Religion . . . in whatever Sect I meet with them.

Franklin went on to say that he admired the "system of Morals" taught by Jesus of Nazareth but had some "Doubts as to his Divinity." However, Franklin saw "no harm" in believing in Christ's divinity if this makes people do good to their fellow creatures.[15] Franklin saw Christianity as useful for supplying America with virtuous citizens, but he himself preferred an Enlightenment faith.

Some American clergy, attracted to the moderate Enlightenment but unwilling to go too far, sought a middle ground. Their compromise position was called "reasonable religion"; it sought to harmonize reason and revelation, nature and scripture. These enlightened ministers revered a benevolent God, who ruled the moral and the natural universe by means of orderly systems (not a sovereign God who wielded arbitrary decrees such as predestination). Rather than overtly rejecting traditional creeds, Scriptures, and sacraments, the enlightened ministers simply downplayed traditional religion in favor of morals and the beauty of nature. It was quietly hoped that antique doctrines, such as the Trinity, could someday be dropped.

Rationalist clergy opposed the Great Awakening, which they said unleashed religious "enthusiasm" (fanaticism). Instead of enthusiasm, the rationalist clergy promoted steady, sober obedience to God's moral system. In this vein, Charles Chauncy (1705–1787), a pastor of First (Congregational) Church in Boston—and a foe of Jonathan Edwards—wrote an anti-revival tract called "Enthusiasm Described and Cautioned Against." Among other things, Chauncy objected to women speaking in public in the revivals; such disorderly conduct could not be of God. Some years later, Chauncy promoted a type of universalism in which all people can save themselves by conforming to the divine moral system.

It was much harder to blend Christianity with the revolutionary Enlightenment, which could be violently anti-Christian. The aim of the revolutionary Enlightenment, according to Henry May, was to overturn the old order to usher in the new. In this view, updating Christianity was not enough; indeed, Christianity was part of the old order, which must be destroyed. An apostle of this view was Thomas Paine (1737–1809). In the American colonies, Paine won fame with *Common Sense* (1776), a pamphlet justifying revolution in the American colonies. Americans who supported the Revolution (including many Christians) hailed Paine as a patriot and a hero. Several years later, Paine promoted the French Revolution in his book *The Age of Reason* (1794, 1796). This time Paine condemned Christianity as part the old regime, which, like the monarchy, must be torn down. Paine condemned the Bible as a book of lies and cruelty.

American Christians liked Paine's zeal for the American Revolution, but they were horrified by his new revelations. Worse still were the excesses of the French Revolution: public executions by guillotine and blatant persecution of the church. All of this provoked a backlash against radical forms of Enlightenment. By the close of the eighteenth century,

Americans needed a way to sift through the various forms of Enlightenment, rejecting what they saw as harmful and keeping only what they could use. They found the help they needed in Common Sense Realism, which Henry May calls "the didactic Enlightenment."

Common Sense Realism (also called the Scottish philosophy) was useful for rejecting extreme forms of Enlightenment. But Common Sense arose well before the French Revolution to rebut yet another form of Enlightenment, namely the radical skepticism of philosopher David Hume. Radical skepticism—doubting everything—is not a reasonable way to live. Indeed, said the Common Sense philosophers, human beings naturally depend on the testimony of others; we are so constituted that we must rely on testimony. The Bible can be accepted as a reliable guide to truth. We need not reject the past (and its religion) in order to make progress in the future.

The great professor of Common Sense Realism in America was John Witherspoon (1723–1794), a Scottish Presbyterian who became the president of the College of New Jersey. Witherspoon applied his philosophy to public life at a pivotal time in the nation's history. A delegate to the Continental Congress from 1776–82, he was the only minister to sign the Declaration of Independence. One of Witherspoon's students at Princeton was James Madison (1751–1836) the political theorist who did much to shape the U.S. Constitution and who later became president.

For nearly a century, Common Sense Realism was the reigning philosophy in American higher education. It was useful for harmonizing religion and science, faith and reason. Common Sense affirmed Christianity in a new way. Rather than appealing to older forms of religious authority, such as bishops or creeds, each person could appeal to common sense and self-evident truths.[16] Common Sense Realism affirmed Christianity as the friend of reason and progress.

Religion in the American Revolution

Historian Paul Johnson writes that "the American Revolution, in its origins, was a religious event" inspired by both the Great Awakening and the Enlightenment.[17] The Great Awakening proclaimed the new birth as God's gift—it was a spiritual declaration of independence from human authorities, civil and ecclesiastical. And the Enlightenment

The Great Seal of the Republic (never officially adopted), 1775 or 1776.

preached progress, even if old institutions had to be overturned. Here the contrast between Europe and America is striking. Europeans of that era typically combined religion with monarchy so that loyalty to the Crown was a religious obligation. For example, in 1775 John Wesley wrote a pamphlet admonishing Christians in the colonies that it was their God-given duty to remain loyal to the Crown. Wesley believed that the king's authority came from God; therefore, rebellion against the Crown was incompatible with Christianity. Likewise, European revolutionaries saw the cross and the Crown as two sides of a coin. In the French and later the Russian revolution, zealots sought to destroy Christianity along with monarchy.

Not so with the American Revolution. Historian Mark Noll writes that "American Christians, despite substantial conflicts among themselves, took for granted a fundamental compatibility between orthodox Protestant religion and republican [non-monarchial] principles of government."[18] Instead of seeing the Christian faith as wedded to royal power, many Americans saw Christianity as their ally *against* monarchy. Nowhere is this stated more clearly than on a national seal devised by

Reverend James Caldwell at the Battle of Springfield
Watercolor by Henry Alexander Ogden

Jefferson, Franklin, and others during the Revolutionary War. The seal pictures the Americans (like the Israelites of old) crossing the Red Sea as Pharaoh's (England's) chariots are destroyed. The motto reads, "Rebellion to Tyrants Is Obedience to God."

In the Revolutionary era and its aftermath, many Americans believed that God was using their struggle to usher in a new phase of history, in which democracy and Christianity would join forces to spread the light of truth and progress throughout the world. By the 1830s, the French observer Alexis de Tocqueville saw that "for Americans the ideas of Christianity and liberty are so completely mingled that it is almost impossible to get them to conceive of the one without the other."[19]

Before the Revolution, Americans feared that an Anglican bishop would be sent to the colonies, strengthening the Church of England here and tightening British control. The slogan "No bishop, no king!" rejected any alliance of monarchy and episcopacy. Back in England, however, the Society for the Propagation of the Gospel pressed for an Anglican bishop to be sent to the colonies. David Holmes, writing on the Anglican tradition in America, says that the bishop issue "may properly be seen as one of the contributing causes of the American War of Independence."[20] No Anglican bishop was sent to the colonies before the Revolution, but the mere prospect rankled many.

When the Revolution came, New England clergy supported independence so strongly that the British called these ministers "the black regiment" (referring to their black ministerial robes). Most New England ministers hewed closely to scriptural themes in their Sunday morning sermons. But in special recruiting services, some preachers came close to making independence from England a kind of salvation, and obeisance to the Crown a kind of idolatry.[21] One of the most popular anthems of the Revolutionary era, written by the Puritan composer William Billings, captures the spirit of the times: "Let tyrants shake their iron rod; let slavery clank her galling chains! We fear them not, we trust in God. New England's God forever reigns."

New Englanders of Puritan stock were not the only religious patriots. Throughout the colonies, ministers from many traditions left their parishes to serve as army chaplains. Chaplains prayed with wounded soldiers and visited the sick. In their preaching, they sought to inspire courage, instill personal discipline, and justify the patriot cause. But preaching to soldiers in camp or before battle was not like preaching in a church; historian Charles Royster notes that drunkenness and profanity were rife in the army. Soldiers were often cold and ill-fed, and many battles brought defeat. Soldiers sometimes showed their contempt for chaplains who said that God was on their side.[22]

Church of England clergy who served in the colonies found themselves in a tough spot. Anglican priests had vowed, at their ordinations, to "maintain the King's supremacy in Church and State." But during the Revolution, a minister who tried to keep that vow (for example, by praying for the king during Sunday worship) risked inciting mob violence. Many Anglican ministers returned to England, while Canada became a refuge for thousands of Anglicans, lay and clergy. Of the colonial churches, the Anglicans had the most to lose in the Revolution. But Anglican loyalty to the Crown was by no means a given. Many Anglicans, especially Virginians and South Carolinians, supported the Revolution, and "more than one half of the signers of the Declaration of Independence were Anglicans."[23]

Meanwhile, some Christians made perhaps the most difficult choice of all: embracing pacifism. Out of religious conviction, such Christians refused to participate in the war except to care for wounded soldiers. Groups with roots in the radical Reformation (Quakers, Mennonites, and others) objected to the war on religious grounds, but patriots often treated them as secret supporters of England.

In contrast to the pacifists and those who remained loyal to England, the Roman Catholics supported American independence with vigor. Catholics were then a small minority of about thirty thousand people. If America became independent, the Catholics—like the Baptists and other suppressed groups—stood to gain religious freedom and full participation in public life. Leading the way was Charles Carroll (1737–1832), a delegate to the Continental Congress and the only Catholic to sign the Declaration of Independence.

Charles' cousin, the priest John Carroll (1735–1815), did much to shape American Catholicism in the Revolution and its aftermath. In 1789 he became the bishop of Baltimore (the first American Catholic bishop) and was made an archbishop in 1808. Carroll worked hard to recruit the leaders (including many priests from France) Catholicism needed to thrive in America. Carroll insisted that Catholics receive equal citizenship and exercise equal participation in government. He believed that all who fought for independence—regardless of their religious belief—had a right to full citizenship. The Revolution gave Catholics an opportunity to demonstrate their patriotism and to make the shift from oppressed minority to equal citizens.

During the American Revolution, congregational life suffered in all churches, regardless of belief or stance toward the war. Many church buildings were abandoned, destroyed, or used for military purposes. Parishes struggled along without pastors as clergy joined the army or fled to Canada or England. Farms were destroyed, households were scattered, and trade was interrupted. In a country that could scarcely feed and clothe its army, resources were scarce. The war years are remembered as a low point for church life in America.

Constitutional Settlement

After independence was won, the new United States needed an official strategy for dealing with religion. The new strategy, articulated in the First Amendment to the Constitution, unhooked religion from government control and support. Ratified in 1791 as the first item in the Bill of Rights, the Amendment ensures that "Congress shall make no law respecting the establishment of religion or prohibiting the free exercise thereof."[24] There would be no nationally established church supported by taxes. Toleration (which granted limited rights to those outside the established church) was no longer adequate; *pluralism* would take its place.

The Constitutional Settlement disestablished religion at the national level; the individual states disestablished according to their own timetables. Religion would henceforth be voluntary in America, sustaining itself without government support or interference. This voluntarism became a major reason why Christianity flourished in America—even as it declined in Europe.

The American experiment in religious freedom drew from Enlightenment thinkers such as John Locke (1632–1704). Locke saw religion as a matter of individual conscience. Since "liberty of conscience" is each person's "natural right," religious belief cannot be compelled by force; it can only be won through persuasion.[25] Locke insisted that for peace to prevail, religion and the civil order must recognize each other's distinct functions: a church cares for souls; the government cares for citizens by securing their civil rights and protecting their property. Neither the government nor church should interfere with the other's work.

Thomas Jefferson, James Madison, and others worked to build Locke's ideas into the foundation of government at both state and national levels. Their first victory came in 1786 when Virginia adopted Jefferson's "Bill for Establishing Religious Freedom." This bill declared that "Almighty God hath created the mind free" and that "truth is great and will prevail" if left to itself. Jefferson believed that any government support for religion violates natural human rights. As the name of Jefferson's bill suggests, the goal was to *establish religious freedom*, not to establish a particular religion. In Virginia, where the Church of England had enjoyed its strongest colonial establishment, this was indeed revolutionary.

Religious freedom was not a child of the Enlightenment only. Jefferson and his colleagues must share the credit with several Christian traditions. The Virginia Bill had political support from Methodists, Baptists, and Presbyterians. Even more significant was the fact that long before Thomas Jefferson lived, Baptists, Quakers, and other dissenters had called for religious freedom. According to historian William Miller, "The most widely held early American idea of the separation of church and state flows from ... *religious* ideas ... not from rationalism."[26] More than a century before the American Revolution, Roger Williams wrote *The Bloudy Tenet of Persecution*, in which he declared that no government has the right to interfere with any person's relationship with God. In the Revolutionary era, Williams' spiritual heirs pushed for the freedom of religion from government control.

One such heir was Isaac Backus (1724–1806). Converted in the Great Awakening under the preaching of George Whitefield, Backus became a Baptist minister. In 1773 he published *An Appeal to the Public for Religious Liberty; Against the Oppression of the Present Day* to protest Massachusetts' tax support of its established religion (Congregationalism). In 1774 a group of Baptists sent Backus to speak in defense of religious liberty to the Massachusetts delegates of the Continental Congress. Backus told them that it is bad enough to pay taxes to support a religious group with which one disagrees; it is even worse to be forced to "render ... to any earthly power" homage that "belongs only to God."[27] Enlightenment arguments centered on human rights, but Backus affirmed human rights *as well as* the claims of God. Put another way, the Enlightenment appeal to human rights was horizontal, with humans as the main point of reference. Backus' appeal was vertical, referring to human relationship with God. Although Backus continued to press for religious freedom, the Congregational Church remained established in Massachusetts until 1833.

The phrase "separation of church and state" has been used sparingly here for a reason. These words do not appear in the Constitution but were used by Thomas Jefferson in private correspondence after 1800.[28] Current invocations of "separation of church and state" that call for complete exclusion of religion from public life do not reflect the founders' intentions. Historian Paul Johnson notes that the first item of the

Bill of Rights is best understood as "an anti-establishment clause"; it was intended to prevent Congress from setting up "a state religion on the lines of the Church of England, 'as by law established.'" Banning religion from public life was not intended. Indeed, the House of Representatives passed the First Amendment on September 24, 1789, and "the next day it passed, by a two-to-one majority, a resolution calling for a day of national prayer and thanksgiving."[29]

Rather than banning religion from public life, the Bill of Rights insisted that no one religion be *established.* Instead of an established religion, there was to be an informal working relationship in which the government guaranteed religious freedom while the churches provided virtuous citizens for the republic. According to historian Gordon Wood, after the Revolution dissolved old bonds of monarchy, gentry, and church hierarchy, something else would have to hold society together. That "something else" was benevolence or public virtue, inspiring citizens to put public good ahead of private power and gain. At the close of the eighteenth century, religion was thought to instill this virtue of benevolence, so necessary for the health of the new nation.

> The importance of this domestication of virtue for American culture can scarcely be exaggerated. It was not nostalgic or backward-looking, but progressive.... It laid the basis for all reform movements of the nineteenth century, and indeed for all subsequent modern liberal thinking. We still yearn for a world in which everyone will love one another.[30]

In the early 1800s, the ideal of benevolence inspired volunteer organizations to improve society, as we shall see in the next chapter. But the ideal of benevolence was soon overtaken by bare-knuckled competition in business, politics, and even religion. Churches had to recruit their own members and pay their own bills without government support. This created a highly competitive environment for religion. But the old fear—that competing religious groups would ignite wars of religion—did not come to pass. The Constitutional Settlement made religious rivalry and competition work *for* the country rather than *against* it. In an informal system of checks and balances, religious competition kept any one church or sect from becoming too powerful. It also generated new churches, schools, and volunteer organizations that helped the new nation thrive.

The Revolution rejected the monarchy, and the Bill of Rights disestablished religion. But slavery, the worst establishment of all, remained. The contradictions between American freedom and African bondage, Christian love and chattel slavery, cried out for resolution. The African American poet Phillis Wheatley wrote in 1774 that "God has implanted a Principle, which we call Love of Freedom," in every human being "and is impatient of Oppression, and pants for Deliverance." Wheatley pointed out that American patriots fought for liberty while wielding "oppressive Power over others."[31] It would take some ninety years and America's bloodiest war to uproot slavery and extend the promises of the Revolution to all Americans.

Suggestions for Further Reading

Books

Gaustad, Edwin. *The Great Awakening in New England* (Peter Smith, 1965). This brief, classic text is one of the best introductions to the Great Awakening.

May, Henry. *The Enlightenment in America* (Oxford University Press, 1978). May separates several strands of Enlightenment so that the reader can learn the themes, goals, and religious outcomes of each. Essential reading for understanding religion in America. The title notwithstanding, this book deals with the Enlightenment in Europe as well as America.

Wood, Gordon. *The Radicalism of the American Revolution* (Vintage, 1993). Wood shows how the American Revolution's assault on monarchy and hierarchy made it much more radical than has been supposed. Religious dimensions of society and politics are explored.

Websites

"Eighteenth-Century America" and "American Revolution." Parts 2 and 3 of an online exhibit by the Library of Congress entitled "Religion and the Founding of the American Republic."

Part 2 shows the appearance of eighteenth-century churches, describes the Great Awakening and Deism, and offers many period illustrations of eighteenth-century religious life: www.loc.gov/exhibits/religion/rel02.html

Part 3 documents the role of religion in the American Revolution with political cartoons, facsimiles of period writings, and portraits of key leaders: www.loc.gov/exhibits/religion/rel03.html

Discussion Questions

1. What populations did missionaries to North America try to reach, and what obstacles did these missionaries face?
2. Describe the message of the Great Awakening and the methods used to spread that message. What were the long-term effects of the Great Awakening?
3. What aspects of the Enlightenment were most attractive to American Christians?
4. "In the Revolutionary era and its aftermath, many Americans believed that God was using their struggle to usher in a new phase of history, in which democracy and Christianity would join forces to spread the light of truth and progress throughout the world" (p. 41). Whether or not you agree with such beliefs, how have these ideas shaped our history?
5. Why did American Catholics so strongly support the Revolution?
6. What did the American founders intend the relationship of religion and government to be? How does that compare to the relationship of religion to government today?

CHAPTER THREE

Christianity in the New Republic

Westward Expansion

After the Revolutionary War, the trickle of settlers crossing the Appalachian Mountains swelled to a flood. Within a few decades the Mississippi Valley—an area comparable in size to western Europe—was settled and organized into states. This settlement was one of "most decisive events in history" because through it the "United States ceased to be a small, struggling ex-colony and turned itself into a major nation."[1] Christians played a strong role in westward expansion. Not only did they carry Christianity with them; they recruited new Christians and convinced many nominal ones to recommit to the faith. They built churches, schools, and hospitals. They organized voluntary societies and distributed literature. All these efforts helped lay the foundations of a new civilization west of the Appalachians.

Native Americans fought to hold back the flood of settlers. But in every conflict east of the Mississippi—from the Seminole War in Florida to the Blackfoot War in Illinois and Wisconsin, Native resistance was crushed. Many Christians thought that Indian removal (to lands west of the Mississippi) was inevitable, but some wanted to live peacefully alongside Native peoples. The way to do this, they believed, was to convert Native peoples and help them to assimilate into American culture. White people tended to see conversion and assimilation as two sides of one coin.

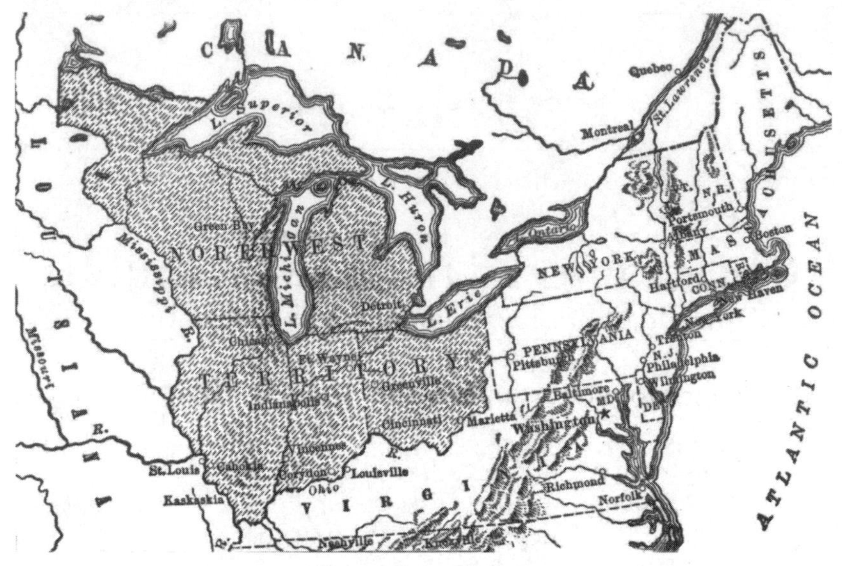

The Northwest Territory

In pre–Civil War America, Christian missions to Native Americans were scattered from New York to Minnesota, with several along the Great Lakes. Other missions clustered south of the Tennessee border and, to the west, in the Oklahoma or Washington territories.[2] Between 1800 and 1860, Catholics and many Protestant groups ran missions that included both a church and a schoolhouse. Mission schools often received federal subsidies because Christianizing the Indians was thought to be in the national interest. But settlers had a relentless appetite for land. The resulting wars and broken treaties made Christianity much harder for Native peoples to accept.

A brief exception was the mission to the Cherokee, who lived in the land we now know as western North Carolina, eastern Tennessee and northern Georgia. Several Christian groups sent missionaries, and the Cherokee slowly and steadily accepted the Christian faith. Historian Mark Noll notes that religious conversion was accompanied by cultural change as the Cherokee "built roads, organized politically in imitation of whites, rendered their language in writing, and began to print their own books and newspapers." Many of the Cherokee adopted white ways in hopes of securing their place in the new United States. But when gold was discovered in northern Georgia, whites clamored for Cherokee land. In 1830 the Indian Removal Act forced the "five civilized tribes" of the South (Cherokee, Seminole, Choctaw, Chickasaw, and Creek) to relocate to "Indian Territory" (Oklahoma). Over a ten-year period, some seventy thousand Native Americans were forced to march west under military guard. Thousands died of disease and starvation along what became known as the Trail of Tears. The missionaries who had worked among the Cherokee "now were forced to watch their country, supposedly the embodiment of Christian civilization, turn violently against a people that had responded to their message."[3] Some of these missionaries went to Oklahoma with the Cherokee. The Native lands were soon claimed by whites, many of whom brought African slaves to help clear the frontier.

So the frontier was always moving. Some said that the frontier was gone when you could see the smoke from your neighbor's chimney, or when the lawyers arrived, or when a church was built. Rough log churches sprang up overnight, only to be replaced with church buildings more like the ones back east. "Churches appeared early and in surprising numbers. Methodists in Pittsburgh established eight congregations during the decade after 1796, and Cincinnati residents could choose among six denominations by 1815."[4] The churches instilled standards of behavior that were the basis for society. But those who preferred lawlessness made havens for themselves in the West, in places like Rogues' Harbor, Kentucky, which traveling Methodist preacher Peter Cartwright described as "a desperate state of society. Murderers, horse thieves, highway robbers, and counterfeiters fled there, until they combined and actually formed a majority."[5] Cartwright would have been hard pressed to gather a congregation there.

Revivalism

More typical on the frontier were the people who grubbed a living from land that had never been cleared or plowed. When a crop failed or a baby died, when winter closed in or sickness swept through a settlement, faith in God helped many a pioneer to hold on. Revivalism was well suited to the stark conditions of frontier life, where death was an ever-present reality. Revival preaching confronted people with sin and damnation, and it promised pardon and release to true believers. Revivalism aimed to "save souls" by bringing people though a spiritual crisis called conversion. Church buildings and highly educated ministers were not needed, for revivals could take place anywhere and be led by preachers who had little or no formal training.

The most famous frontier revival took place in 1801 at Cane Ridge, Kentucky. Thousands of people came from places like Ohio and Tennessee and camped out for several days at Cane Ridge. These multitudes were divided into smaller crowds so that everyone could hear a preacher. And the preachers—Presbyterian, Methodist, and Baptist—pleaded with people to turn from sin and embrace Jesus. Religious excitement swept through the camp at Cane Ridge, taking forms that surely would have scandalized the more respectable folk back east. Converts began to sing, dance, and faint. Some laughed uncontrollably, barked like dogs, or got "the jerks."

Barton W. Stone (1772–1844), a Presbyterian who later became a founder of the Christian Church (Disciples of Christ), was a leader of the Cane Ridge revival. Inspired by the religious ecstasy of earlier revivals, Stone wanted Cane Ridge to be like a new Pentecost—a dramatic outpouring of the Holy Spirit. Indeed, religious "exercises" were so wild that Cane Ridge came to occupy a place in the annals of revivalism not unlike the place of Woodstock in the annals of the 1960s counter-culture.

Frontier camp meetings, however, were only one type of revivalism. Colleges had revivals, too, such as the one that began at Yale in 1802 and converted many a student from "infidelity" (deism and skepticism) to Christianity. At Rochester, New York, a revival took place among shopkeepers and merchants in 1830–31. Even bankers and businessmen in New York City, Philadelphia, and Boston were caught up in the urban "prayer meeting revival" of 1857–59. Revivals reached across the divides between the frontier and long-settled areas, urban and rural places, educated and uneducated people.

The nineteenth-century revivals had much in common with the Great Awakening of the 1740s. Both revival epochs centered on the new birth, used traveling preachers as agents of salvation, and sparked conflicts with traditional forms of Christianity. Yet the nineteenth-century revivals differed from the Great Awakening in important ways. Where the older

Camp meeting at Eastham, Massachusetts
Reprinted from *Gleason's Pictorial Magazine*, 1851

Awakening saw revivals as heaven-sent, nineteenth-century revivalists declared that human beings could make revivals happen. In colonial times, a theology of divine sovereignty held that God decides each person's eternal destiny; but in the nineteenth century, more and more preachers exhorted people to choose salvation for themselves. The Great Awakening had begun with the old colonial traditions—Congregational (Edwards), Presbyterian (Tennant), and Anglican (Whitefield). But in the nineteenth century, upstart groups like the Methodists, Baptists, and Disciples took center stage.

The differences between these two eras of revivalism point to a significant change: in the United States, Christianity was becoming less European and more American. The move toward a distinctively *American* form of Christianity is examined by historian Mark Noll,[6] who describes three major ingredients in this new synthesis of American Christianity. First is evangelical Christianity, with conversion (rather than sacraments, confessions, or clergy) as its hallmark. Second is "Common Sense Realism," which encourages people to draw their own conclusions rather than looking to traditional authorities. Third is representative government and democracy: Christians increasingly saw themselves as "voting"

Charles Grandison Finney
Photo courtesy of Oberlin College Archives

for their own religion through conversion, rather than inheriting the faith of their forbears. If people could interpret Scripture for themselves, then traditional religious authorities were less important—perhaps irrelevant. In nineteenth-century American revivalism, the freedom of the individual was more important than the sovereignty of God.

No one pushed harder for this change than Charles Grandison Finney (1792–1875). Finney was an apprentice lawyer in upstate New York when a vivid conversion experience moved him to "plead the cause of the Lord Jesus Christ." Finney began preaching in newly settled areas, such as upstate New York; later he refined his style to suit more sophisticated crowds in Boston, New York City, and London. In 1835 Finney was called to teach at what is now Oberlin College, where he later served as president.

Finney was famous for the techniques he used in revivals. These techniques, called "the new measures," were spelled out in Finney's *Lectures on Revivals of Religion* (1835). Just as a farmer plants seeds to reap a harvest, Finney declared, so Christians conduct revivals to make converts. The most famous new measure was the "anxious bench" (front row) in a revival meeting. People seeking conversion would come to the anxious bench to be preached and prayed over the threshold of conversion. The anxious bench helped induce labor for the new birth.

The use of techniques like the anxious bench signaled major changes in theology. Instead of a sovereign God who arbitrarily chooses ("elects") some people for salvation and others for damnation, Finney preached that God is the Supreme Moral Agent, reasonable and benevolent. It would be unreasonable for God to demand conversion if people are not able to change their own hearts. Finney saw people as free moral agents, able to be good citizens in God's moral government and to be saved *because they choose to be.* Finney blended Enlightenment views of progress, reason, and morality with an evangelical zeal for conversion. This faith in human potential led him to exhort Christians to seek moral and social perfection—they should never be "satisfied until they are as perfect as God."[7]

Finney urged new converts and mature Christians to enlist in God's campaign against sin and suffering.[8] Many people joined voluntary or "benevolent" societies. In the early nineteenth century, there were hundreds of societies, each with a specific agenda. The most important cause was the abolition of slavery; other projects included temperance (limiting the use of alcohol), Bible and tract distribution, education, and Sabbath observance. Benevolent societies formed a vast network of members, donors, and leaders collectively known as "the benevolent empire." By 1834 the combined budgets of the leading benevolent societies "rivaled the major expenditures of the federal government."[9]

Christian activists sought to rid the world of sin and evil to prepare the world for Christ's return. Finney preached that if Christians would make themselves useful to the highest degree, revivals and reforms would bring in the millennium (a thousand-year period in which sin and Satan are banished; Revelation 20:1-6). Christ was expected to return *after* the millennium (hence the term "post-millennialism"). Christians could hasten the millennium and speed the return of Christ by making converts and by ridding the world of sin. Charles Finney saw slavery as blocking the millennium, because slavery was sinful and Christ would not return to a sinful world.[10] The vision of a future free from sin (including social sin such as slavery) blended Enlightenment faith in progress with Christian belief in the second coming of Christ. Although it may seem far-fetched today, in the first half of the nineteenth century, this grand optimism inspired Christians to combine evangelism and social reform—two aspects of Christian life that later generations would pull apart.

Methodists and the Baptists

Finney's revival techniques owed much to the Methodists and Baptists, two groups which enjoyed phenomenal growth in early nineteenth-century America. The Methodists were founded in England by John Wesley (1703–1791) as a renewal movement within the Church of England. The Methodists urged people to experience God directly and personally and to live the Christian life with discipline and joy. They took their message to factory towns and coal mines and other places seldom reached by the Church of England. The Methodists loved singing. Their hymns, especially those written by Charles Wesley, spread the movement. Organization was another key to their growth. John Wesley sent traveling preachers out on routes ("circuits") and created a system of small groups ("classes") that involved every Methodist in fellowship and service. The Methodists reached the American colonies by the 1760s.

American Methodists officially separated from the Church of England in 1784 at the "Christmas Conference" in Baltimore. At least two things compelled the American Methodists to make this break. First, the Methodists in America needed a new identity. In the wake of the Revolution, they could ill afford to be associated with the Church of England, and they were embarrassed by John Wesley's opposition to American independence. The second concern was mission strategy. Unlike the Church of England, whose educated ministers served in settled parishes, the American Methodists needed traveling preachers who could speak the language of frontier people. So many Americans were leaving their old communities behind and moving west beyond the Appalachian Mountains. For people on the move, it was a conversion experience, not a particular congregation or tradition, that defined their faith. The Methodist strategy of circuit riders who preached for conversion was much better suited to the frontier than the traditional Anglican system.

At the helm of early American Methodism was Francis Asbury (1745–1816). Sent from England by John Wesley in 1771, Asbury later assumed the title of bishop—against Wesley's wishes. So strong was Asbury's command over his preachers that critics charged Methodists with "popery" and monarchy. But Asbury asked nothing of his preachers that he himself was not willing to endure: he traveled the wilderness for decades, never marrying or acquiring wealth. Asbury understood his authority as a bishop to come from his apostolic sufferings. Thus, his "Episcopal vision, premised on Jesus' saying that 'the first shall be last,' was a radical inversion of worldly power"[11] that won respect on the frontier.

Asbury demanded that his preachers "itinerate" (travel) rather than "locate" (settle down). Itinerancy was a mark of the apostolic church, Asbury believed. Following Wesley's strategy and Asbury's orders and example, Methodist preachers were "circuit riders." The ideal circuit rider was self-taught, young, and single. (Marriage made preachers want to settle down, and married preachers needed money to support their families.) Like the medieval mendicant (begging) orders, circuit riders relied on the kindness of common people for food, clothes, and shelter. Often they slept out in the cold; many died from exposure and fatigue. But their circuits reached everywhere. So aggressive and so thorough was the Methodist advance that other preachers lamented "The Methodists always get there first."

The spectacular rise of Methodism—from a fledgling renewal movement to the largest Protestant group in the U.S. by 1850—owed much to its message. "Early Methodism," notes Mark Noll, offered people "a loving God able to touch people with his Holy Spirit, able to enfold them into supportive fellowship with others who had also felt the touch of justifying grace, and able to nerve them for lives of self-disciplined sacrifice to others."[12] American Methodism, however, changed along with the frontier. Its ministry gradually became more settled. Education came to be more highly valued. By 1860 the Methodists had founded many schools, including those known today as Wesleyan, DePauw, Northwestern, and Boston universities. Church buildings became more sophisticated. And although conversion remained a strong emphasis for much of the nineteenth century, Christian nurture slowly became the preferred means for securing the next generation of Christians. In time, those who longed for the fervor of early Methodism separated to form "holiness churches."

The Baptists also grew dramatically in the nineteenth-century revivals. Like the Methodists, the Baptists preached for conversion and spoke the language of the common people. However, Methodists and Baptists differed in several important respects—above all, in their understanding and practice of baptism. For Baptists, baptism was a public testimony to grace already received; conversion came before baptism. Following New Testament accounts, baptism was done by immersion. The Methodists, in contrast, practiced infant baptism as a means of grace that prepares one for conversion. Following the practice of their parent church, the Church of England, Methodists usually baptized only the person's head. Frontier legends of Methodist and Baptist rivalries abound, usually with the mode of baptism as the flash point. But Methodists and Baptists also differed in their modes of ministry. In contrast to the Methodists with their circuit riders under a bishop's control, Baptists tended to call their preachers from within each congregation, and preachers supported themselves by farming. When Baptists went west, they often brought their own preacher with them.

Methodists and Baptists differed theologically. Methodists strove for sanctification (perfection or freedom from sin's power), a goal most Baptists rejected as unreachable due to original sin. Methodists believed that Christ's death on the cross gave *all people* the potential to embrace Christ through repentance and conversion; but some (not all) Baptists believed that God elects *particular individuals* to salvation. Among themselves, Baptists could differ in theology and practice. In time, the Baptists surpassed the Methodists as the largest Protestant group in the United States.

We should not give the impression that revivalism was just for Protestants. Nineteenth-century Roman Catholics had a form of revivalism called the "parish mission," in which traveling priests preached for repentance. Those who were brought to conviction by the preacher were directed to the confessional, where a priest would absolve them of their sins. According to Catholic historian Jay Dolan, the parish missions gave people the opportunity of "getting religion and setting oneself straight with God as the church had traditionally instructed."[13] Catholic revivals caught on in the 1840s and '50s and for decades remained an important means of recruiting immigrants and transforming nominal Catholics into devout, active ones.

This widespread use of revivalism helped to make Christianity more democratic and, hence, more American. According to Nathan Hatch, popular religious movements of the early republic were militantly democratic in spirit. "They denied the age-old distinction that set clergy apart as a separate order." Instead of traditional religious authority, revivals promoted the religious experiences of ordinary people. Revivalism became the religious counterpart of the quest for political, economic, and social equality in America.[14]

Pioneers of social equality included female preachers among Methodists, Baptists, and other new groups. In the period between 1790 and 1845, according to historian Catherine Brekus, "none of these women were ordained and, technically, they were not even licensed.... Nevertheless, clerical leaders wrote women letters of recommendation giving them official permission to preach."[15] African Methodists and Baptists also had female preachers, such as Jarena Lee (1783–1850), who was for thirty years an itinerant preacher.

Gains for women, however, were hard to sustain. Some evangelical groups sought social respectability and began to develop a professional ministry. Since ministerial training and systems of church governance were for men only, female preachers often found themselves excluded from the very groups that had briefly tolerated (if not welcomed) them. During the 1830s, ministers of several groups passed "a flurry of resolutions forbidding women to pray aloud, lecture or preach."[16] Some female preachers responded by seeking religious frontiers where regulations and social constraints had not yet closed in. For example, Brekus documents at least twenty-two female preachers among the Millerites—a revivalist group that expected Christ's immediate return.[17]

In pre–Civil War America, a famous female religious leader was Phoebe Palmer (1807–1874).[18] Inspired by the writings of John Wesley, Palmer sought to rekindle the fervor of early Methodism. She preached at hundreds of camp meetings and revivals in the U.S., Canada, and Great Britain. Palmer was an early advocate for the religious leadership of women. She also supported ministries for the urban poor. Most important, she pioneered the holiness movement that later contributed to modern Pentecostalism.

Critiques of Revivalism

Revivalism had many critics. For example, John Williamson Nevin (1803–1886), a German Reformed theologian, saw revivalism as sectarian and individualistic. In his 1843 book, *The Anxious Bench*, Nevin charged that revivalism glorified personal conversion at the expense of Christian community and the sacraments. A second critic was Horace Bushnell (1802–1876), a Congregationalist pastor and leader in Christian education. In his 1847 book, *Christian Nurture,* Bushnell urged Christians to bring up their children so that they would never know a time when they were not Christians. Bushnell insisted that the family (not the revivalist) should bring people into the faith and that a gradual shaping of character (not a crisis experience of conversion) was the best way for people to become Christians. A third important critic of revivalism was Charles Hodge (1797–1878), a Princeton seminary professor and staunch defender of "Old School Presbyterianism." Hodge was open to revivals and conversions if they were theologically grounded in the grace of God, given by Christ and his cross. Hodge rejected Finney's perfectionism and Finney's view of human free will. Hodge insisted that people are not the agents of their own salvation.

By promoting the sacraments, Christian nurture, and classical theology, these critics of revivalism were dealing with largely mainstream issues. But while these debates were going on, a new set of movements was growing, movements that would make even Charles Grandison Finney look tame.

New Movements

One such movement was "Restorationism," so named because it sought to restore the church to its New Testament purity. As far as the Restorationists were concerned, any development of Christianity that took place after the New Testament—such as creeds, confessions, and a formal ministry—should be purged away. Historian Brooks Holifield notes that Restorationism sprang from Baptist and Presbyterian origins and appealed to a populist spirit: old hierarchies were to be cast aside and religious power vested in the people.[19]

An early leader of Restorationism was Barton W. Stone (1772–1844), noted earlier for his role in the Cane Ridge revival. Although he had roots in the Presbyterian Church, Stone later embraced "primitive" Christianity and rejected denominations; his followers simply called themselves "Christians." A second key leader of Restorationism was Alexander Campbell (1788–1866). Born in Ireland and nurtured in the Scottish Presbyterian church, Campbell became a traveling preacher in America. He took the Bible as his sole authority and rejected denominations and creeds. Campbell preached that each person should simply decide to be a Christian and then be baptized for the remission of sins. Campbell's followers were known as "disciples." When he denounced all churchly forms (including denominations, synods, and ministerial ordination), Campbell made enemies. He also rejected the doctrine of the Trinity because he did not find it in the Bible. Musical instruments were not to be used in worship, since they are not mentioned in the New Testament. All of this and more followed Campbell's motto: "Where the Scriptures speak, we speak. Where the Scriptures are silent, we are silent."

In 1831 many followers of Stone, Campbell, and others formed the Christian Church (Disciples of Christ). The new church enjoyed rapid growth, claiming about one million members by 1900. But this movement, which began as a call for unity and simplicity, split apart and added three new groups to the list of American denominations.

Restorationists and other revival converts were among the early followers of Joseph Smith (1805–1844), founder of the Latter-day Saints, popularly known as Mormons.[20] Smith began his religious movement in upstate New York—an area called the "burned over district" because of the religious fervor that blazed through that region in the early 1800s. But Smith led his disciples beyond Christian primitivism into a new religion, with its own unique theology and scriptures, worship and ethics.

Joseph Smith was a man of great personal charisma. As a youth, Smith had a vision in which Christ warned him not to join any denomination, since none of them represented true Christianity. Further instructions came some years later: Smith claimed that an angel led him to a hillside near Palmyra, New York, and showed him where to dig for golden plates. These plates, according to Smith, were inscribed with scriptures written in an ancient language. Smith translated the text by means of two "seer" or "peep" stones, a form of folk magic. In 1830 this work was published as the *Book of Mormon.* Smith's new revelation claimed that ancient tribes of Israel had migrated to America, where Christ appeared to them in person. Critics dismissed the *Book of Mormon* as a fraud, but to Smith and his followers, its publication signaled that God was about to restore the true church and gather believers into an American Zion.

Not long after the *Book of Mormon* was published, Mormon settlements sprang up in Ohio, Missouri, and Illinois. In each place, violence flared and "Gentiles" (non-Mormons) forced the Latter-day Saints out. A simple explanation for these events is religious persecution. But the Mormons themselves did much to alarm their Gentile neighbors. For example, Mormons could swing local elections by voting in large blocks as Smith directed. Some of the Mormon leaders seem to have engaged in bank fraud, real estate scams, and counterfeiting.[21]

In Missouri, both Mormons and Gentiles formed vigilante groups, vandalizing, stealing from, and killing each other. Large in Mormon memory is the Haun's Mill Massacre of 1838, in which some two hundred armed Missourians murdered seventeen Mormons—including old people and children—and dumped the bodies down a well. This atrocity may have been an attempt to carry out Missouri governor Lilburn Boggs's decree that Mormons must leave that state or be exterminated. After issuing the decree, Boggs himself barely survived an assassination attempt, probably carried out by Joseph Smith's bodyguard.

Forced out of Missouri, the Mormons settled in Commerce, Illinois, and renamed it "Nauvoo." There the Mormons drained swamps, established farms and businesses, and began work on an impressive temple overlooking the Mississippi River. Smith appointed himself the commander of the Nauvoo Legion, a fighting force of some four thousand men. Rumors of polygamy began to spread, angering both Gentiles and many Mormons who could not believe that their leaders would take multiple wives.

When a disgruntled Mormon in Nauvoo published an exposé of polygamy, Joseph Smith ordered the offending printing press to be destroyed. Smith's contempt for freedom of the press enraged the governor and many citizens of Illinois. In July 1844, Joseph Smith and several Mormon leaders were jailed in Carthage, Illinois, on multiple charges. When the jail was conveniently left unguarded, a mob shot and killed Joseph Smith and his brother Hyrum. After Smith's assassination, conflict over who would succeed him as prophet and revelator split the Mormons into several factions. The largest group trekked to the Utah Territory under the leadership of Brigham Young (1801–1877). As we shall see in a later chapter, the move to the Utah Territory made it possible for Mormons to thrive as an independent religious movement, far beyond the mainstream of American Christianity.

Communal Experiments

Pre–Civil War America became a laboratory for religious experiments. Even though the great majority of people stayed within more conventional forms of Christianity, there were always some who thought they could discover, restore, or invent true religion. Available land helped to make these experiments possible.

Take, for example, the Shakers. Their movement began in England with "Mother" Ann Lee (1736–1784), who was one of the "shaking Quakers" (people who shook with fervor in worship). Mother Ann's children died in infancy, and in her grief she received visions that she believed were from God. In these visions, she saw herself as a female incarnation of God, a counterpart to Jesus. Ann Lee came to believe that sexual intercourse was the source of all sin and that the family was based on carnal lust. Therefore, the perfect community must practice celibacy, which alone could bring equality between the sexes. When Mother Ann preached in public, she was attacked by mobs and imprisoned.

Ann Lee came to America in 1774 with only eight or nine followers. The group began to attract revival converts who sought a radically new way of life; the Shakers also grew by adopting orphans. The Shakers fit into larger patterns of early nineteenth-century revivalism: conversion, striving for perfection, and intense faith in Christ's second coming. Yet the Shakers were distinctive in their insistence on celibacy and their attitude toward property. Their basis for Christian community was the village, where property was held in common and all duties were shared. They built villages in which men and women lived separately and everyone contributed to farmwork or crafts. Shakers marketed products such as cloth, furniture, and seeds, and the proceeds helped to support their communities.

The Shaker rule of celibacy freed women from childbearing and childrearing, but it also meant that without new converts or the steady adoption of orphans, the movement would eventually die out. At their high point, the Shakers had perhaps as many as five thousand members living in villages scattered across New England, New York, Ohio, Indiana, and Kentucky. But revivals receded, and industrialization decreased the demand for Shaker products. At the close of the twentieth century, only one Shaker village remained, with just a few believers.

Another experimental group linked to revivalism was the Oneida Community, founded by John Humphrey Noyes (1811–1886). Noyes was a revival convert who believed that Christ had already returned and that true Christians (such as himself) were sinless. Noyes envisioned the perfect society as holding everything in common, including property, industry, and spouses. In 1846 in Vermont, Noyes instituted "complex marriage," in which any adult male in the community could have sexual relations with any adult female. Children would be raised communally. Outraged neighbors forced Noyes and his followers to flee. After moving to Oneida, New York, the community grew to about two hundred members, supporting themselves through logging, farming, and the manufacture of steel traps. Another Oneida community excelled in the crafting of fine silverware, by which the Oneida name is still widely known. In 1879 Noyes fled to Canada to escape lawsuits. Oneida community members abandoned complex marriage in favor of monogamy. Both the Shaker and the Oneida communities attempted to redefine or do without family and private property. These communal experiments were religiously based, but for the vast majority of Americans, religion was a support to traditional forms of community.

Changing Fortunes: The Older Protestant Churches

While revivalism spread westward, the older churches had to find their way forward. Of the former colonial churches, none faced greater challenges than the Episcopal Church (formerly the Church of England). Loyalty to England and its monarchy had been a hallmark of the Anglican Church in colonial times. After the Revolution, Americans of this tradition could hardly continue as "the Church of England." They began to use the phrase "Protestant Episcopal" to express their religious identity without emphasizing loyalty to England. The word "Episcopal" referred to a threefold ministry structure stemming from bishops and also including priests and deacons. As in the Church of England, the Episcopal worship was based on the Book of Common Prayer.

To continue as a viable religious community in the new United States, Episcopalians had to secure their own bishops. No longer could they, as in colonial times, be dependent on English bishops to ordain priests for America. It was necessary to have an American bishop who could ordain priests in the United States while still maintaining the continuity of apostolic succession as understood by that tradition. The Episcopalians therefore arranged to have their first bishop consecrated in Scotland (under the apostolic succession) before he came to the U.S. This made it possible to retain the apostolic succession without depending on English bishops. Another step toward autonomy was the founding of General Theological Seminary in New York in 1819.

The Protestant Episcopal Church grew very slowly in the first half of the nineteenth century. The departure of the Methodists did not help. And then there was money. Historian David Holmes notes that Episcopalians had grown used to state support and were not accustomed to fully funding their churches. "Once religion had been disestablished, the Episcopalians had to pay for clergy salaries, church building and upkeep on a voluntary basis." Nor was frontier mission a strong suit for the Episcopalians, since "most Episcopal clergy came from reasonably comfortable backgrounds [and] the frontier mission field held relatively little appeal for them."[22] There were exceptions, of course—including a few Episcopal circuit riders who preached conversion and gathered frontier congregations. In general, however, Episcopalians thrived in urban areas, where they attracted educated, well-to-do members. Episcopal leaders worked hard to rebuild old congregations and organize new ones "back east." By 1820 the Protestant Episcopal Church was slowly growing, so that by 1830 about 5 percent of American Christians were Episcopalians.

In the early nineteenth century, there were at least two ways to be Episcopalian in America. In the tradition of George Whitefield, the Anglican revivalist of colonial times, there were "evangelicals" who preached for conversion. In contrast, the "high church" party emphasized liturgy, episcopacy, and sacraments. By mid-century the high church party received fresh inspiration from the Oxford movement, which arose in England in the 1830s to renew the church by returning to Catholic tradition. In America, the Oxford movement grew in importance after the Civil War—not only among Episcopalians but among several other Protestant denominations.

To follow this theme of how the once-dominant colonial churches fared in the new United States, we turn now to the Congregationalists and Presbyterians, heirs of Puritanism. In 1800 these two groups held a much larger share of the Christian population than they do today. They had the prestigious schools of Harvard, Yale, and Princeton. The heirs of Puritanism still enjoyed cultural dominance—especially in New England. But as the nineteenth century progressed, a very significant change took place. Historian Mark Noll describes this change as "the eclipse of Calvinist pre-eminence."[23] Internal conflicts, cultural changes, and competition from new religious groups all helped to reduce this once-powerful tradition to a shadow of its former self.

The most spectacular internal conflict took place among Congregationalists. The flash point was Unitarianism (named for its rejection of the Christian doctrine of the Trinity and its affirmation that God is one person, not three). Unitarianism has its roots in Enlightenment religion, and made its American debut in colonial Boston. More was at stake than the doctrine of the Trinity. The Unitarians believed in human morals and a reasonable, benevolent God. They rejected classic Calvinist doctrines such as original sin and predestination. Meanwhile, Congregationalists who clung to doctrinal orthodoxy were losing ground as Harvard College and many of the oldest churches in eastern Massachusetts became Unitarian. Battles for control of these venerable institutions rocked New England Congregationalism and severely weakened it.

An early leader of Unitarianism in the nineteenth century was William Ellery Channing (1780–1842), a Harvard graduate. Channing led Boston's prestigious Federal Street Church from Congregationalism to Unitarianism. Channing did not see humans as depraved sinners in need of salvation. Rather, he thought that people already have "the seeds of the same excellence" as God. Therefore "true religion consists in...a growing likeness to the Supreme Being."[24] Another leading Unitarian minister was Theodore Parker (1810–1860). An early voice for American Protestant liberalism,[25] Parker insisted that creeds, confessions, and theology were transient—while the ethical teachings of Jesus and the goodness of human nature were permanent.

But Unitarianism soon morphed into another movement, called transcendentalism. A cadre of Unitarian ministers and writers found Unitarianism too formal, cold, and rational. They created a romantic literary ethos called transcendentalism, with Ralph Waldo Emerson (1803–1882) as their most famous bard. As a young Unitarian minister, Emerson found that he could no longer in good conscience preside over the Lord's Supper or lead in public prayer. He left the ministry to launch a literary career that had deeply religious themes. For example, in his 1838 address to the senior class of Harvard Divinity School, Emerson proclaimed that religion "cannot be received second hand."[26] Emerson allowed that old rituals may once have expressed heartfelt religion, but now these dead forms were keeping people away from God. And God, said Emerson, is not to be found in scriptures, creeds, or sacraments, but within the self and in nature.

Unitarianism and its runaway child, transcendentalism, were too radical for most heirs of Puritanism. What moderate Congregationalists and Presbyterian leaders sought was a way to update their tradition and still hold on to core beliefs. Nathaniel William Taylor (1786–1858), professor of theology at Yale Divinity School, paved the way. True to the spirit of the times, Taylor valued moral reform and human ability to do the right. He worried that the old Calvinist belief in total depravity might excuse people from striving for a better society. In his address *Concio ad Clerum* (Advice to Clergy), Taylor told ministers to move their hearers to good works—not give them reasons to be passive. Instead of being born in sin, he said, people *become* sinful by their own acts and choices. At the same time, however, we *do* have the power not to sin and we can do our duty before God. In the age-old conflict between sin and free will, Taylor wanted to have some of each.

Putting Taylor's theology into action was one of the most influential ministers of the early nineteenth century. Lyman Beecher (1775–1863) served Presbyterian and Congregationalist churches. He was a revivalist and seminary president who raised a family of preachers and reformers. Beecher fought to keep Unitarianism from spreading. But later in his life, he himself was tried for heresy by staunch Calvinists who accused him of tinkering with Puritan doctrine.

Meanwhile, the Congregationalists faced the practical issue of how to expand westward. In colonial New England, educated ministers might spend decades serving the same church. But frontier religion called for self-taught preachers who could "itinerate." Congregationalists hoped that they could move westward more effectively by joining forces with the Presbyterians. In 1801 the Congregationalists and Presbyterians entered into a "Plan of Union." Under this plan, these two denominations could have their members join each other's churches; they could also share clergy and cooperate in founding new congregations and schools. By 1835 some 149 "Presbygational" churches had been planted in the Western Reserve[27] and several colleges as well. Eventually many of these churches became Presbyterian.

Compared with the Episcopalians and the Congregationalists, the Presbyterians were in the best position to thrive in the early nineteenth century. Their rate of growth in the first half of the 1800s puts them just behind the Methodists and the Baptists.[28] The Presbyterians did not suffer disestablishment. They did not have to redefine their identity, as did the Episcopalians. The Presbyterians had theological conflicts, but they also had a ministry and an administrative structure that could deploy itinerant or settled ministers as needed. In the early 1800s, Presbyterians were gathering congregations in Pennsylvania, Ohio, Kentucky, and Tennessee. "By 1850 they had founded churches in every state east of the Mississippi River, as well as [territories] bordering it on the west, with additional congregations in Texas and California."[29] All of these factors counted, but perhaps the biggest reason for Presbyterian growth was revivalism.

Revivalism brought conflict as well as converts. As we have seen, several of the great religious entrepreneurs of the early nineteenth century (Alexander Campbell, W. Barton Stone, and Charles Finney) started out in Presbyterianism but decided to leave. Through it all, Presbyterians insisted on having pastors who were firmly grounded in Presbyterian theology. Princeton Seminary was founded in 1812, close to the older Princeton University. Princeton Seminary was a stronghold of Old School Presbyterianism. Indeed, one of its most famous professors, Charles Hodge, declared that no new ideas came from Princeton. For Hodge, "theological truth [remained] in static categories which were not influenced by historic development."[30] Though not so immune from change as it claimed to be, Princeton Seminary prepared faithful ministers who served not only in the East but in the South and in the growing Midwest as well.

The churches that had been so powerful before the Revolution (Anglicans, Congregationalists and Presbyterians) found themselves in a changed world. The frontier, revivalism, and theological revisions all played a part. And so did the arrival of millions of Europeans who were not part of the Anglo-Protestant tradition.

Catholics and Lutherans

Catholics and Lutherans were not likely to view each other as fellow travelers in early nineteenth-century America; they tended to see each other more as different religions than as fellow Christians. Yet the similarities between Lutheran and Catholic experience are considerable. Neither of these groups belonged to the Anglo-Protestant culture. Catholics were the consummate outsiders. And Lutherans, though Protestant, long remained on the margins, set apart by language and by theological heritage.

Both groups experienced tensions around "Americanization." Some wanted to adapt to American ways and forge a distinctively American Catholicism or Lutheranism. But others wanted to stay "pure" from the corrupting influences they observed in their new homeland. Both groups grew rapidly from immigration. Between 1815 and 1860, about five million people immigrated to America; a great many of these were English and Irish, with a large portion from Germany as well. Lutherans and Catholics came from many ethnic groups, so that *keeping* the Catholics together under one umbrella and *bringing* the Lutherans together comprised a significant part of each group's efforts in America. With these parallels between Catholics and Lutherans in mind, we will turn to each group separately.

As the nineteenth century began, Catholicism *was* Christianity in Mexico, the Southwest, and much of Canada. But in the U.S., Catholics were a small minority concentrated in Maryland. In 1830 Catholics comprised about 4 percent of Christians in the U.S. But by 1890 more than 30 percent of all American Christians were Catholics.[31]

As Catholics settled in America, they created institutions to sustain their faith and to build community. The key institution was the parish. "In a local community, the parish is a particular representation of the Church universal; this is where the local Catholic community manifests its beliefs."[32] So the parish was more than a church building. It was people: the priest, the nuns, and the families. It was also a complete network of schools, businesses, and charities. The parish was a community for celebrations, mutual aid, and devotion: a Catholic subculture in a Protestant nation.

In the late eighteenth century, Catholic parishes tended to be defined by location, not by a particular ethnic or language group. But in the nineteenth century, the huge immigration began to change things:

> Even though they might have lived in the same area or city, German and Irish Catholics were not willing to worship in the same church. Each group wanted to worship and pray in its own language and according to the tradition and custom of the Old World; as more diverse groups of Catholic immigrants arrived in the United States, the problem became even more acute.[33]

The solution was the national or ethnic parish (German, Irish, and so on), which became the center of life for immigrant Catholics.

Conflicts over authority roiled many a Catholic parish in the nineteenth century. Traditional, European-style Catholicism ran on a chain of command, in which authority flowed from the pope to the bishops to the priests. At the parish level, the laity were expected to "pay, pray, and obey." But things could be different in America, where Catholic laity took it upon themselves to construct the church buildings and organize parishes in hopes of securing a priest—probably a priest from Europe. Meanwhile, American ideals of self-government influenced Catholic as well as Protestant church life. Representative government was the new ideal, and many American Catholics wanted a voice in their parishes as well as in politics. Each church, whether Catholic or Protestant, was required by law to have a board of trustees responsible for church property. Thus, among American Catholics, a system called "trusteeism" arose in which trustees (laymen) made decisions for the parish. In matters of governance, Catholic parishes run by trustees had much in common with their Protestant neighbors.

Trusteeism did not have the last word in American Catholic life; traditional authority made a comeback as more priests became available and immigration reinvigorated old worldviews. Catholic historian Jay Dolan, whose work informs this section, notes that Catholics in the nineteenth century had more conflicts over authority than over doctrine. Nor did the conflict fall neatly with priests on one side and laity on the other. There were priests—usually Americianized ones—who encouraged lay leadership. And there were laypeople—usually recent immigrants—who expected the priest to run the parish. The traditional authoritarian model became a way of expressing Catholic identity and may have helped limit the number of ethnic schisms.

American Catholics faced internal conflict over authority in the parish. More ominous were the external threats. Anti-Catholic prejudice seemed to grow along with immigration. It was one thing for Catholics to be a small minority in places like Baltimore or Philadelphia. But when Catholics began arriving in large numbers, organizing parishes in Michigan, Ohio, upstate New York, Kentucky, and Missouri, many Protestants were alarmed. To be sure, the Constitution formally guaranteed religious freedom. But many Americans assumed that God intended the United States to be a Protestant country. They typically saw

Ruins of Ursuline Convent in Charleston, Massachusetts, after anti-Catholic rioters burned it in 1834.
Reprinted from *Some Events of Boston and Its Neighbors*. Boston: State Street Trust,1917.

Protestantism as the ally of representative government and Catholicism as the ally of papacy and monarchy. In the nineteenth century, many Protestants thought that Catholics, because of their loyalty to the pope, could not be good citizens in a democracy.

The relationship of Catholicism to democracy was addressed by Alexis de Tocqueville (1805–1859), a French philosopher who traveled extensively in the United States. Tocqueville, himself a Catholic, observed that "the Catholics are very loyal in the practice of their worship and full of zeal and ardor for their beliefs. Nevertheless, they form the most republican and democratic of all classes in the United States." Tocqueville saw Catholicism and democracy as a good combination for the United States for several reasons. First, as a minority, Catholics were bound to support religious freedom. Second, Catholics were obedient in matters of faith, but in politics they were open to "free investigation." Third, Catholicism encouraged faithful obedience to the priest and equality among all people, while "Protestantism in general orients men much less toward equality than toward independence."[34] In other words, a democracy needs people who see themselves as equal participants in a community—at least as much as it needs individualists.

Tocqueville's insights were ahead of his time; much more common were anti-Catholic sermons and tracts. Lurid tales of sexual abuse in convents or confessionals sold very well. The most notorious was *Awful Disclosures of the Hotel Dieu Nunnery of Montreal* (1836), purportedly written by an ex-nun named Maria Monk. The document was a fraud, and a very popular one indeed.

Anti-Catholicism found political expression in a movement called "nativism"—named for its intent to protect the interests of "native born" whites by keeping political power and jobs away from Catholic immigrants and other newcomers. Nativists held rallies that sometimes turned into violent riots, as in Philadelphia in 1844, when "two Roman Catholic churches and dozens of Irish homes were burned, militia fired point-blank upon advancing crowds, a cannon was turned against the soldiers guarding Saint Philip Neri Church, and for three days mob rule prevailed in the city." A few days later in New York City, local police refused to provide protection, so a Catholic bishop stationed "large numbers of fully armed men around every Catholic church" and thus prevented a repeat of what had happened in Philadelphia.[35]

The most powerful nativist party was nicknamed the "Know Nothings" because its members, if questioned about their beliefs and activities, were instructed to reply, "I know nothing." In 1855 the Know Nothings elected more than one hundred of their candidates to Congress. The party dissolved as secession and slavery took center stage, but after the Civil War, anti-Catholic prejudice took on new forms.

American Catholics were determined to keep a firm hold on their religious identity and demonstrate good citizenship. They built hospitals, schools, and orphanages. Sometimes these efforts were a direct response to prejudice in places where Catholic priests were not allowed to make pastoral calls in hospitals or where anti-Catholic attitudes pervaded schools. However, in other places, community needs rather than prejudice[36] were the chief motivation for building new institutions. Many non-Catholics benefited from Catholic hospitals and schools.

Lutherans did not have to contend with prejudice as ugly as anti-Catholicism, but in the decades following the Revolution, they did face threats from several directions. The Enlightenment convinced some Lutheran leaders to make reason and morals (rather than the Scriptures and the Lutheran Confessions) the center of faith. For example, in 1792 the Pennsylvania Ministerium omitted all reference to the Lutheran Confessions from their constitution; and in New York a new Lutheran catechism denied "the inspiration and authority of the Bible and the validity of the Apostles Creed and the chief Lutheran Confessions."[37] In some places it was possible to become a Lutheran pastor without making any commitment to the Lutheran Confessions.

Assimilation into other Protestant groups was a danger for Lutherans. In frontier areas with few resources and a shortage of clergy, Lutherans often joined forces with other Protestant neighbors, building churches, sharing ministers, and even worshiping together. "Union" congregations were formed in several places as Lutherans combined with Presbyterian, Reformed, or Episcopalian Christians. According to historian Abdel Ross Wentz, early nineteenth-century unionism "meant the decline of denominational consciousness, and for a time the new American impulse to union threatened the very existence of the [Lutheran] church in this country."[38] The situation illustrates how difficult it can be to have both unity and identity.

Language posed yet another challenge for Lutherans. Each German-speaking congregation had to decide whether—and when—to switch over to English. Successive waves of Lutheran immigrants (German, Swedish, Norwegian, Finnish, Danish, Slovak, and Icelandic) would face the same problem. In hindsight, the change to English seems inevitable. But making the transition was painful, for language connects people to culture, faith, and community. Many congregations split over language. Advocates for the continued use of German warned that much could be lost in translating the Confessions, hymns, and German Bible; false teachings might creep in. Meanwhile, those who called for the use of English warned that young adults would leave if the church clung to German. Indeed, Wentz reports that "thousands of young people" left the Lutheran churches over the language issue.

Beset by such challenges, the Lutherans had to gain a firmer footing. At the close of the eighteenth century, they organized new synods (regional bodies) to support and strengthen congregations and to secure faithful pastors—many of whom came from Germany. Some Lutherans rejected any other form of church besides the congregation or the regional body, but many others wanted to create a national organization. Thus, in 1820 the General Synod was formed as the first national Lutheran body. Its authority was limited, but it could initiate and support projects to strengthen American Lutheranism. The General Synod moved quickly to create the first permanent American Lutheran seminary, which opened in 1826 in Gettysburg, Pennsylvania. This was a major step for Lutherans in America. If Lutheran pastors could be trained at a Lutheran seminary in America, their church would be less dependent upon clergy imported from Europe or trained in seminaries of other denominations.

The Lutheran seminary's first professor and chief architect was Samuel Simon Schmucker (1799–1873), who also served as the seminary president. Schmucker wrote theological books and articles and addressed social issues. He opposed slavery and is said to have hidden runaway slaves in his home on the seminary campus. Schmucker called for equal treatment under the law for free African Americans in Pennsylvania. As he prized freedom, he also longed for Christian unity. Schmucker had studied at Princeton Seminary, and he identified with several forms of American Protestantism. In 1838 he published his *Fraternal Appeal to the American Churches*, which is remembered today as a forerunner of the modern ecumenical movement.

For the sake of evangelism and unity, Schmucker wanted to bridge the gap between Lutherans and Anglo-Protestants. He wanted American Lutherans to have a confession that expressed their current beliefs and practices, which he perceived as different from those of sixteenth-century German Lutherans. He worried that waves of Lutheran immigrants would set back the progress Lutherans had made in America. For all of these reasons, Schmucker made a bold—and disastrous—move. In 1855 he revised the Augsburg Confession. (The Augsburg Confession of 1530 was and is the cornerstone of Lutheran theology and the chief symbol of Lutheran identity.) Schmucker's edited version, with his explanations for the changes, was called the "Definite Platform."

Surrounded for the most part by like-minded people, Schmucker underestimated his opposition. The backlash against the Definite Platform caught him off guard. He had hoped to stem the rising tide of

Lutheran Confessionalism, which he called "Old Lutheranism." Many of these Old Lutherans were immigrants from Germany, but there were also American-born Lutherans who wanted to strengthen Lutheran identity and recommit to the Lutheran theology of the Reformation. Several streams fed into Lutheran Confessionalism in America, but in general it may be said that Confessionalists rejected American evangelicalism and had little use for ecumenism. Instead, they prized the German language and heritage, championed the ministry of Word and sacraments, and revered the Lutheran confessions not merely as a cultural symbol but as a theology to be proclaimed and lived. Schmucker wanted Protestant unity, but the Confessionalists prized Lutheran identity. Their differences were irreconcilable. Instead of providing a way for Lutherans to become more like other American Protestants, the Definite Platform became a catalyst for Lutheran rejection of outside influences.

New leaders arose to champion Lutheran confessionalism. Charles Porterfield Krauth (1823–1883) had studied under Schmucker but rejected his former professor's "American Lutheranism." A second Lutheran seminary opened in Philadelphia with Krauth at the helm. His book, *The Conservative Reformation and Its Theology*, fortified many Lutheran pastors in their theology and preaching. Meanwhile, in the Midwest, a strong confessional movement was led by C. F. W. Walther (1811–1887). A German pastor and theologian, Walther arrived in the United States in 1838 with a large German Lutheran immigration. He became the leader of what is now the Lutheran Church–Missouri Synod and president of Concordia Seminary in St. Louis. Walther wrote and published to defend confessional theology and to reject any influence that might corrupt Lutheranism. Walther hoped that the twin barriers of language and doctrine would preserve a pure form of Lutheranism. But while Walther sought to defend Lutheranism from outside influences, a much larger storm was brewing, leading the nation to civil war. The walls of language and theology would not keep Lutherans, Catholics, or others from being swept up in that great conflict.

Suggestions for Further Reading

Books

Brekus, Catherine. *Strangers and Pilgrims: Female Preaching in America 1740–1845* (University of North Carolina Press, 1998). Long before women's ordination, women were preaching. Brekus carefully documents the lives of female preachers with attention to their message, their ways of life, and their strategies for dealing with barriers to their leadership.

Hatch, Nathan. *The Democratization of American Christianity* (Yale University Press, 1989). This study probes the effects of democracy on Christianity in early nineteenth-century America. Religious authority was redefined in terms of individual rights and popular movements.

Noll, Mark. *America's God: From Jonathan Edwards to Abraham Lincoln* (Oxford University Press, 2002). This comprehensive study of American religious thought shows how Christian theology adapted to (and helped shape) a distinctly American environment. Noll examines the relationship between public life and religious thought and gives significant attention to the uses of the Bible in the crisis over slavery.

Websites

"Religion and the New Republic" Part 3 of an online exhibit by the Library of Congress entitled "Religion and the Founding of the American Republic." Brief descriptions and many graphics of camp meetings, the African American church, Mormonism, and benevolent societies: www.loc.gov/exhibits/religion/rel07.html

"Catholicism: Reaction and Radicalism." Primary sources in nineteenth-century Catholicism, including "On the Condition of the Working Classes (*Rerum Novarum*)." This section is part of the much larger "Internet Modern History Sourcebook" of Fordham University: www.fordham.edu/halsall/mod/modsbook37.html

Discussion Questions

1. At least by the early 1800s, Christianity in the United States was becoming more American and less European. Name three ingredients of this distinctively American Christianity.
2. Why did the Methodists and Baptists grow so fast in the first half of the nineteenth century?
3. How did American Christians blend revivalism and social reform in the nineteenth century? What may be learned from their example, positively or negatively?
4. Select *one* of the "new movements" or "communal experiments" described in this chapter. What was the appeal of this movement or experiment? Would it attract followers today? Why or why not?
5. What challenges did the former leading churches of colonial times (Congregational, Presbyterian, and Episcopal) face in the nineteenth century? Give one or two examples of how they responded to these challenges.
6. Can an immigrant group to adapt to American life without losing its identity? Give an example from the past or present to support your response.

CHAPTER FOUR

Slavery and Civil War

African American Christianity

Slavery is central to American history and to the story of Christianity in America. The so-called "peculiar institution" was so deeply imbedded in American life that it took a civil war to end it. Both slavery and the Civil War had religious dimensions, which are described in this chapter. For our purposes, the best place to begin is with African American Christianity. In the period leading up to the Civil War, three major factors shaped black Christianity: African heritage, slavery, and evangelical Protestantism.

Some aspects of African heritage were noted in chapter 1. But in contrast to colonial times, it was illegal after 1808 to bring African slaves into the U.S. Demands for slave labor were met mostly by "natural increase" and the internal slave trade. Historian Albert Raboteau notes that for American slaves, the "memories of Africa grew fainter with each passing generation." In the Caribbean, the slave population was continually "re-Africanized" through newly arriving slaves; but in the United States, the black population in the U.S. increasingly forged a religious faith among those born in North America.[1] Yet African heritage ran deep. Whites overhearing African Americans at worship reported a sharp sense of "otherness." For example, one white woman, "listening to the slaves on her plantation singing at a praise meeting, called their songs 'mostly a sort of weird chant that makes me feel all out of myself when I hear it way in the night, too far off to catch the words.'"[2] African dancing, though suppressed, lived on in the "ring shout," a circle dance in which people chanted and shuffled in "states of religious trance." Preaching was African, with the preacher and people using call and response to invoke God's presence.[3] Whites forbade the use of drums, but chanting and clapping preserved "the rhythmic drive of the drums that was so crucial in African worship."[4] This worship was deeply African: it was communal; it quickened body, mind, and emotions; it was alert to the spirit world.

African American Christianity was forged in the crucible of slavery. The experience of bondage called for a faith that could help people to endure with dignity, even as they longed for justice and deliverance. The outward conditions of slavery varied greatly. Huge numbers of slaves worked on large plantations, growing cash crops such as tobacco, rice, sugar cane, or cotton. These "field hands" lived in the slave quarters—rows of cabins or shacks set apart from the master's "big house." Other slaves did domestic work—cooking, cleaning, and childcare—sometimes living in the big house. On smaller farms, a white family might own just one or two slaves, and it was not unknown for blacks and whites to work the fields together. A smaller number of slaves were skilled in carpentry, blacksmithing, or other trades. Such slaves might "hire out" and work off the plantation, and their earnings would be paid to the master. A few slaves were allowed to save their wages and buy their own freedom.

But the vast majority of slaves had no exit. They struggled to endure, finding subtle ways to assert their own humanity under conditions that often were degrading and brutal. Many turned to Jesus for strength and hope, as in the words of the spiritual: "Nobody knows the trouble I see, nobody knows but Jesus."

Slavery and race were so deeply joined in America that it took an immigrant to state the obvious: Philip Schaff, a nineteenth-century German Reformed theologian, observed, "Of all the forms of slavery the American is the most difficult to dispose of, because it is not only a question of domestic institution and political economy, but of race. *The negro question lies far deeper than the slavery question.*"[5] Thus, even free blacks lived with the daily reality of slavery; and when slavery ended, the root problem of racism lived on.

Illustration used broadly in English and American anti-slavery campaigns
Photo © Snark/Art Resource, NY

Owners believed that the slaves were duty-bound not merely to work but to show obedience and deference to the master at all times. The master/slave relationship was based on paternalism, which historian Eric Foner describes as "a sense of obligation based on mastership over an inferior."[6] Masters felt entitled to the slaves' gratitude; after all, masters had purchased the slaves and provided them with food, clothing, and shelter. Even where genuine affection existed between master and slave, and where conditions were relatively humane, paternalism "undermined the slaves' sense of self-worth as black people and reinforced their dependence on their masters."[7]

Masters wanted Christianity to reinforce paternalism by teaching slaves to be grateful, obedient, and submissive. Christianity was often twisted to this purpose, but even so, many slaves sensed that Christianity was at odds with slavery. Christianity taught that all believers are children of the Most High God, redeemed ("bought back") by Christ. If one were bought by the blood of Christ, how could one still be owned by a human master? Many black Christians felt the contradiction between the claims of slavery and the claims of Christ.

Evangelical Protestantism was the third basic ingredient of African American religion before the Civil War. In evangelicalism, conversion is essential. It changes one's life and marks one as belonging to God. Albert Raboteau describes conversion in the context of slavery as a complete "reorientation of the convert's life." Converted blacks felt their "infinite worth as children of God, no matter what slaveholders thought and taught. For those facing the brutal conditions of slavery—the daily physical, psychological and emotional attacks against their worth as a person"[8] conversion was God's guarantee of their worth as human beings.

New converts received spiritual powers—public baptism, spiritual discipline, the support of other Christians, and the Bible. In most of the South, it was illegal to teach slaves to read, but they learned the Bible through preaching, storytelling, and singing. African American Christians revered the Bible as "a source of prophecy, magic, conjuring, and dreams... a dramatic, narrative book... [and] a volume of grand, inspiring themes instead of ethically oriented verses."[9] The Bible was a world of people who walked with God. The most important person they met there was Jesus, who though he was the Son of God, took the form of a servant, humbled himself to die on the cross, and rose again in glory. Next to Jesus was Moses, who led his people out of slavery into freedom. The slaves sang, "Go down, Moses, way down in Egypt-land. Tell old Pharaoh to let my people go."

Some African Americans found in the Bible the inspiration to revolt—just as whites feared. Some two hundred slave revolts took place in the United States; in these uprisings, "religion played a significant role, reflecting its status as a pillar of the slave community and a source of antislavery values among the blacks," notes Eric Foner. The largest rebellion was led by Nat Turner (1800–1831), a slave preacher who saw "visions in the sky: black and white angels fighting, the heavens running red with blood. He became convinced that he had been chosen by God to lead his people to freedom."[10] Turner and his followers went to farmhouses in Southampton County, Virginia, killing every white person they could find. By the time it was over, fifty seven-whites, nearly all women and children, were dead. Within a day, local militia captured or killed most of the rebels, but Turner remained at large for several weeks while roving bands of white people murdered blacks who had not joined the rebellion. After about two months, Turner was caught, tried, and executed.

Very few blacks took part in slave rebellions, but the whole South was affected by them. After Nat Turner's rebellion, "slave codes" (laws to control blacks) became stricter all over the South. Fearing that black worship services would encourage rebellions, many whites thought that blacks should not be allowed to worship without white supervision.

Forms of Black Worship

Since colonial times, slaves and masters had often worshiped together in the same church. A common pattern was for the white minister to lead the worship service while blacks sat in the back or listened from outside through open windows. On remote plantations, where churchgoing was infrequent, worship could be held on-site. Household servants might attend these services with their owners, but those who lived in the slave quarters were far less likely to worship with their white masters—if, indeed, the whites held worship services at all! In the early nineteenth century, many African Americans still had little or no contact with Christian faith and worship.

To address that need, Charles C. Jones (1804–1863), a Presbyterian minister and educator, led a campaign to evangelize slaves. This "plantation mission" extended "the missionary efforts beyond selected household slaves to all enslaved Africans."[11] Preachers of several denominations took part. To gain access to plantations, they had to persuade the masters that Christianity offered salvation without undermining the institution of slavery. The missionaries could also exhort white masters to treat their slaves kindly and provide for their needs.

The plantation mission was not the only way for slaves to hear the gospel, nor was all the preaching done by whites. Some plantations had their own black preacher or were served by a traveling black preacher—perhaps one licensed by Methodists or Baptists. It was not unheard of for a white master to be converted by a black preacher.

More typical was the tug-of-war in which "the whites of the Old South tried to shape the religious life of their slaves, and the slaves overtly, covertly, and even intuitively fought to shape it for themselves,"[12] according to historian Eugene Genovese. Africans sifted what they heard, rejecting the false message that God willed Africans to be slaves and accepting the gospel that declared them to be children of God. Ex-slaves later recalled that many a plantation sermon consisted of warnings not to steal chickens from the henhouse or hams from the smokehouse. Ex-slaves also recalled hearing blacks preach about freedom when whites were absent. No wonder many blacks felt the need to worship without white supervision.

Slaves thus gathered in secret, meeting in "brush arbors" or "hush harbors" tucked back in the woods. Even then, they had to be wary of informers. Those who were caught in a secret meeting could be punished by whipping. Slave Christians often led a double life: they appeared to accept religion as presented by whites, but most preferred a faith proclaimed by and for their own people. To survive, they learned to communicate on several levels at once. For example, if a slave sang "Steal Away to Jesus" while working in the field, the white overseer might hear just another song, while the other slaves might hear it as a signal for a secret prayer meeting to be held later that night. The "peculiar institution" of slavery made it necessary for Christian slaves to develop an "invisible institution" or secret church.

Meanwhile, in the North and in some southern cities, another form of black church arose: the independent African congregation. For example, the First Baptist Church of Savannah began in the early 1780s with the preaching of a slave named Andrew Bryan (1737–1812). Bryan and some of his congregants were severely whipped by whites who feared slave rebellions. Bryan refused to quit preaching. He was finally permitted to hold worship services for Africans and was ordained in 1788. After his master died, Bryan was able to purchase his freedom. By 1794 his congregation had erected their own church building. This church gave rise to two more Savannah congregations led by Africans. Many other independent churches arose: perhaps "more than two hundred Black Baptist churches" existed "mostly in the South, with a [combined] membership of close to five hundred thousand."[13] These black-led churches were subject to persecution or closure if whites suspected a slave conspiracy.

In the northern states, African Americans could worship together with whites, but very seldom as equals. Many churches had segregated seating; in some places the Lord's Supper was for whites only. Racial discrimination (then called "persecution") sometimes provoked African Americans to form their own separate congregations. The most famous instance occurred in Philadelphia in 1787. In that city, St. George's Methodist Episcopal Church, faced with a growing black constituency, added a balcony where blacks were expected to sit apart from the whites. One Sunday after the balcony was completed, Absalom Jones (an African American) knelt near the front of the church for the opening prayers as was his custom. A white usher told Jones to move to the balcony. When Jones asked to finish his prayers, the usher threatened to remove him by force. Then Jones, together with the other black Christians, walked out of the church in protest.[14]

Among those who left St. George's that day was Richard Allen (1760–1831). While a young slave in Delaware, Richard Allen was converted by a Methodist preacher and soon began sermonizing on his own. So powerful was Allen's message that his owner converted to Christianity and allowed Allen to buy his own freedom with wages earned away from the plantation. From 1781–86, Allen preached on Methodist circuits. He worked with others to create the Free African Society, a mutual aid group that "helped provide moral guidance and financial assistance as part of living a Christian life."[15] After the walk-out from St. George's in 1787, the Free African Society began to worship in a blacksmith shop.

So began the Bethel African Methodist Episcopal Church. In 1816 Bethel and similar churches from the mid-Atlantic region formed a new denomination: the African Methodist Episcopal (AME) Church. Bishop Francis Asbury (who had encouraged Allen's circuit preaching and ordained him into the ministry) also consecrated Allen as the first Bishop of the AME. Richard Allen decried the persecution that blacks suffered while worshiping with white Methodists, yet he also declared that the Methodists were "the first people that brought glad tidings to colored people. I feel thankful that ever I heard a Methodist preach. We are beholden to the Methodists, under God, for the light of the Gospel that we enjoy."[16] Like so many other African Americans Christians, Allen saw a clear difference between the gospel of Jesus Christ and human prejudice.

Anti-Slavery Movements

Today people often assume that before the Civil War, everyone in the North opposed slavery. The truth is harder. In the North as well as the South, many whites saw slavery as a positive good; others saw it as a necessary evil. Either way, slavery was deeply embedded in the nation's economy, politics, and society. Abolitionists (anti-slavery activists) were regarded as dangerous radicals, hated almost as much in the North as in the South. And the abolitionists did not agree among themselves as to how best to get rid of slavery. Some were gradualists, and others demanded immediate abolition. Most anti-slavery campaigns were peaceful, but a few (including slave rebellions and the raids conducted by John Brown) were violent. Both blacks and whites were involved in abolitionist activities. Abolitionism took many forms, as anti-slavery Christians sought to address the great issue of their time.

African American Christians fought slavery on many levels. During the Civil War, about 180,000 blacks enlisted in the Union Army. But long before the war, northern black churches opposed slavery by participating in abolitionist societies and hiding fugitive slaves. Northern black ministers preached and published against slavery. The most famous black abolitionist, however, was not a minister. Frederick Douglass (ca. 1817–1895) escaped from slavery in 1833 and won international fame as an anti-slavery author and orator. Douglass fearlessly confronted his audiences to show how slavery contradicted true Christianity and democracy. In his 1852 address, "What to the Slave Is the Fourth of July?" Douglass castigated the Christian "Divines" (ministers) who proclaimed "that a man may be a slave; that the relation of slave to master is ordained by God" and that the duty of every Christian is to return a runaway slave to bondage—and he decried the fact that "this horrible blasphemy is palmed off upon the world for Christianity."[17]

While Douglass and other abolitionists worked the lecture circuit, still others labored in secret to help runaway slaves escape via the Underground Railroad, a network of routes and hiding places for fugitive slaves heading north to freedom. The most famous "conductor" on the Underground Railroad was Harriet Tubman (1821–1913), a member of an African Methodist Episcopal Church. Born into slavery and forced

Frederick Douglass
Photo courtesy of William L. Clements Library

to do hard labor in the fields, Tubman escaped in 1849 and made her way to Philadelphia. Tubman returned often to the South, conducting about three hundred slaves to freedom. Admirers called her the "Moses of her people," but enemies offered to pay $40,000 for her capture, dead or alive.

While the Underground Railroad helped to move fugitive slaves northward, the American Colonization Society wanted blacks to move eastward, to Africa. Under the assumption that blacks never should have been forcibly taken from Africa in the first place, the Colonization Society raised money to buy people out of slavery and then pay their passage to Africa. It was hoped that these former slaves would spread Christianity in West Africa. Several thousand went to West Africa; Liberia was founded by ex-slaves in 1822. But many abolitionists, black and white, saw colonization as a pipe dream and rejected it. What really needed to happen, they insisted, was for blacks to gain freedom and equality in the U.S., the country their hard labor had done so much to build.

Colonization generated limited interest compared to the mass appeal of the evangelical revivals. Some revivalists felt called by God to denounce slavery and to demand its abolition. Charles Finney, for example, castigated Christians and churches for supporting slavery and warned of divine judgment. Finney's revival preaching converted Theodore Dwight Weld (1803–1895) and made him an apostle for abolition. Speaking in the style of a revivalist, Weld convicted his hearers of sin (slavery), converted them to faith (anti-slavery), and enlisted them in the good fight for a holy life (abolition). Weld worked for the American Anti-slavery Society. Founded in 1833, this organization soon had hundreds of local chapters throughout the northern states. The society sponsored public lectures, held anti-slavery rallies, distributed literature, and circulated petitions—all part of a larger attempt to turn public opinion against slavery.

Most white Northerners preferred to ignore the issue of slavery, but that became impossible after 1837. In that year, a mob in Alton, Illinois, destroyed an abolitionist printing press and murdered its editor, Elijah Lovejoy. Publishing anti-slavery literature was a dangerous business, even in a free state. Lovejoy's death put the nation on notice that people were willing to kill each other over the issue of slavery and that the cherished constitutional right of freedom of the press was in danger.

Lovejoy, the murdered editor, was a Presbyterian minister, and several great abolitionist leaders were Christian. But not the editor of the most famous abolitionist paper, *The Liberator.* William Lloyd Garrison (1805–1879) all but rejected Christianity. He declared reason, not the Bible, as his authority on slavery and all other issues.[18] Garrison condemned churches and political parties as props for the slave system. He said that it was not enough to make slavery illegal; there must be complete social and political equality for blacks throughout the United States. And if that were not radical enough, Garrison declared that women were little better off than slaves, since women could not vote and were legally subject to men.

When in 1848 the first women's rights convention was held in Seneca Falls, New York, many who attended were abolitionists. Their activism had forced them to confront "the woman question," as it was then called. An example is Lucy Stone (1818–1893), a graduate of Oberlin College.

To give lectures against slavery, Stone also had to defy taboos against women speaking in public. No wonder the more radical abolitionists wanted to combine anti-slavery with women's rights. Still others wanted to add pacifism and other reforms to the mix. This alarmed moderates, who wanted to focus on slavery as a single issue. The moderates (unlike Garrison) did not condemn the churches and political parties but sought to work with them to achieve abolition. These conflicting agendas and strategies meant that abolitionists needed more than one organization.

American churches could not stay together either. Tensions over slavery festered and erupted in denominational schisms along North/South lines. In 1837, the year of Lovejoy's murder, the Presbyterians divided. Methodists split in 1844 and Baptists in 1845. A study of these schisms led historian C. C. Goen to observe that "the division of America's popular churches into sectional factions several years before the political break . . . painfully exposed the deep moral chasm between North and South" and contributed to the eventual disruption of the Union.[19]

As in religion, so in politics: by midcentury, the compromises that cobbled together free and slave states were coming undone. The Fugitive Slave Law of 1850 was a turning point. That law required Northerners to assist in the capture and return of runaway slaves in the north—or face fines and imprisonment. People who had thus far remained silent on slavery became activists. Many otherwise law-abiding citizens gave food and shelter to fugitive slaves, vowing to disobey human laws in order to keep God's "higher law."

The Fugitive Slave Law outraged Harriet Beecher Stowe (1811–1896) and inspired her to write an anti-slavery novel, *Uncle Tom's Cabin.* Stowe came from a prominent New England family of preachers and reformers, and she saw slavery as a deeply religious issue. On an intimate level, the death of her little child in a cholera epidemic made her grieve for slave mothers whose children were sold away. Stowe's vivid prose brought slavery into the parlors of America in what now would be called an "up close and personal" way. The novel features Tom, a black Christ figure, who is brutally murdered for refusing to obey an unethical command of his white master. The novel shows both the suffering and the dignity of the slaves, while revealing that whites were also enslaved to the "peculiar institution." First published in book form in 1852, *Uncle*

Harriet Beecher Stowe, ca. 1855
Engraving by Francis Holl, Smithsonian Institution. Photo © ArtResource, NY

Tom's Cabin became an overnight sensation. It sparked such public outcry against slavery that when Abraham Lincoln met Stowe in the White House in 1862, he is said to have called her "the little woman who wrote the book that started this great war."

Stowe hoped for a peaceful end to slavery, but John Brown (1800–1859), by all accounts a religious fanatic, called for holy war. For a time Brown helped runaway slaves escape along the Underground Railroad. But he felt called by God to take more extreme measures. He found an opportunity when the 1854 Kansas-Nebraska Act declared that people within those territories would decide for themselves whether to keep or abolish slavery. This strategy (called "popular sovereignty") set the stage for guerilla warfare between pro- and anti-slavery factions. "Bleeding Kansas" was the perfect venue for John Brown, who arrived there in 1855 to carry out his mission. Of many atrocities, he is best remembered for leading his accomplices in the brutal murder of five pro-slavery settlers at Pottawatomie Creek in 1856.

Brown vowed to bring the fight into the heart of the Old South. With financial backing from Boston abolitionists, he laid plans to instigate a slave revolt in Virginia. In the fall of 1859, John Brown and his band of twenty-one men captured the federal arsenal at Harper's Ferry, Virginia. But the slaves in the area did not rise up. Instead, U.S. Marines stormed the arsenal, killing or capturing Brown and his followers. Brown's raid on Harper's Ferry inflamed southern fears of slave rebellion and confirmed their worst suspicions of northern treachery. Indeed, many Northerners hailed John Brown's cause as righteous. Henry David Thoreau, addressing a crowd just days before Brown's execution, compared Brown to Jesus Christ and called him an "angel of light." Brown was put on trial and found guilty of murder, treason, and conspiracy to incite insurrection. On the day of his hanging, he wrote, "I John Brown am now quite certain that the crimes of this guilty land will never be purged away; but with Blood."[20]

Civil War

When the war finally came, it seemed to abolitionists like the day of divine judgment for the sin of slavery. No one expressed this more powerfully than Julia Ward Howe (1819–1910). A Unitarian, Howe was also a feminist, author, and social reformer. In 1861 she visited a Union Army encampment near Washington, D.C.; the massing troops reminded Howe of apocalyptic images from the book of Revelation. Thus inspired, she wrote the "Battle Hymn of the Republic": "Mine eyes have seen the glory of the coming of the Lord; he is trampling out the vintage where the grapes of wrath are stored; he hath loosed the fateful lightning of his terrible swift sword; his truth is marching on." The last verse of the hymn includes the words, "As [Christ] died to make men holy, let us die to make men free, while God is marching on." This conclusion to the "Battle Hymn," according to Ernest Lee Tuveson, calls for "spiritual liberty [to] be completed by political freedom."[21] For many Northerners, the "Battle Hymn of the Republic" expressed the religious meaning of the war.

But even for those who saw the war as God's work, army life was no church picnic. The army was a theater of "spectacular profanity, gambling, drunkenness, sexual licentiousness, and petty thievery" where young recruits quickly picked up the behavior of more seasoned troops.[22] Many soldiers gambled away their pay and had nothing to send back home. Armies took food and firewood from lands they passed through, and the line between foraging and looting was thin. Stealing from civilians and wantonly destroying their property were common occurrences. Researching letters from the Civil War era, historian Steven Woodworth found that devout soldiers wrote home about their struggles to live a Christian life in the army.[23] As the war progressed, the death toll had a very sobering effect. Revivals became common among northern and southern soldiers as they tried to prepare for death by "getting right with God."

Chaplains—usually civilian clergy who volunteered—played important roles in army life. Sometimes they preached revival services, but their regular duties were to provide religious support in camp life and over the long marches. During and after a battle, the chaplains comforted the dying and helped remove the wounded from the field. Some chaplains were assigned to army hospitals, where they ministered to wounded soldiers and wrote letters home to inform families that loved ones had died.

On the home front, civilians mobilized into voluntary societies. Two large organizations must be noted: first, the United States Sanitary Commission, led by the Unitarian minister Henry Bellows (1814–1882). Primarily a reform group, the USSC sought to improve sanitation and diet in hospitals and army camps; it also purchased and distributed medical supplies. The second group was the United States Christian Commission, sponsored by George H. Stewart (1816–1890), a Presbyterian businessman. Primarily an evangelistic group, the USCC mustered over five thousand volunteers to distribute Bibles and religious tracts among the northern troops. The volunteers also cared for wounded men on battlefields and in hospitals and wrote letters on behalf of disabled or illiterate soldiers.[24] Both of these large voluntary societies had strong religious dimensions, and both eventually had full, official cooperation from the U.S. government and military. Countless smaller organizations, usually connected with churches, gave humanitarian aid during the war. Ladies' aid societies raised money and sent supplies and volunteer nurses to hospitals. Many women worked long hours as hospital or battlefield nurses; some traveled with armies to assist with food and sanitation.

As a confederacy of sovereign states, the South did not have national societies on the same scale as did the North to help in the war effort. But southern Christians also sent Bibles, medical supplies, nurses, and humanitarian workers to their soldiers. Churches of all denominations sent clergy to be chaplains in the southern armies, while church women zealously prayed for their soldiers and sent them clothing, bandages, and food whenever possible. Christian civilians in both the North and the South were deeply involved in the war effort, which many saw as a religious cause.

Soldiers were not the only ones in need of support from Christian volunteers. A refugee crisis ensued when thousands of slaves left plantations and followed the Union Army. These former slaves dug ditches for the army or sought work as farm laborers. Because their status was unclear, these people were called "contrabands of war," and it was decided that they should not be returned to slavery. Contrabands lived in miserable makeshift camps, where many died from hunger, disease, and exposure. Northern churches, both black and white, organized relief efforts to bring food, clothing, and medicine to these former slaves. Some volunteers began teaching the contrabands to read and write. Eventually the U.S. Freedmen's Bureau, formed in 1865, took responsibility for assisting ex-slaves to make the transition to freedom. But churches continued to work with former slaves for several years after the war.

To be sure, not all Christians supported the war. The peace churches, including Mennonites, Brethren, the Society of Friends (Quakers), Shakers, and others, refused military service. Neither the North nor the South had a unified plan for dealing with pacifism as a religious response to the war. One solution was for a religious objector to serve in a military hospital or other noncombatant position. But some chose to go to jail rather than support the war effort in any way. At the end of 1863, United States Secretary of War Edwin M. Stanton paroled all conscientious objectors.

For most Christians of that generation, the Civil War was a religious event. Historian James Moorhead notes that "America in the nineteenth century was a culture drenched in the images of the Bible. The minister's ability to justify war in the name of the sacred Book did much to mobilize support" for the war. Preachers on each side declared that their cause was

Abraham Lincoln, ca. 1865
Photo: Adoc-photos/ArtResource, NY

holy and that God would punish those who failed in their duty. Some likened the war to a "baptism of blood" through which God would cleanse the nation and usher in a glorious new era.[25] Since Northerners and Southerners firmly believed that God was on their side, patriotic sermons were common fare at Sunday morning worship in the North and in the South. The Civil War diarist Mary Chestnut describes her reaction to a sermon she heard at a Presbyterian church in Columbia, South Carolina, in 1864. "The preacher stirred my blood. My very flesh crept and tingled. A red-hot glow of patriotism passed through me. Such a sermon must strengthen the hearts and the hands of many people. There was more exhortation to fight and die [like] Joshua, than meek Christianity."[26]

The most profound religious view of the war came not from a preacher or a theologian but from a lawyer turned politician: Abraham

Lincoln. Although he did not belong to a church and may never have been baptized, Lincoln was steeped in the language of the Bible. Central for Lincoln was the doctrine of providence: that God's will is done through nature and history. Historian Allan Guelzo writes that over time, Lincoln seems to have moved from a remote and mechanistic view of God's providence to a much more personal and unpredictable one. "Lincoln had come, by the circle of a lifetime and by the disasters of the war, to confront once again the Calvinist God who could not be captured or domesticated . . . the voice out of the whirlwind."[27] Such a God did not belong to either side.

Lincoln's two most famous speeches were deeply theological. The Gettysburg Address (1863), delivered at the dedication of a battlefield cemetery, spoke of redemptive suffering and a new birth of freedom. His Second Inaugural Address (1865) invoked a God whose purposes were beyond the claims of either North or South. Both sides, said Lincoln, "read the same Bible, and pray to the same God; and each invokes his aid against the other." Nevertheless, "the Almighty has His own purposes." The war was God's judgment on the whole nation—not just the South—for the sin of slavery. Echoing the biblical prophets, Lincoln finished with a call for healing and peace:

> With malice toward none, with charity for all, with firmness in the right, as God gives us to see the right, let us strive to finish the work we are in; to bind up the nation's wounds; to care for him who shall have born the battle, and for his widow, and his orphan—to do all which may achieve and cherish a just and a lasting peace, among ourselves, and with all nations.

Not long after Lincoln gave this speech, southern armies were collapsing and the war was ending. Lincoln traveled to fallen Richmond, once the proud capital of the Confederacy, where freed blacks hailed him as their liberator. Lincoln returned to Washington, D.C., where on April 14, 1865, he was assassinated by a southern sympathizer. In life, Lincoln had often been mocked for his homely appearance and backwoods manners, but now a nation in mourning honored him as their fallen savior. The fact that he was shot on Good Friday was not lost on a religious public.

After the Civil War

At a very high cost, the Civil War preserved the Union and ended slavery. At least 620,000 soldiers died in the war—not only "in glorious battle for a sacred cause" but from disease and disaster. The South lay in ruins, and the future of some four million freed slaves was unknown. As the smoke lifted and the dead were buried, Americans sought a religious meaning for the war. For example, Christian educator Horace Bushnell saw the bloodshed as creating a new America, "God's own nation." Bushnell believed that the Civil War prepared the United States for a redemptive mission in the world. This view provided a religious and moral framework for American foreign policy through the two world wars.[28]

But few southern whites could accept the "nation reborn" interpretation of the war; after all, *their* nation, the Confederacy, was no more. Nor could southern defeat be explained merely on the basis of Union military might, since southern armies had won many a battle against Union forces superior in numbers to the Confederates. One explanation that gained currency in the South was this: the southern practice of slavery had failed to meet biblical standards, and therefore God allowed white "stewardship" over slaves to be taken away.[29] Southern society would soon find ways to assert white claims to supremacy, but without the institution of slavery.

After winning the war, the federal government now had to win the peace. That meant bringing the southern states back into a Union without slavery. This transition, called Reconstruction, lasted from 1865 to 1876. There was conflict over what Reconstruction should do. Lincoln's successor, President Andrew Johnson (a Tennessean) wanted the southern states to reenter the Union on easy terms, leaving whites in control. But "radical Republicans" in the North insisted that the federal government must define and protect the rights of freed slaves. Ulysses S. Grant, elected president in 1868, was more sympathetic to the radical program of economic, social, and political reform.

Reconstruction brought the passage of the Fifteenth Amendment to the Constitution in 1870, guaranteeing the right of male citizens to vote regardless of race, color, or previous condition of servitude. The Civil

Rights Act of 1875 declared that all persons should have "equal enjoyment" of public accommodations. (This legislation was only sporadically enforced, however; not until the 1950s and 1960s would there be a widespread campaign to desegregate hotels, restaurants, theaters, and public transportation.) The Reconstruction Radicals also wanted to prosecute those whites accused of whipping black workers—a practice common during slavery, which after the war became a crime. The Radicals wanted the "freedmen" (ex-slaves) to help build a southern Republican Party by running for political office. In the North, many Christians supported the Radical Republicans, seeing the campaign to reform race relations in the South as "an extension of the anti-slavery crusade."[30]

During Reconstruction, northern missionaries—including blacks as well as whites, women as well as men—poured into the South. They found a destitute region where "towns and cities lay in ruins, innumerable schools and churches had closed, and thousands of refugee families returned to find their farms, plantations, and communities in shambles."[31] Churches that still held worship on Sunday had no money to pay teachers or buy supplies.

Illiteracy presented a great challenge to the northern missionaries. Few of the four million newly freed black people could read, and neither could a great many poor to middling whites. Teaching people to read was a top priority, both to help prepare blacks for citizenship and to give them direct access to the Bible.

With so many children working the fields during the week, Sunday was the time for teaching people to read. Sunday schools spread quickly throughout the South during Reconstruction. Start-up costs were low, because teachers and lesson materials usually came from the North. Postwar southern Sunday schools met in private homes, barns, or storefronts, or outdoors. These groups often gave rise to new congregations. According to historian Sally McMillen, from whose work this information is drawn, the Sunday schools played a significant role in bringing literacy and hope to southern communities.

As the Sunday schools spread throughout the South, blacks were forming their own churches, independent from white churches. We have already noted that racially mixed worship was common before the war. But afterward, great numbers of blacks left the white-controlled churches, to form congregations where they could worship as they pleased and follow their own leaders. Historian Eric Foner notes that this "wholesale withdrawal of blacks from biracial congregations redrew the religious map of the south" so that the independent black church became the most dramatic religious change after the war.

In the postwar South, the church was *the* institution led by blacks for blacks. The house of worship was also a school and a community center where blacks managed their own affairs and developed their own leaders. There was no artificial separation of religion and politics: African American preachers ran for public office during Reconstruction because they were respected leaders, often the most literate persons in their communities. The independent black church became the hub for community concerns, with religion, politics, education, and social progress intertwined. It has been said that the modern black community was born during Reconstruction.[32]

And so was the Ku Klux Klan. Founded in Tennessee in 1866 by former Confederate officers, the KKK arose "to keep Negroes in their place." Its members dressed in white robes, like ghosts of the Confederate dead, and rode forth at night to intimidate African Americans and any whites known to be supportive of blacks. With slavery now abolished and black men voting and running for political office, and Yankee Republicans running the state and local governments, *someone* had to defend the old ways—so said the KKK, who saw themselves as exercising vigilante justice. In truth, however, the KKK was what would now be called a terrorist group, fueled by rage at southern defeat and by fears that blacks would move up from the bottom rung of society. Many Southerners did not approve of the Klan, and it was more powerful in some places than in others. But where it had a strong following, the Klan became "in effect . . . a military force serving the interests of the Democratic party, the planter class, and all those who desired the restoration of white supremacy."[33]

In its early phase, the Klan murdered hundreds of people; in some places, the Klan was so powerful that federal troops were brought in to crush it. Although Klansmen sometimes killed at random, more often they targeted blacks who ran for political office or who showed any sign of economic or social progress. Blacks were the primary targets, but whites who worked with or encouraged blacks also were harassed and sometimes killed. There was a religious dimension to the KKK, insofar as its members believed that God willed whites to rule society. Anyone who challenged white supremacy by daring to "advance the Negro" committed "the supreme Radical [Republican] sin,"[34] which the Klan, as the self-appointed agent of divine wrath, stood ready to punish.

Reconstruction ended in 1877. It became a political bargaining chip for the election of the Republican candidate, Rutherford B. Hayes, to the presidency: in exchange for southern electoral support, federal troops were withdrawn from southern states. More broadly, however, Reconstruction was doomed both by southern resistance and by waning northern commitment. Southerners quickly dismantled Reconstruction and passed a whole new series of laws to enforce white superiority. The bright hopes of emancipation were all but extinguished, not to be fully rekindled until the civil rights movement of the 1950s and 1960s—a movement that drew deeply from the black churches.

Suggestions for Further Reading

Books

Genovese, Eugene. *Roll, Jordan, Roll: The World the Slaves Made* (Vintage, 1974). This book is rich in primary sources, documenting how slaves found ways to assert their humanity. Of particular interest are the sections on the Christian tradition and slave religion.

Guelzo, Allen. *Abraham Lincoln: Redeemer President* (Eerdmans, 1999). This biography probes the role of ideas in Lincoln's life and politics. Religious themes receive careful attention, especially Lincoln's belief in and use of the doctrine of providence.

Raboteau, Albert. *Slave Religion: The Invisible Institution in the Antebellum South* (Oxford University Press, 2004). From the African heritage to the faith of blacks in bondage, Raboteau explores the role of religion for African slaves—both those who endured and those who rebelled.

Stowe, Harriet Beecher. *Uncle Tom's Cabin* (various printings). First published in book form in 1852, this anti-slavery novel helped turn public opinion. Today it still attracts attention as a key text for women's literature and history as well as black history.

Websites

Uncle Tom's Cabin and American Culture. This multimedia archive from the University of Virginia is a treasure trove of primary source material related specifically to *Uncle Tom's Cabin* and, more broadly, to the anti-slavery movement: www.iath.virginia.edu/utc/

"North American Slave Narratives." A special collection within the larger website, "Documenting the American South," University of North Carolina. This collection includes narratives of fugitive and former slaves published as broadsides, pamphlets, or books in English up to 1920. Biographies of fugitive and former slaves and some significant fictionalized slave narratives are also available here: http://docsouth.unc.edu/neh/

Discussion Questions

1. Several Christian denominations split over the slavery issue. Why could they not resolve their differences? What did these church splits imply for the nation at large?
2. According to historian Eugene Genovese, "The whites of the Old South tried to shape the religious life of their slaves, and the slaves…fought to shape it for themselves." Specifically, how did African Americans fight to shape their own religious lives in the period before the Civil War?
3. Name several different ways in which anti-slavery people (whites and blacks) protested against slavery and/or sought to end it. How did religious belief inform their actions?
4. How did religiously motivated civilians participate in the Civil War and its aftermath? What might be the role or responsibility of Christian civilians in wartime today?
5. What did Lincoln's second inaugural address suggest about his understanding of the war? About his view of God?
6. After the war was over, what religious explanations were offered to give meaning to that conflict? Do you find any of these persuasive? Explain your response.

CHAPTER FIVE

Moving People

Newcomers

Twenty-five million immigrants came to the United States in the years between the Civil War and the First World War. During this period, the first waves of immigrants came from the British Isles and then from Germany and Scandinavia; these groups of immigrants settled much of the Midwest and later the Great Plains. But from about 1890 to 1914, immigrants began arriving in large numbers from countries such as Poland and Russia, Italy and Greece. This latest influx of newcomers had less opportunity to buy land, so they gravitated to large cities where they sought work in factories or the trades.

Americans often compared the United States to a "melting pot,"[1] which would render all foreigners into Americans speaking one language and sharing the same culture. Melting, that is, exchanging an old identity for a new one, was thought to be inevitable—even if it took more than one generation. Some immigrants eagerly embraced all things American, but others had no intention of "melting." Indeed, many people came to the United States in the hope that here they could preserve their culture, retain distinctive beliefs, or practice worship in ways that had not been welcome in Europe. In any event, the immigrants made America—and religion in America—more diverse than ever before. A country once defined by Anglo-Protestantism acquired a growing Catholic population of many languages. Orthodox Christians

On board an immigrant boat. England, 1871
Photo © Snark/ArtResource, NY

and Jews arrived, as did a goodly number of Lutherans. Many of these groups put a long-lasting stamp on neighborhoods or entire regions where they lived.

Immigrants naturally sought out people of common language and religious faith, whether in a tenement in New York or a sod hut on the prairie. Chain migration, in which people from the same family, town, or region in Europe relocate near each other, was common. Ethnic churches quickly sprang up. These churches for a time preserved European languages and customs and thus could offer newcomers oases of familiarity in a strange land. Many people who had not been active Christians back in the old country found the immigrant churches to be centers of community, where they could reconnect with Christian faith.

But the ethnic parish could be a storm center as well as an oasis. Rivalries flared up among nineteenth-century American Catholics. Since Italians, Germans, and Poles (and many others) wanted to practice Catholicism as they had back home, they might resist the control of an Irish or American priest. One way to deal with Catholic diversity was to gather parishes according to nationality, with priests of that nationality if at all possible. A large city like New York or Chicago might have several ethnic parishes that overlapped geographically but were worlds apart culturally. Most of these ethnic parishes stayed within the larger Catholic fold instead of breaking away to form a new denomination.

Lutherans also grew dramatically. By 1910 they were "the third largest Protestant denominational grouping, after the Methodists and the Baptists."[2] Like the Catholics, Lutherans had many ethnic groups—German, Danish, Finnish, Swedish, Norwegian, Slovak, and Icelandic. But unlike the Catholics, Lutherans had no overarching structure. They were a patchwork of older synods, fledgling denominations, and independent congregations. Nor was nationality the only thing that distinguished one Lutheran group from another. There were also different foci for religious faith. Probably a majority of the newly arriving Lutherans were Pietests, for whom personal religious experience and evangelism were vital. Lutheran Confessionalists, in contrast, were above all committed to the doctrines expressed in the Lutheran Confessions. Still other Lutherans found their religious identity in a kind of culture Protestantism, or formal religion, as they had known it in some of the European state churches. Such typologies can be misleading, of course. Lutherans could and did combine the elements of their heritage in various ways. For example, Pietists often were theologically informed by the Confessions, and Confessionalists often had some Pietist tendencies.

Once in America, Lutherans confronted new issues—such as whether and how to interact with other American Christians (as we saw in the previous chapter with Samuel Simon Schmucker). Some Lutherans strove hard to keep out unwanted influences that might corrupt Lutheran teaching. For example, in 1875 the General Council (Lutherans primarily in the eastern U.S.) adopted the "Galesburg Rule," which stated that Lutheran pulpits were for Lutheran ministers only, and Lutheran altars were for Lutheran communicants only. Any exception was a privilege and not a right, to be decided by the judgment of pastors.[3] Lutheran identity was more important than Protestant unity.

Theology mattered in the way Lutherans related to non-Lutherans and in the way Lutherans related to each other. In the late nineteenth century, several Lutheran groups, mostly in the Midwest, broke into bitter conflict over predestination. At issue was the understanding of salvation by grace through faith, particularly the relationship of faith (human response to God's grace) to election (God's choice of whom to save). The dispute never was resolved, but it fractured Midwestern Lutherans for decades. The "melting pot" did not seem to be an apt metaphor for Lutherans. Over time, however, many Lutherans sought consolidation. A long series of mergers began in the early twentieth century, with Lutherans gradually forming larger denominations and seeking ecumenical relationships beyond Lutheranism. Some Lutheran groups, however, chose not to participate.

While Catholics, Lutherans, and other immigrants were addressing their own internal issues, "native born" Americans worried that the new immigrants might change life in the United States beyond recognition. What if the melting pot did not work? What if European forms of Christianity clashed with American forms? To be sure, immigrant labor was needed to run the factories, build the railroads, and plow the prairies. But newcomers (it was feared) had beliefs and loyalties and customs that seemed "un-American" and might pose a threat to democracy. What if immigrants did not embrace American life and culture? Can any nation safely harbor millions of people who do not share its basic ideals? These were sobering questions for many Americans by the end of the nineteenth century.

In an earlier chapter, we discussed "nativism," noting the violence it inspired. However, it would be simplistic to lump all the concerns of "native born" Americans under the heading of prejudice, since there were, in fact, some significant differences between the older-stock Americans and the new arrivals. For example, historian Jon Gjerde, whose scholarship on immigration informs this section, notes a major tension between *pluralism* and *particularism*. The United States was becoming an increasingly pluralistic society in which even religion was a matter of personal opinion. But "many groups of immigrants streaming westward were taught that they, as true believers" had the particular truth, and should therefore "segregate themselves from the godless throngs."[4] The Midwest and later the West gave immigrants the space to inhabit their own islands of particularism in a sea of pluralism. Some of these islands were quite large, thanks to chain migration and available land.

Bisbee Lutheran Church, Bisbee, North Dakota
Immigrant church built in 1903
Photo courtesy of Region 3 Archives of the Evangelical Lutheran Church in America, Luther Seminary, Saint Paul, Minnesota

Gjerde also notes a tension between *American individualism* and *European collectivism*. European immigrants often arrived as extended families and lived collectively. The family determined where its members would live and work and whom they would marry. The pastor or priest (in turn representing a collective faith tradition) determined what was to be believed.[5] For a great many immigrants—especially in the first generation—life was communal and survival depended on mutual support of a family or ethnic group. In contrast, the "American ideal" was for individuals to make their own way in the world. Personal choice was more to be prized than the will of the family or the church. Nor have these tensions entirely melted away. To this day some Lutherans criticize evangelicals for being "too individualistic," while evangelicals (if they know about Lutherans at all) are puzzled by Lutherans' apparent lack of concern for personal salvation.

Many immigrants believed strongly in education as the best way to preserve their traditions and to help their children and grandchildren succeed in America. Therefore, in the Midwest and the West, Protestant and Catholic immigrants founded colleges to serve their own language and faith communities. Although some of the schools were short-lived, many grew to become first-rate colleges and universities that served constituencies far beyond the original ethnic or religious community; an example is Notre Dame University, founded in 1842 near South Bend, Indiana, by French priests.

Theological education also changed because of immigration; between 1860 and 1890, more than twenty-five new seminaries were founded, mostly by immigrants in the Midwest. "In these schools only gradually did the language of instruction move from the native languages to English."[6] Thanks in part to the newcomers, theological education diversified beyond the older Anglo-Protestant schools.

African American Migration

Another great movement of peoples took place between 1890 and 1930, as African Americans left the rural South. Responding to economic hardship and racial discrimination, 2.5 million blacks moved to northern and western cities. Many who remained in the South abandoned farming and moved to southern cities. Historian Albert Raboteau observes that this huge migration "disrupted rural and urban congregations, transplanted Southern religious customs North and West, strained the resources of urban churches, and formed in black city neighborhoods new opportunities for religious creativity."[7] For thousands of blacks arriving in cities, the churches became a spiritual home away from home and a place to work on political and social concerns. A common pattern was for newcomers to join African Methodist and Baptist churches in the cities. But there were other options. Some blacks joined religious groups that had not been available in the rural South, while others started new churches known for spirited, freestyle worship, and still others forged new religious groups by combining elements of Christianity and African identity.

River Baptism
Howard Norton Cook, 1936

The great black migration made African American religion—and American life generally—more diverse than ever before. It also contributed to the settlement of the West: an African Methodist presence grew in California and in scattered areas west of the Mississippi;[8] by 1885 African Methodist groups had a solid presence also in parts of the old North and the Midwest.

We saw in the previous chapter how the civil rights of black people were abandoned along with Reconstruction. This was true not only in the South but throughout the country. In 1883 the Supreme Court invalidated the Civil Rights Act of 1875 and declared that private organizations and individuals were not prohibited from practicing race discrimination; thus, railroads, hotels, theaters, and other public accommodations could and did enforce racial separatism. In 1896 the court ruling *Plessy v. Ferguson* approved the principle of "separate but equal," claiming that blacks were not deprived of equal rights if accommodations were equal. But in practice, accommodations were not equal. Schools for blacks were underfunded, completely neglected, or nonexistent.

The eighty-some years between Reconstruction and civil rights have been remembered as a long night of despair in the quest for racial justice. Segregation affected all areas of life, from housing to education to jobs. Lynching and other crimes against black people often went unpunished. Yet African Americans were determined to build a better future. They continued to shape American Christianity and culture despite relentless racial discrimination. Among their many achievements in the late nineteenth century were independent congregations and the rise of black colleges and trade and professional schools, to be described later in this chapter.

Manifest Destiny and the West

Even as immigrants poured into the United States and black people migrated to American cities, the population was also expanding west of the Mississippi River. This westward movement had a religious dimension: many Americans believed that God destined the United States to occupy all the land between the Atlantic and the Pacific oceans. The term for this was "manifest destiny," popularized by journalist John O'Sullivan, who wrote in 1845, "The American claim is by right of our *manifest destiny* to overspread and to possess the whole of the continent which Providence has given us."[9] Manifest Destiny helped to justify the Mexican-American War (1846–48), which resulted in the United States' acquisition of territory in the Southwest; it also helped to justify innumerable wars with and the forced relocation of Native American tribes onto reservations.

Even before the Civil War, the West lured people who were seeking God or mammon. As we have seen, the Mormon migration drew to Utah thousands who strove to establish God's kingdom on earth; and the California gold rush of 1849 attracted people who wanted to strike it rich. After the Civil War, several changes sped up westward migration:

the conflict over slavery in the western territories was over; a growing network of railroads made it easier for people to go west; and tribal peoples, after decades of resistance, were gradually defeated in battle or subdued through starvation, then confined to reservations. In 1890 the U.S. Census Bureau declared the frontier "closed" because there were no longer clear boundaries between settled and unsettled lands.

Some Christian leaders saw that the wildest people in the West—those most in need of taming—were white folk. The story is told, for example, of John Dyer, a Methodist preacher who preferred hymn-singing to gun-slinging. In the mining town of Breckenridge, Colorado, Dyer faced down a mob of anti-Chinese rioters by singing "All Hail the Power of Jesus' Name" at the top of his lungs. Then he began preaching of God's love for all humanity until the crowd disbursed. Another intrepid leader was Sheldon Jackson, a Presbyterian minister who gathered congregations throughout the West. In Alaska, Jackson started several schools. He became an advocate for Native peoples who were being exploited by white traders of alcohol.[10]

The first evangelists in Alaska were not American Protestants, however. In 1794 Russia sent ten monks to evangelize Alaskans. A successful Orthodox mission was established by Ivan Venyaminov (1797–1879), a Russian missionary. After Alaska became U.S. territory in 1867, Orthodox Christianity persisted with more than ten thousand communicants among Native peoples. Encroachment by new settlers did not undermine the work of the missionaries as swiftly as in other regions.

Probably the most lasting contribution Christians made to western settlement was the building of infrastructure needed for their society. According to historians Szasz and Szasz, both the churches and Sunday schools "promoted social stability while reining in local violence."[11] In other words, the churches played a key role in civilizing whites on the frontier. Many western churches began with Sunday Bible schools, which grew into congregations. Closely connected with the churches were schools. Ministers and their wives often did double duty by serving as schoolteachers and church leaders. Higher education spread westward as Christian denominations founded colleges in newly settled areas. Alongside religion and education, Christian groups sought to provide medical care in the West. Many of the first western hospitals relied on Catholics or Protestant denominations for funding and personnel. Catholic priests sometimes traveled back east to recruit nuns to staff new western hospitals. Other social services, such as orphanages and homes for the aged, were started with church support; Jews, Mormons, and nonreligious groups also made substantial contributions in these areas.

There was, however, a Christian presence in the Southwest long before U.S. settlement. This Christian presence was Catholic, originally planted by Spanish missionaries and carried by people from Mexico moving north. Over time, a blend of Spanish, Mexican, and Native traditions shaped a type of Catholicism distinctive to the Southwest. In contrast to European-style Catholicism—which centers on the mass conducted by a priest in a church building—southwestern Catholicism thrived on outdoor religious festivals. Saints days were celebrated with processions and feasting. The most adored of all saints was the Virgin Mary, and southwestern Marian devotion centered on reported appearances of the Virgin of Guadalupe (near Mexico City) in 1531.

In addition to this blend of cultures, southwestern Catholicism was shaped by the scarcity of priests. The people developed their own religious life with relatively little influence from clergy. Mass was infrequent, and it was not unusual for people to conduct their own baptisms, weddings, and funerals. Instead of the parish run by a priest (the standard European style), the southwestern Catholics had confraternities: "fraternal and spiritual organizations formed to promote devotion to a particular saint or religious practice," according to Jay Dolan. Confraternities often built private chapels that were beyond the control of a priest. Thus, "when the southwest became a part of the [Catholic] Church in the United States, the people had become accustomed to a great deal of independence in religion."[12] This southwestern or Hispanic Catholicism remained culturally strong in Santa Fe, New Mexico, and other areas.

Hispanic Catholics came into the United States in the nineteenth century as the nation acquired lands through war and purchase and statehood. Texas was admitted to the Union in 1845; the War with Mexico in 1846–48 resulted in the acquisition of California and New Mexico; over fifty thousand square miles of southwestern lands were purchased from Mexico a few years later.

Part of the story of Christianity in the West concerns this meeting of two very different types of Catholicism: the indigenous type of the

Sisters of the Incarnate Word and Blessed Sacrament, Victoria, Texas, c. 1900
Photo courtesy of Catholic Archives of Texas

Southwest, and the Catholicism of Europe and the eastern United States. Rome did not officially "cease to regard the Catholic Church in the U.S. as a mission field" until 1908.[13] Meanwhile, Catholics whose families had lived in the Southwest for generations "had to face the reality of being 'Mexican in an Anglo society.'"[14] Catholics from "back east" wanted their co-religionists in the Southwest to accept the authority of bishops and priests, make the mass central to faith, organize the church around parishes, and discard much of southwestern folk piety. Bishops were assigned to administer the various regions. The bishops recruited priests from places like France and Italy for service in places like Texas and New Mexico. However, many places remained without priests and kept their local traditions. Given this clash of cultures, "it is a marvel that the

Catholic Church survived without ethnic schism."[15] Willa Cather's novel *Death Comes for the Archbishop* treats in fictional form this southwestern encounter between two different kinds of Catholicism.

Mormons

The Mormons played a vital role in western settlement. Earlier we noted that after the death of Joseph Smith, Brigham Young led the "exodus" of Mormons moving to the Utah Territory. This Mormon migration began in 1846 and continued for several decades, drawing "saints" from the Midwest and also from England and Sweden, where Mormons had evangelized. By 1877, the year of Brigham Young's death, up to 150,000 people[16] lived in the Salt Lake Basin—an amazing feat for the time before railroads spanned the West. Early Mormon pioneers crossed prairie, desert, and mountain on foot or in wagons. Some pushed all their worldly goods along in handcarts. Many died of disease, hunger, and exhaustion. But the Mormons strove to help each other along the way. They improved trails and cached supplies; some groups planted crops to be harvested by others coming after them, and leaders in Salt Lake sent emergency relief teams to help stragglers. The trek to Utah became sacred history to the Mormons; it defined them as a people who saw themselves in the biblical story of the Israelites leaving Egypt for the Promised Land.

Like the Puritans of seventeenth-century New England, the Mormons sought to build a complete theocracy (rule of God) in the West, and for a while they succeeded. Thanks in part to the prolonged crisis over slavery and the Civil War back east, the Mormons enjoyed many years of relative isolation to build their "Zion" in Utah. The Latter-day Saints had a unique religion, a self-contained economy, and a "political party that voted as a bloc in accordance with directions delivered from the pulpit."[17]

But their isolation could not last. Utah became a territory of the United States. In 1857 the federal government sent soldiers to Utah and installed a non-Mormon territorial governor. Expecting armed conflict, the Mormons temporarily abandoned their settlements and moved to the backcountry. The shooting didn't start, but tensions remained high.

Meanwhile, non-Mormons ("Gentiles") were passing through Mormon territory on their way west. In 1857 Mormon vigilantes, reportedly disguised as Native Americans, attacked a wagon train and killed more than one hundred people. According to Richard and Joan Ostling, motives for the massacre may have included "fear of war and invasion as well as a desire for revenge"[18] for the death of Joseph Smith and for other Gentile violence against Mormons. But nothing could stem the tide of westward settlement. The splendid isolation of those first years of Mormon settlement could not last. Statehood for Utah became more desirable, but first Mormons would have to move closer to the mainstream of American society.

The biggest obstacle was polygamy. In a previous chapter, we saw that Mormon founder Joseph Smith claimed to have received a divine directive to take more than one wife.[19] At first, this practice of "plural marriage" was kept secret—only top Mormon leaders knew about it. But Brigham Young and others carried plural marriage to Utah, where it became an open practice. It was not unusual for a man to marry two women; Young himself had at least twenty wives. Polygamy directly challenged the bedrock of nineteenth-century American morals: marriage between one man and one woman. Also troubling to outsiders was the Mormon theocracy, in which the church controlled every aspect of life, including how individuals should vote. Non-Mormons saw the Latter-day Saints as a direct threat to democracy and to Christianity.

Back east, "evangelical Protestants pressured the government to act"[20] against Mormon plural marriage. Here we will note only two highlights from the prolonged legal battle against polygamy. First, the Supreme Court (*U.S. v. Reynolds*, 1879) ruled that although "laws cannot interfere with mere religious beliefs and opinions, they may [interfere] with practices." The ruling said that some things—such as polygamy and human sacrifice—cannot be permitted even in the name of religious freedom. In such cases, government interference is justified. Second, the U.S. Congress passed the Edmunds-Tucker Act in 1887; this denied the vote to polygamists, legally dissolved the Mormon Church, and confiscated much of its property. Federal agents went to Utah and jailed heads of polygamous households.[21] It has been said that the Edmunds-Tucker Act brought the Mormon Church to its knees.

Mormons believe in continuing revelation, and so in 1890, Wilford Woodruff, who was then the Mormon president, was inspired to issue a manifesto banning plural marriage. With polygamy officially ended and the Mormon political party disbanded, the way was clear for Utah to become a state in 1896. Polygamy did not vanish overnight, however; families who chose not to obey federal law or the new LDS directive simply slipped farther into the backcountry. The Church of Jesus Christ of the Latter-day Saints condemns polygamy, but even today there are small sects that practice plural marriage[22] in several western states and in a few places in Canada and Mexico.

Native Americans and Religion

Today, nineteenth-century missionaries who sought to reach Native peoples are often disparaged. In fairness, however, it must be noted that some missionaries sought to protect Native peoples from white encroachment on tribal lands and to hold whites accountable for the promises made in treaties. For example, Episcopal bishop Henry Benjamin Whipple (1822–1901) became an advocate on behalf of the Sioux, Ojibwas, and other peoples. Whipple met with Abraham Lincoln to press for reforms in the federal conduct of Indian affairs; throughout his lifetime, Whipple continued his advocacy for Native Americans.

The efforts of Whipple and other well-intentioned missionaries could not, however, offset the effects of disease, warfare, treaty breaking, and removals to reservations. Those harsh realities, according to historian Henry Warner Bowden, "always interfered with evangelical efforts and changed them before they could operate as intended."[23] Insofar as they saw Christianity as the "white man's religion," Native peoples were hard pressed to take the claims of Christianity at face value.

American expansion ended an entire way of life for Native Americans west of the Mississippi. As traditional ways of life were crumbling, the Plains Indians experienced a revival of religion in the 1880s. Inspired by the Paiute prophet Wovoka, a new religion called the "Ghost Dance" was born. It awakened the hope that life could return to the way it was before the coming of the whites. The Ghost Dance invoked the spirits of the dead and sought to bring about their return. Some said that the Ghost Dance was a peaceful religion; others hoped it would "bring about a day when [Native peoples] were "strong enough to wage an all out war against the whites."[24] The Ghost Dance spread through several reservations, including Pine Ridge and Rosebud in the Dakota territories. It promised a better future than the one offered "by missionaries, the Office of Indian Affairs, and the United States Army—a future in which the only way to survive" was to give up their distinct cultures and assimilate.[25] Ghost Dance shirts were believed to have the power to stop bullets of the white soldiers. But the Ghost Dance shirts did not protect anyone on December 29, 1890. On that day, federal troops, expecting an uprising, massacred more than two hundred Miniconjous Sioux who were camped at Wounded Knee Creek. Old men, women, and children were shot down; some of the victims were wearing Ghost Dance shirts, which soldiers stripped off to keep as souvenirs. Wounded Knee is remembered as the last official engagement between the U.S. Army and Native Americans.

Settlers continued moving west as tribal peoples were increasingly confined to reservations. The federal government enlisted the aid of various Christian denominations, which were to send missionaries to reservations. The missionaries were expected to help transform native peoples into Christian farmers. Missionary teachers started boarding schools on reservations to get Native children to "travel the white road" by adopting the language, religion, and culture of the whites. Toward this end, children were separated from their families and forbidden to speak their own languages, wear Native dress, and practice tribal religions. (Not until 1978, with the passage of the American Indian Religious Freedom Act, were Native Americans guaranteed the right to practice their traditional religions.)

The problem of tribal land became acute in the late nineteenth century. Many tribes had been given lands, but whites kept pressing to settle on these reservations. Access to and attitudes toward land were intimately tied to the survival of Native cultures. Many whites felt that tribes would never assimilate as long as they held land communally. So "by the 1880s, in near unanimity, government officials, military officers, congressional leaders and Christian reformers agreed that ... reservations should disappear along with Indian identity."[26] Therefore, the Dawes

Act of 1887 forced several tribes to give up their communal land and become individual property owners. Land not designated to private Native owners was sold to whites.[27] Given this long and tragic history, it seems little short of a miracle that some Native Americans did become Christian. Yet there were (and continue to be) Native American congregations on many reservations. Over time, the Native American church developed a blend of Indian religious practices and basic Christian teachings. Such a faith does not ignore the wrongs of the past but manages in many instances to transcend them.

Overseas Missions

While the U.S. was closing its western frontiers, a new frontier of global mission was opening up. For a long time, America had been primarily a receiver of missionaries; many churches imported priests and pastors from Europe. Rather early in our history, however, Americans began sending as well as receiving missionaries. In 1810 the American Board of Commissioners for Foreign Missions was founded. By the late nineteenth century, the U.S. was a major sender of missionaries; and by 1920 "North America had become the principal source of missionaries."[28] In the progressive era of the late nineteenth century, the mission movement sought to spread both Christianity and democracy around the world. Mission societies sprouted up everywhere. Some of these were denominational; many were ecumenical. The Student Volunteer Movement (SVM) was the largest ecumenical mission society, deploying thousands of American missionaries around the world.

No less important were the mission societies of local congregations. These groups raised money and gathered supplies to build churches, schools, hospitals, and orphanages overseas. Local mission societies cultivated strong relationships with missionaries, supporting them both materially and spiritually. Mission scholar Andrew Walls notes how these mission societies had a practical, problem-solving approach: they would "identify a task to be done, find appropriate means of carrying it out; unite and organize a group of like-minded people for the purpose."[29] Walls further observes that this was an activist American Christianity with the resources and the will to plant itself around the world. The mission societies were designed "to direct the resources of Christians in one country to the preaching of the gospel and the establishing of churches in another country.... The design was essentially for one way traffic."[30] Not until the late twentieth century would some American Christians begin to sense a need to receive help from African, Asian, or Latin American Christians.

The nineteenth-century missionary movement affected people at home as well as abroad. Church women became organizers, fundraisers, and public speakers in support of mission. A few women, inspired by missionary speakers, entered medical schools in the States in order to serve abroad as missionary nurses or doctors. For example, Ida Scudder (1870–1960) was a Christian missionary who founded a hospital in Vellore, India; she was one of the first female graduates of Cornell School of Medicine. Overseas mission gave women the opportunity to enter professions that were all but closed to them in the United States.

Overseas mission also built relationships between American and African blacks. In the nineteenth century, many black Christians desired to bring the gospel message to Africa. Albert Raboteau notes that "the challenge of African missions loomed large in the consciousness of black Christians.... Symbolically, the mission to redeem Africa confirmed the importance of African Americans as a people."[31] One of the greatest black leaders of mission to Africa was Alexander Crummell (1819–1898). After studying for the priesthood in the Episcopal Church, Crummell took holy orders in England because racial prejudice precluded his ordination in the U.S. Crummell became a missionary educator in Liberia. After many years, he returned to the U.S. to work for black education, civil rights, and solidarity with Africa. Thus, the global missionary movement had important effects at home as well as abroad, as American Christians, many of them blacks and women, became missionary leaders.

Education

Christian missionaries felt called by God to serve in faraway places; many Christian educators felt just as strongly called to work here in the United States. Throughout much of the nineteenth century, a strong sense of religious mission infused education in the United States, from the Sunday schools to the colleges and even to the beginning of some universities.

For Protestants, a key institution was the Sunday school. In an earlier chapter, we noted the importance of Sunday schools in the reconstruction of the South. Among southern Christians especially, hymns, Bible verses, and prayers shaped the culture. Children were encouraged to seek conversion as the entry point into Christian life—especially in Baptist, Methodist, and Presbyterian Sunday schools. And the Sunday school was vital not only in the South but throughout most of the United States. Sunday schools began in late eighteenth-century England as a means to rescue factory children from a life of poverty. The American Sunday School Union, founded in 1824, started thousands of Sunday schools. Historian Anne Boylan notes that by the late nineteenth century, the Sunday school, with its annual picnics, attendance awards, and memorization contests, became "an agency of cultural transmission" that "almost rivaled in importance the nineteenth-century public school."[32]

Over the course of the nineteenth century, Sunday schools shifted their goals from social reform and literacy to the conversion of youth and finally to Christian nurture. By the late nineteenth century, many Christian educators were aiming for "growth, not conquest."[33] The new ideal, advanced by Horace Bushnell, was that young people should never know a time when they were not Christian. Families and ministers increasingly relied on Sunday school teachers to impart Christian faith to the young and to offer Bible classes for adults. Outreach to non–church members did not vanish entirely; yet in general, Sunday schools focused on nurturing insiders rather than evangelizing or serving those who were not already in the church.

In the nineteenth century, Sunday schools and public schools (also called common schools) worked together to form the minds and characters of children. In those days, public schools were said to be non-sectarian (which meant "generically Protestant") because they did not teach the specialized beliefs of Baptists, Presbyterians, or Methodists; instead, public schools simply took for granted the core beliefs shared by most Protestants. The role of the public schools was to teach basic academics and virtues; the role of the Sunday school was to impart the specific beliefs of each church.

Most Protestants felt at home in the public schools. A Protestant current still flowed through public education by the late 1800s, although that current was slackening. For example, historian and educator John Westerhoff researched the changes in *McGuffey's Reader*, a standard text in nineteenth-century schools. With each subsequent revision of *McGuffey's Reader*, the old-time religion of sin and salvation gradually gave way to "cultural beliefs, attitudes and values that under-gird American civil religion."[34] As the decades passed, the public schools were becoming culturally independent from the churches.

The fading of explicit Protestant teaching from the public schools, however, did little to improve conditions for Catholics. Among Protestants the notion persisted that Catholicism was incompatible with American citizenship. Public school texts and teachers still used words like "papist," "superstitious," and "unpatriotic" to describe Catholics.

No wonder a great many Catholics chose private schooling, even though it meant they had to "pay twice" for education—once for taxes to support the public school and again to finance their own Catholic school. Catholic schools proliferated, offering education free from anti-Catholic bias and inculcating Catholic faith. Many parochial schools offered instruction in languages other than English—a necessity for new immigrants. These parochial schools received a boost when Catholic bishops met in Baltimore in 1884 and called for a parish school to be built near every church. Catholic parents were told "to send their children to the parish school."[35] Priests could punish noncompliant parents by withholding the sacraments. To be sure, many priests and bishops deplored such tactics, and some were open to having Catholic children attend public schools.[36] Not all Catholics were in a position to choose among schools, but for those who did have school options, their choices expressed both religious identity and community concerns.

Thus far we have noted the importance of the Sunday school, the changing role of religion in the public schools, and the rise of Catholic parochial schools. We now turn to the field of higher education. For much of American history, private colleges funded by churches were by far the most prevalent form of higher education. In pre–Civil War America, most colleges were explicitly religious: daily chapel attendance was required, and campus revivals were common. The older church colleges sought to provide a classical education (including Greek and Latin) and to form the character of each student. There were many seminaries in the United States, but in general students who desired professional or advanced training beyond the college level had to go to European universities.

American higher education began to change with the rise of universities. Several universities may be traced back to the Morrill Land Grant Act (1862), which gave states acreage to be used for "land grant colleges." These land grant colleges offered practical subjects such as agriculture and engineering along with traditional courses. This new form of higher education had productivity as its goal, rather than character formation. Meanwhile, most of the older colleges were still linked to Protestant denominations. As universities began to open, "the old-time colleges became liberal arts colleges"[37] within a more diversified system of higher education.

Today the phrases "secular university" and "Christian college" stand in sharp contrast. But that contrast took time to come into focus. Many nineteenth-century Christian educators and donors to higher education saw the new universities as serving humanity—a goal consistent with Christianity. Historian George Marsden, on whose work we here rely, observes that the grand stone chapels on several university campuses testify to the central place Christianity was expected to have. Before 1900, required chapel attendance was common even at universities. Christian pastors, educators, and philanthropists took the lead in founding Johns Hopkins University (the first American school to specialize in graduate and professional education). The University of Chicago had older roots in a Baptist university. There are many more examples of Christian roots in the early history of universities. But Christianity did not maintain a controlling influence. "The universities themselves, as well as the vast majority of their disciplines, were defined according to a new professional scientific bias for which religion was considered irrelevant."[38] It was increasingly assumed that religion had no place in a university dedicated to science, objectivity, and productivity.

In a related development, some Christian colleges, such as Syracuse and Vanderbilt, decided to become universities. To reach a broader range of students, they not only had to expand their offerings; they had to loosen (if not terminate) the control of the founding denomination over the school. In situations in which a church college developed into a university, Christian beliefs gradually merged into "non-sectarian, or perhaps 'interfaith' liberal cultural ideals." Religion was regarded as private and therefore was not allowed to interfere with the work of the university.[39] Thus, in many institutions of higher learning, Christianity moved from the center to the margins.

An exception to this trend was Catholic University of America. American Catholic bishops wanted a university for research and graduate and professional education. The school was to be avowedly Catholic in character and purpose. The university's first rector, Bishop John Joseph Keane, described the new university as "a living embodiment and illustration of the harmony between reason and revelation, between science and religion, between the genius of America and the church of Christ."[40] In the tradition of Aquinas, reason and revelation were expected to work together in a living synthesis. The opening of Catholic University in Washington, D.C., in 1889 strengthened the university movement among American Catholics, building on a tradition pioneered by Notre Dame.

Many African American colleges and professional schools were founded in the years between the Civil War and World War I. Denied entrance to American colleges and universities, blacks created their own institutions of higher learning. Because African Americans did not segregate religion from education, most of these colleges were explicitly Christian, and many have remained so to this day. An early example was Fisk University, which began in Nashville shortly after the war, with sponsorship of the American Missionary Association and with several pastors as founders. Money for the first permanent building was raised by the Fisk Jubilee singers, who toured the Northern United States and Europe performing slave songs and spirituals. Other examples include Allen University (named for Richard Allen, founder of the AME Church), which opened its doors in 1870 in Columbia, South Carolina; Morehouse College in Augusta, Georgia, founded by a Baptist minister to prepare African American men for the ministry; and Atlanta's Spelman College for women, which began in 1881 in the basement of a Baptist church, receiving start-up funds from the women's American Baptist Home Missionary Society.

American blacks hoped that education could lead to a better future. Yet African American leaders had very different ideas about what the future should look like and how best to get there. Booker T. Washington (1856–1915), founder of Tuskegee Institute in Alabama, took a separate-but-equal approach that did not directly challenge segregation. Tuskegee Institute trained its students in skills and trades; Washington believed that hard work and self-improvement were a wiser strategy than direct conflict with racism.

On the opposite side of the spectrum was W. E. B. DuBois (1868–1963), a philosopher, social critic, and university professor who became the founder of the National Association for the Advancement of Colored People (1909). Dubois charged Washington with promoting black compromise and submission to whites. Black youth, said DuBois, should not settle for vocational training.[41] Education should do more than help people learn a trade; it should teach young people to examine society and inspire them to change it through political action.

African Americans moved out from under the shadow of slavery. Meanwhile, European immigrants moved across the ocean to take up a new life in the United States. Americans were moving in other ways too, as they confronted urban poverty and responded to new ideas in theology and science. The next chapter explores Christian responses to modernity in an industrial age.

Suggestions for Further Reading

Books

Dolan, Jay P. *The American Catholic Experience: A History from Colonial Times to the Present* (Doubleday, 1985). This book is an excellent introduction to the history of American Catholicism. See especially the several chapters under the heading "The Immigrant Church."

Gjerde, Jon. *The Minds of the West: Ethnocultural Evolution in the Rural Middle West, 1830–1917* (University of North Carolina Press, 1999). This book examines the immigrant experience as newcomers redefined their relationships to family, church, and nation. It also explores the dynamics between newcomers and people with older roots in the United States.

Ostling, Richard and Joan. *Mormon America: The Power and the Promise* (HarperSanFrancisco, 1999). This is a thorough yet readable introduction to the Mormon movement, past and present. For the westward migration, see especially the chapter entitled "The American Exodus."

Websites

"The Church in the Southern Black Community." A special collection within the larger website, "Documenting the American South," University of North Carolina. An excellent source for primary writings on African American churches during Reconstruction and on the role of women in these churches: http://docsouth.unc.edu/church/

"The Immigrant Experience." A special exhibit that is part of the official Ellis Island website. Includes six stories of immigration and a timeline of immigration with narrative descriptions for several historical periods: www.ellisisland.org/Immexp/index.asp

Discussion Questions

1. How did American Catholics deal with the ethnic diversity that came with late nineteenth- and early twentieth-century immigration from Southern and Eastern Europe?
2. Jon Gjerde contrasted individualist forms of religion with collective (communal) forms. What are the strengths and weaknesses of each?
3. In what specific ways did Christians contribute to the settlement of lands west of the Mississippi?
4. Why did the United States become the biggest "sender" of missionaries to foreign lands by the early twentieth century?
5. How did the goals and methods of Sunday schools develop over time?
6. What has been the role of religion in higher education? How has this changed since the mid-nineteenth century? What role, if any, do you think religion should play in higher education?

CHAPTER SIX

Responses to Modernity

Religious Unity, American Style

Four centuries after Columbus first made landfall in the New World, the Columbian Exposition was held in Chicago. This exposition was housed in the the "White City," a gleaming complex of buildings especially built for the purpose on the shore of Lake Michigan. In today's language, the White City might be called a theme park. The theme was the forward march of civilization—with the United States at the vanguard. Among the many exhibits and events at the Columbian Exposition, the most significant for Christianity in America was the "World Parliament of Religion." Lasting for seventeen days, the Parliament gathered delegates from around the world to present papers on religious themes ranging from theology to mission to unity among world religions. Muslims, Hindus, Buddhists, and others were invited to the Parliament—a radical step for the 1890s. This was a significant public acknowledgment that non-Christian religions were to be taken seriously. Indeed, the World Parliament of Religion is regarded as the beginning of the worldwide interreligious movement.[1]

The Parliament also signaled that religious pluralism in America was changing. As historian William Hutchison explains, religious pluralism in America has gone through several phases. For a long time, pluralism meant *toleration*, in which a dominant group allows other groups to exist relatively free of persecution. The new kind of pluralism, demonstrated at the Parliament of Religion, according to Hutchison, was a pluralism of inclusion[2] that goes beyond mere toleration and actually involves people or groups (who had not been part of the mainstream). For example, women were strong participants in the Parliament by the standards of that time. And according to historian Richard Seagar, Catholics who spoke at the Parliament were able to "gain a wider hearing in the Protestant dominated mainstream"; while the Jewish delegation "emphasized the contributions of Judaism to western religion and theology, Jewish views on social issues, and Jewish/Christian relations."[3] Even though the Parliament of Religion was shaped by Anglo-American Protestants who sometimes treated representatives of non-Christian groups as exotics, it nevertheless marked a growing awareness of global religions.

Christians in the Progressive Era

The Columbian Exposition with its World Parliament of Religion was the crowning glory of the progressive era. In light of its many achievements since Columbus, America seemed poised to lead the world into an age of peace and prosperity. In reality, however, industrialization confronted the U.S. with a daunting set of problems. Millions of factory workers lived in poverty, while a few business tycoons grew spectacularly rich. Several big-city governments were corrupt "machines" run by "bosses" who dispensed favors in return for votes. Rural life also had its problems; farmers tried to adapt to a changing economy, only to find themselves at the mercy of railroad companies to ship their produce to faraway markets. During this era, three presidents—Theodore Roosevelt, Robert Taft, and Woodrow Wilson—sought reforms; but the "progressive era" was by no means limited to politics. Historian Robert Crunden describes progressivism as a "climate of creativity, religious to the core." Progressivism tried to "restore the proper balances among Protestant moral values, capitalistic competition, and democratic processes, which the expansion of business in the gilded age seemed to have changed in alarming ways."[4] The religious dimension of the progressive era was the "social gospel," and it expressed Christian themes.

Some Christian leaders sought to reform society at the national level. They supported labor unions, worked to pass laws prohibiting child labor, and lobbied to secure public education for all children. But the two great pillars of progressive reform at the national level were Prohibition (the attempt to ban alcohol from society) and women's suffrage. Many reformers believed that a national ban on alcohol would help to alleviate urban poverty and that extending the vote to women would instill compassion and virtue into public life.

At the local level, city churches were on the front lines of the battle with urban poverty. Although some churches sold their downtown property and fled to the new suburbs, many of those who stayed in the city were committed to serving in poor neighborhoods. A new Protestant strategy in the progressive era was the "program church," which offered programs such as English language training and various forms of recreation to make city life more humane. Food pantries, clothing shelves, and shelters for the homeless were among the ministries of city Protestant churches.

Catholic parishes also responded vigorously to urban poverty. For emergency relief, they ran charities—such as the Society of St. Vincent de Paul—that gave food and clothing to the destitute. Anticipating the modern insurance companies, Catholic mutual benefit societies offered a shelter against poverty by having families "pay in and take out" for medical or funeral expenses. Catholic parishes improved their neighborhoods by building hospitals and schools. Thanks to prodigious fundraising and to nuns who worked for next to nothing, these institutions offered education and health care to those who would not have been able to afford it.

Catholic workers needed labor unions but were at first forbidden to join them. In the late nineteenth century, a great many Catholic immigrants worked in factories, in mines, and on the railroads. A growing American labor movement sought fair pay and safety for workers. "Catholic laymen and women, the Irish especially, were heavily committed to this call for reform."[5] But Catholic labor activism was blocked by an 1884 Vatican pronouncement barring Catholics from joining the Knights of Labor. The pope saw labor unions as secret societies, whose rituals competed for the devotion of the faithful. Moreover, the Vatican at that time condemned socialism, with which labor unions were associated. American Catholic leaders, however, saw that their people needed the labor movement, just as the labor movement needed the Catholics.

A breakthrough came when several American bishops, led by James Cardinal Gibbons, persuaded Pope Pius to change his position and allow Catholics to join labor unions. Another milestone occurred in 1891 when Pope Leo issued the encyclical *Rerum Novarum* ("On the Condition of Workers"). This document declared that the church has a duty to speak on social and economic issues. It defended workers' rights to receive fair pay and to organize into unions; and it encouraged Catholics to address social problems, particularly the conditions of workers in an industrial society.

The labor movement was not the only strategy for getting out of poverty. Three new strategies—the settlement house, the YMCA, and the Salvation Army—started in England and spread to the United States. We shall look at each of these in turn.

Although some were in rural areas, settlement houses were mostly inner-city dwellings that gave short-term help and long-term hope to poor people. Settlement houses took many forms, but the most famous one was Hull House in Chicago. The founder of Hull House was Jane Addams (1860–1935), a social reformer of Quaker and Presbyterian background. Hull House was a mansion in an old Chicago neighborhood, donated upon the death of its owner. Addams secured public support from prominent Chicago clergy for Hull House to be made into a settlement house. Here Addams would work to raise the awareness of the middle and upper classes, a goal that she saw as at least as important as offering assistance to the poor.[6] Middle-class and wealthier Americans needed to discover firsthand what life was like for those who struggled to survive. Hull House went beyond charity to what a later generation would call "consciousness raising." Hull House and other settlement houses inspired new leaders—including many women—to pioneer the fields of social work, advocacy, and urban studies.

The Young Men's Christian Association (YMCA) was a second strategy for dealing with the urban crisis. It was founded in London in 1844 by George Williams (1821–1905), a rural youth who became a Christian through a conversion experience. When Williams went to take a job in London, he found himself surrounded by "pickpockets, thugs, beggars, drunks, lovers for hire and abandoned children running wild by the thousands."[7] Williams saw that inexpensive, clean housing and Christian fellowship in the city could help keep young men from falling into a life of crime. With a group of like-minded laymen, Williams founded the YMCA to offer clean rooms and to conduct evangelism. From the beginning, the YMCA was explicitly Christian, nondenominational, and open to people of all classes.

After the Civil War, the Y caught on in many American cities. By the 1890s, its mission was defined as a service to "spirit, mind, and body." Bible studies and evangelism addressed the needs of the spirit. For the mind, Ys ran libraries and sponsored lectures; sometimes these educational offerings grew into colleges or trade schools. For the body, the Y offered swimming pools, bowling alleys, and gyms. To meet the need for vigorous sports that could be played indoors without an athletic field, volleyball and basketball were invented. Each Y had a dormitory to provide safe, low-cost housing.

The first Y for blacks was founded in 1853 in Washington, D.C., by a freed slave named Anthony Bowen. Many more black YMCAs would follow, and in a later generation YMCA leaders supported civil rights. In South Dakota, "Indian Association" Ys began in 1879 and became community centers for many Native Americans. Ys were also founded in San Francisco to serve the large Chinese population there. In some places, women could join or at least use YMCA facilities. The Young Women's Christian Association (YWCA) was organized in 1866 as an independent organization, run on principles quite similar to the YMCA. For a great number of city people who otherwise would have had no access to housing and recreation, the YMCAs and YWCAs made American cities livable. In the early days, this effort was strongly motivated by Christian evangelism.

A third Christian strategy for responding to urban poverty was the Salvation Army, founded in London in 1865 by William and Catherine Booth. The Booths had a passion to save the "untouchables" of the late nineteenth century: prostitutes, drunks, and criminals. In the early days, the Salvation Army's brass bands would hold forth outside of factories at closing time—or blare out their hymns outside of bars (much to the dismay of the owners). When a crowd had been gathered, the preacher proclaimed salvation to rowdy folk who were more likely to throw rocks and eggs than to repent of their sins. Salvation Army preachers were sometimes jailed for disturbing the peace. The Booths used street preaching and music to draw street people into a homeless shelter called a mission. There the destitute could be instructed in the Christian faith and receive short-term emergency help. The Salvation Army was ridiculed as a "slum brigade," but it spread to cities around the world, with many missions in the United States.

William Booth saw himself as fighting against the forces of evil for the soul of the city. Accordingly, he organized his followers in military-style ranks, complete with uniforms. New converts quickly were enlisted to save others. Women preached as well as men, and many became high-ranking officers. The Salvation Army's advocacy for women's leadership began with Catherine Booth. A powerful preacher in her own right, Catherine wrote and published in favor of full leadership of women. The Booths' daughter Evangeline became the "commander" of the Salvation Army in the United States. Under her leadership from 1904 to 1934, the Salvation Army strove to help orphans, single mothers, and alcoholics. The Salvation Army demonstrated female public leadership long before "respectable" churches ordained women.

We have noted several strategies that addressed urban poverty from a Christian perspective. Overshadowing them all was the Prohibition movement, a campaign to make the manufacture and sale of alcohol illegal. Later generations dismiss Prohibition as the work of petty moralists, who wanted to spoil everyone's fun. But a closer look reveals a movement striving to address issues of poverty and women's rights. Social reformers on the left as well as the right wings of progressivism supported Prohibition.

Alcohol abuse was linked to issues of poverty and domestic violence. In the late nineteenth century, few jobs were open for women and women's wages were very low. Public welfare was practically nonexistent. If a husband drank up his wages, the family would run out of food and clothes. Without money to buy coal or wood, tenement dwellers shivered through cold winters. Paying a doctor's fee for a sick child was out of the question. Women who were trapped in such conditions had no easy way out. The desperate straits of women and children in urban slums led reformers to connect the dots between alcohol and poverty, of which women and children were so often the victims. Alcoholism was a plague,

"Woman's Holy War"
Currier & Ives lithograph, c. 1874
Photo courtesy of Library of Congress, Prints and Photographs Division

and it was hoped that a cure could be found in Prohibition. Not surprisingly, many of the leaders in the Prohibition movement were women.

The Prohibition movement carried on where the pre–Civil War temperance movement left off. To put matters in context, it helps to recall that by 1830 "U.S. consumption of distilled spirits (hard liquor) reached a rate of five gallons per capita, nearly triple that of the latter part of the twentieth century."[8] The temperance movement used moral suasion to get individuals to use alcohol moderately or abstain from it on a voluntary basis. In contrast, the late-nineteenth-century prohibitionists aimed to make teetotalism (total abstinence from alcohol) mandatory by means of a constitutional amendment. Even before the national amendment went into effect in 1920, many counties and some states had already "gone dry."

The most powerful organization in the Prohibition movement was the Women's Christian Temperance Union (WCTU). Founded in 1874, it was led from 1879 to 1898 by Frances Willard. Willard was a Methodist, deeply committed to evangelical Christianity. For a time she was a lay preacher affiliated with Dwight L. Moody, the era's most famous evangelist. Willard also served as Dean of the Woman's College of Northwestern University in Chicago, but found her life's calling as a social reformer. Willard had a flair for packaging radical reforms in conventional language, which appealed to a broad swath of Americans. For example, she advocated woman's suffrage on the grounds that women must have the right to vote in order to protect the home. As her biographer Ruth Bordin notes, Frances Willard was the most famous reformer of the late nineteenth century, but she is now all but forgotten along with Prohibition.[9]

The Social Gospel

The story of Prohibition and women's suffrage will be continued in the next chapter. Both of these movements had roots in pre–Civil War evangelicalism, which combined revival and social reform. But by the late nineteenth century, revival and reform were parting ways, like a river diverging into two distinct streams.

One of these streams was the Social Gospel, which aimed to save society through social reform. Centuries earlier, Puritans had labored to achieve a godly society. And the pre–Civil War decades bristled with schemes to rid the world of sin. But unlike these earlier movements, the Social Gospel had little interest in saving souls. Instead of converting individuals, the Social Gospel strove to convert society. Instead of targeting individual sinners and changing lives one by one, the Social Gospel condemned corporate sins of greed and competition and sought to instill a Christlike character into the society, especially the economy.

What made the Social Gospel distinctive was its "elevation of social salvation."[10] At issue was the nature of the church's mission in the world. Individual salvation does little to help society, according to the Social Gospel. Indeed, too much emphasis on individual salvation only distracts people from social concerns; in the words of an old gibe, "Religion makes you so heavenly minded that you're no earthly good." Advocates of the Social Gospel called for the salvation of society to take precedence over the salvation of individuals—for as long as the "the church continued to fix its attention on saving sinners one by one," society would never change.[11] Thus, Social Gospel advocates drove a wedge between personal salvation and social reform.

Walter Rauschenbusch (1861–1918) was a prophet of the Social Gospel movement. While serving for several years as pastor of a church in "Hell's Kitchen," a New York City slum, Rauschenbusch was deeply moved by the plight of the urban poor. A study leave in Germany allowed him to immerse himself in the new liberal theology (described below). Later, while teaching at Rochester Seminary in New York, Rauschenbusch wrote *Christianity and the Social Crisis* (1907). This book used portions of the Hebrew prophets and some of Jesus' teachings as the foundation of the Social Gospel. Rauschenbusch declared that "the fundamental purpose of Jesus was the establishment of the kingdom of God, which involved a thorough regeneration and reconstitution of social life."[12] The church must carry out the ministry of Jesus by changing the social order. The trouble was that business and the economy were based on selfishness and competition. So the masses suffered poverty while a privileged few reveled in wealth. Rauschenbusch warned that unless Christians could lead the way to a new social order, violent revolution would destroy much of Western civilization. The only hope was for Christians to apply love, cooperation, and justice to public life.

German liberal theology deeply informed Rauschenbusch and the American Social Gospel movement. Here the word "liberal" refers to a specific movement in nineteenth-century German universities. It has been said that liberal theology aimed to adapt Christianity to modernity, using insights from the new social sciences. Of special importance to the American Social Gospel was the German theologian Albrecht Ritschl (1822–1889). Ritschl's theology centered on the kingdom of God, which he believed was started by Christ and must be completed by humanity. Ritschl disparaged individual salvation, insisting that Christianity must be social and communal. Society will change only when Christians recover the ethical, social dimension of the gospel.

Walter Rauschenbusch
Photo courtesy of the American Baptist Society,
American Baptist-Samuel Colgate Historical Library, Rochester, New York

A second German mentor of the American Social Gospel movement was the historian Adolf von Harnack (1851–1930), who taught that dogma (official church teaching) develops in history. Each new generation must shuck off the dead husk of dogma to find the grain of wheat, or gospel, inside. In his famous book, *What Is Christianity?* (1900), Harnack taught that the gospel consists of three things: the coming kingdom of God; the fatherhood of God and the infinite value of the human soul; and the higher righteousness and the command to love.[13] The Social Gospel took the teachings of theologians such as Ritschl and Harnack and adapted them to American contexts. In time, it became embedded in the structures of several denominational headquarters, whose leaders saw revivalism as a relic of a bygone era.

Revivalism and Dwight L. Moody

But revivalism was not going away. Far from it, for a great many American Christians continued to prize individual salvation as central to Christian faith. Their champion and the leading revivalist of the era was Dwight L. Moody (1837–1899). Converted to Christianity as a young adult, Moody felt called to work among inner-city immigrants. Many of his early activities were compatible with the Social Gospel: Moody organized Sunday schools, held prayer meetings, offered English classes, and opened a church for immigrant families; he also served as president of the Chicago YMCA. Then the Chicago Fire of 1871 left much of the city in ruins.[14] Thereafter, Moody resolved to pour all his energies into evangelistic preaching. YMCA connections helped him get speaking engagements in the British Isles, where his tour was so successful that he was invited to preach in the largest cities in the United States.

Moody updated revivalism for the late nineteenth century. Working closely with him was Ira Sankey, a musician who used solos and gospel hymns to prepare audiences for Moody's message. Unlike many revivalists of earlier times, Moody did not preach hell and damnation, but offered Christ's love for sinners. Sentimental stories carried his messages. As for theological issues that divided one denomination from another, Moody simply sidestepped them. Critics called him a theological lightweight. When asked why his preaching converted so many people (despite Moody's lack of theological acumen), Moody is said to have replied "God likes the way I do evangelism poorly, better than the way you do evangelism not at all." In the era before radio and television, up to one hundred million people heard Moody—a former shoe salesman who did not attend seminary and was never ordained.

Moody remains a watershed figure for the history of American Christianity—in part because he lived on the verge of a great divide in American Protestantism. One part of his legacy flows toward world evangelism. Not only did Moody inspire people to become missionaries; he also "produced and mobilized Christian businessmen, who munificently supported missions at home and abroad."[15] Believing that missionaries must cooperate across denominational lines to spread the gospel, these protégés of Moody helped to lay the foundations for the modern ecumenical movement. For

Dwight L. Moody
Photo courtesy of the Billy Graham Center Archives

example, the Student Volunteer Movement (SVM) was the evangelistic arm of the YMCA. Formed in 1888 under the inspiration of Moody, the SVM aimed to "evangelize the world in this generation." Toward that end, it recruited and trained some twenty thousand college students for missionary work. The leader of SVM was John R. Mott (1865–1955), a Methodist layman deeply influenced by Moody. Mott went on to help organize the Edinburgh Missionary Conference of 1910, which eventually gave rise to the World Council of Churches, of which Mott became the first president.

The other current of Moody's legacy, however, flows toward fundamentalist separatism. Around the time of Moody's death in 1899, a fundamentalist movement was beginning to coalesce in reaction to evolution, liberalism, and new methods of biblical study. Like other conservatives, Moody disliked these new trends; but he "lacked one trait that was essentially 'fundamentalist'—he was unalterably opposed to controversy."[16] Nevertheless, as historian George Marsden demonstrates, Moody's ministry nurtured the fundamentalist movement by updating revivalism, promoting holy living, and creating Moody Bible Institute to promote a particular view of biblical authority.

Recall that as a young man in Chicago, Moody combined evangelism and social work. But after the Chicago Fire—which must have seemed like the end of the world—Moody focused on winning souls. He came to believe that individuals can be saved, but society cannot be saved (the opposite of the Social Gospel movement). The world can only get worse until Christ returns for the final judgment. Comparing this world to a sinking ship, Moody famously declared, "I look upon this world as a wrecked vessel...God has given me a lifeboat and said to me, 'Moody, save all you can.'"[17] Moody felt a great urgency to convert individuals to Christianity before the end of the world and Christ's return.

Such convictions led Moody to support the prophecy conference movement. In opposition to the Social Gospel movement (which believed that society can progress toward the kingdom of God) the prophecy movement said, in effect, "We can't get there from here," because the world is doomed to judgment and destruction. Only after a great cataclysm will God bring in the kingdom. The prophecy movement read the Bible and human history according to a system called "dispensationalism." In the dispensationalist view, all of human history is laid out on a time line, marked by distinct chapters or dispensations. Each dispensation ends with human failure to live up to God's expectations. The whole system culminates with the world's destruction, the return of Christ, and the last judgment. Biblical prophecy is understood to predict future events along the dispensational timeline. Dispensationalists expected "unprecedented wickedness and unbelief" as the end drew near. Bible schools, prophecy conferences, and print media spread this message so effectively that "by 1900 dispensationalism had become a bedrock doctrine for vast numbers of conservative Protestants."[18]

The prophecy movement was under way long before Moody. Its chief architect was John Nelson Darby (1800–1883), a minister of a sect called the Plymouth Brethren. Darby lived in England and traveled several times to the United States and Canada to promote dispensationalism.

The key to his system was the "rapture"—a miraculous event in which Christians are taken up into heaven. The rapture signals that the return of Christ and the final judgment are at hand. Darby's system was based not only on the book of Revelation but on his reading of 1 Thessalonians 4:16-17 and on key passages in the Old Testament book of Daniel. All of Scripture had to be configured in such a way as to support his reading of these few passages.

Darby's ideas circulated in prophecy conferences and received a great boost from the publication of the *Scofield Reference Bible* (1909), which has been called the single most important publication in the history of fundamentalism. This Bible has an elaborate system of footnotes that helps the reader to interpret all of Scripture according to the dispensational system. These reference notes were prepared by Cyrus Scofield (1843–1921), a man well qualified to dwell upon the end of the world since he himself, as a Confederate Civil War soldier, had already experienced it.

Not all conservatives were dispensationalists, however. For example, the Presbyterian theologians of Princeton Seminary rejected dispensationalism as a modern innovation. Neither dispensationalism nor the rapture was included in the 1910 list of essential doctrines approved by the Presbyterian General Assembly. This list became known as the five points of fundamentalism: the inerrancy of Scripture, the virgin birth of Christ, Christ's substitutionary atonement (Christ died in our place), the resurrection of Christ, and the authenticity of miracles.[19] These beliefs were not to be compromised at any price.

Meanwhile, *The Fundamentals* tried to articulate traditional Christian teaching and defend it from attack. This important series of pamphlets—published between 1910 and 1915—set forth what its writers regarded as core Christian teachings. Rejected were evolution, German liberal theology, and new methods of Bible study. American and British scholars wrote articles for *The Fundamentals*, while wealthy businessmen paid for publication and distribution. Because of the pamphlets that bore this name, the term "fundamentalist" was applied to Protestants who resisted adapting Christianity to modernity.

American Protestantism was polarizing into liberal and conservative camps. Each side fought for control of key institutions. One famous battle in this war was the heresy trial[20] of Charles Briggs (1841–1914). A

Presbyterian pastor whose education included a stint at the University of Berlin, Briggs was appointed to be the chair of biblical studies at Union Seminary in New York. In his inaugural speech in 1892, Briggs denied biblical inerrancy—a particular view of biblical authority that insists on the literal truth of the Bible in all things. Briggs was tried for heresy, and in 1893 the Presbyterian General Assembly suspended him from its ministry. Union Seminary then severed its ties with the Presbyterians and kept Briggs on its faculty. Briggs separated from the Presbyterians and became Episcopalian. Briggs and Union were on the liberal end of the spectrum; but in decades to come, separation became a common conservative response to the conflicts over modernization.

Modernity challenged Catholics, too, but the overall response was different. Catholics, instead of separating from each other, to a large degree separated "intellectually from modern American culture and focused on strengthening the institutions of the church."[21] In Catholic America in the progressive era, theological liberals did not even establish a beachhead—much less gain control of key institutions. Instead, traditional believers remained firmly in charge of parishes, clergy, and schools. In 1899 Leo XIII issued a papal letter, *Testem Benevolentiae*, condemning the whole constellation of ideas labeled "Americanism." The prevailing winds in Catholicism at this time were anti-modern. There were, however, a few American Catholic intellectuals who questioned the nature of church authority and asked whether doctrine, like plants and animals, can actually evolve. This movement to reconcile Catholicism with modernity was snuffed out in 1907 by a papal encyclical that condemned all efforts to modernize Catholic theology.[22] These issues were largely suppressed until the Second Vatican Council, in the 1960s.

New Movements

While the older Christian groups responded to modernity in various ways, several new religious movements arose. Some of them appeared for the first time, and others built on foundations laid before the Civil War. While these movements differ from each other in important ways, they are all, in the words of historian Paul Conkin, "American Originals."[23] One of these movements, the Latter-day Saints (Mormons), has already been described. Other uniquely American faiths include Adventism, Christian Science, and Pentecostalism; these are introduced below.

Adventism takes its name from the word *advent*, which means "coming" or "arrival." Advent refers to the return of Christ, a belief affirmed by the Apostles' and Nicene creeds and proclaimed in several places in the New Testament. Many forms of Christianity keep this belief on the margins, but the Adventists make the return of Christ central. Throughout Christian history, the return of Christ has been understood in many ways, both literal and symbolic. As we have seen, the Social Gospel looked for a symbolic return of Christ, through a kingdom that comes gradually as society increasingly reflects Christian values. In contrast, dispensationalists expect a literal and sudden return of Christ in the near future. Adventists also expect a literal return of Christ, but the Adventist movement has its own unique story.

The largest Adventist group is the Seventh-day Adventists. It has roots back in the 1830s and '40s, when William Miller (1782–1849), a self-taught Bible student who later became a Baptist minister, started a new movement. Miller's study of Bible prophecies led him to calculate that Christ would return around 1843 or 1844. He began preaching and lecturing to persuade people of "the appointed time." Miller's message gained a wider hearing thanks to his colleague Joshua Himes (1805–95), a Christian Connection minister with a talent for publicity. By the hundreds and then thousands, people heard Miller's lectures and saw his apocalyptic charts. Many were persuaded by Miller's sincerity and the logic of his interpretation, which involved charting history along a prophetic timeline. According to some estimates, up to one million people believed Miller's message at the height of the movement.

William Miller won followers among Baptists, Methodists, Disciples, and other groups. Like the Restorationists, he longed to unite all churches to prepare them for the Lord's return. But unity was elusive: some followers of Miller (Millerites) left their churches in order to worship with like-minded Christians, while others were expelled from their churches. Still the movement spread. Miller came under great pressure to name specific dates for Christ's return, which he did with some reluctance. The last and most significant date was October 22, 1844. To prepare for the Great Day, many Millerites ceased farming; others signed away their businesses and divested themselves of all worldly goods. When the appointed time came, believers gathered to hear the last trumpet and to see the Lord "appearing on the clouds." When the next day dawned and Jesus had not appeared, the faithful suffered a "Great Disappointment." Newspapers made great sport of the non-event, publishing satirical cartoons of Millerites wearing white robes, waiting on hilltops or rooftops for their ascension. Readers were advised to return to business as usual.

Of several Adventist leaders who tried to salvage the movement, the most successful was Ellen White (1827–1915). White had been a follower of William Miller, but after the Great Disappointment, she worked with her husband and several others to reorganize the former Millerites. In 1863 these efforts took shape as the Seventh-day Adventist Church.[24] White's first priority was to explain the Great Disappointment in such a way that believers could still expect Christ's return. This she achieved by means of her heavenly sanctuary doctrine—which taught that Christ *did* return in 1844, not to this earth but to his heavenly sanctuary. In heaven, said White, Christ is now forgiving sins and cleansing people in preparation for his final return to earth. In other words, the Millerites had been right about the October 22, 1844 date; they were only mistaken about the location. According to White, Christ's advent was to the heavenly sanctuary, not to this earth.

The Seventh-day Adventists refrained from naming a precise date for Christ's return to earth. They did, however, insist that believers get ready. Ellen White claimed to receive visions, which told her followers how to prepare for Christ's return; her husband published accounts of these visions in books and pamphlets. One of White's most important visions directed the faithful to observe the Sabbath on the "seventh day" (Saturday), a practice that still distinguishes Adventists from other Christians. White also directed her followers to abstain from alcohol and tobacco, meat, and caffeine. Many Seventh-day Adventists revered White as a prophet with a direct line to God, while other Adventists were reluctant to ascribe special powers to her. In any case, White's advice on holy living was widely read beyond the Adventist fellowship, making her one of the best-selling religious authors of her generation.

As part of their commitment to holy living, Adventists invented dry breakfast cereal—which became a favorite American food and a big business. Both Kellogg and Post cereals originally had ties to the Seventh-day Adventists in Battle Creek, Michigan. There Dr. John Harvey Kellogg "helped perfect a method of turning cooked grains into dried flakes."[25] For a time Kellog was head of the Western Health Reform Institute, which practiced natural therapies for illnesses and explored diet as a strategy for preventative health care. The Adventists pioneered modern health foods and anticipated some alternative therapies. Today the Seventh-day Adventists report close to thirteen million members worldwide.[26]

Healing and female leadership were themes shared by another new religious group that arose at roughly the same time: the Church of Christ (Scientist). This movement claimed to use spiritual forces to achieve physical healing. It was founded in 1879 by Mary Baker Eddy (1821–1910). In her youth Eddy suffered from many ailments; she reported being cured by Phineas P. Quimby (1802–1866) through his techniques of mesmerism and hypnotism. Some years later she claimed to have healed herself of a back injury; this experience showed her that "all healing should be accomplished by the spirit and the mind without the aid of drugs." This revelation inspired the Christian Science movement to proclaim "mind over matter" for healing.

Mary Baker Eddy gained about one hundred thousand followers within her lifetime. She built the "Mother Church" in Boston and founded the Massachusetts Metaphysical College to train healers. She wrote *Science and Health*, which, alongside the Bible, functions as scripture in the Church of Christ (Scientist). Eddy also built a "media empire" with the *Christian Science Monitor* as its flagship publication. Historian Stephen Prothero, from whose work this information comes, notes that theologically, Mary Baker Eddy either rejected or radically reinterpreted basic Christian doctrines. For example, instead of a traditional view of sin and salvation, she taught that evil, "sickness, pain and death are illusions that can be manipulated by mental and spiritual means."[27] Mary Baker Eddy did retain some residue of Christianity in her teachings. Some of her early disciples, wishing to move further away from Christianity, left Eddy's movement to form "New Thought" strategies for health and success. In the twentieth century, Norman Vincent Peale popularized a formula for success known as "the power of positive thinking," which in some ways resembled the teachings of Mary Baker Eddy.

Pentecostalism

The modern Pentecostal movement erupted in Los Angeles, California, in 1906 when a revival broke out in a warehouse church on Azusa Street. The Azusa Street revival has been called the most important religious event in the United States in the twentieth century. The original revival blazed on long enough to draw people from about town, across the country, and around the world. Pentecostal fire quickly spread from Los Angeles to Chicago and Miami, and then to places like Rio de Janeiro, Seoul, and Johannesburg.

Pentecostalism is the fastest-growing form of Christianity in the world. Take, for example, the Church of God in Christ (COGIC), the largest African American Pentecostal church. It was founded by Charles Mason (1866–1961), who received Spirit baptism at Azusa and brought it back to his already existing network of holiness churches in Memphis. By the year 2005, COGIC had about 5.5 million members in the United States. The Assemblies of God, which also has historic ties to the Azusa Street revival, was approaching three million members in the U.S.

The early Pentecostals did not expect the world to last long enough for later generations to remember their revival. Indeed, they believed that the return of Christ was at hand, for not since the first Pentecost had the Holy Spirit descended with such power. This power came in many forms, but the experience of "speaking in tongues" was called the "sign gift." Tongues speaking, also called "glossolalia," is a form of ecstatic speech that can be translated only by someone with another spiritual gift—that of interpretation. Related to this was "xenolalia," the gift of instant fluency in known languages (see Acts 2:6). Early Pentecostals who claimed to receive this gift felt that the Spirit was equipping them to evangelize the world before Christ's return. Also reported at Azusa were miraculous healings and dramatic gifts of preaching, prayer, and song.

Perhaps the greatest miracle was that in the warehouse on Azusa Street, blacks, whites, Hispanics, and Asians worshiped together. This was a scandal in the "Jim Crow" era when laws barred blacks from riding in the same train cars as whites, drinking from the same fountains, or eating in the same restaurants. But at the Azusa street revival,

> what seemed to impress—or disgust—visitors most...was...the fact that blacks and whites, men and women, embraced each other at the tiny altar as they wept and prayed. A southern white preacher later jotted in his diary that he was first offended and startled, then inspired, by the fact that, as he put it, "the color line was washed away by the blood [of Jesus]."[28]

Critics used racial slurs common in that era to ridicule the revival. But to those who were caught up in the Spirit, the coming together of races was miracle, gift, and sign of the end times all rolled into one.

The key leader of the Azusa Street revival was William Seymour (1870–1922). Seymour embodied several ingredients of Pentecostalism, the first of these being African American heritage. Born to former slaves in Louisiana, Seymour came from a background rich in spontaneous prayer and preaching.

As a young adult, Seymour worked in various cities and became involved in holiness groups—a second basic ingredient of Pentecostalism. Many of the holiness groups stemmed from the Methodist movement started by John Wesley in eighteenth-century England. A much-debated aspect of Wesley's teaching was sanctification (also called holiness or perfection), which meant living a holy life by the power of God's love. Early Methodists were regarded by many as extremists. Over time, as Methodism became more mainstream, many small holiness groups arose to rekindle the zeal that they felt had been lost. One such group was the Evening Light Saints, a radical Wesleyan group whose teachings included complete holiness, "divine healing...and the promise of a worldwide Holy Spirit revival"[29] heralding Christ's return. Seymour belonged to this group for a time in Cincinnati.

Seymour picked up a third ingredient of Pentecostalism from Charles Parham (1873–1929), a white holiness teacher sometimes credited with founding Pentecostalism. This third ingredient was speaking in tongues (as described in Acts 2:6–8) as the sure sign of Holy Spirit baptism. In his Bible schools in Topeka and Houston, Parham encouraged his students to seek the gift of tongues; he also linked spiritual gifts to biblical prophecies of the end times.

William Seymour, leader of the Azusa Street Mission

Studying under Parham, Seymour had to listen from the hallway—since blacks were not allowed to sit in the same classroom with whites. Nevertheless, Parham convinced Seymour to seek the gift of tongues as a sign of Spirit baptism. Not yet having received that gift, Seymour traveled to Los Angeles in 1906 to work in a holiness church there. But the leaders rejected Seymour's message about speaking in tongues. Seymour then joined a small group of like-minded seekers. After much fasting and prayer, Seymour and others finally received the gift of tongues. Soon so many people came to hear Seymour preach that a larger space was needed. The fellowship rented an abandoned building on Azusa Street in an African American neighborhood.

This became the scene of an exuberant, round-the-clock revival, which lasted for about three years. Seymour's former teacher Charles Parham visited Azusa Street. There Parham found the "holy ghost bedlam" offensive, and the mixing of the races alarming. The tongues speaking he heard sounded like gibberish to him rather than like the actual foreign languages he expected. Historian Paul Conkin notes that Parham "tried to control the revival and was quickly rebuffed by local leaders."[30] Seymour himself suffered a setback when one of his co-workers absconded with the mailing list for Seymour's *Apostolic Faith Magazine.* The loss of this database deprived Seymour of having a direct voice in the growing

Pentecostal movement.[31] As the original revival abated, Seymour became a local pastor toiling in an urban mission. Some years after Seymour's death, the old warehouse-church on Azusa Street was torn down, leaving no physical trace of the birthplace of Pentecostalism.

Early Pentecostalism was fraught with internal tensions. The races that had mixed so freely at Azusa street soon divided into the mostly white Assemblies of God and the largely black Church of God in Christ, not to mention a host of smaller groups. Disputes flared up over biblical prophecy and spiritual gifts. But these conflicts did not stem Pentecostal growth; indeed, each new group scattered more sparks across the religious landscape, spreading Pentecostal fire. For "despite doctrinal controversies and schisms, the central appeal of Pentecostalism has never been an issue of belief but a special quality of experience."[32] Early Pentecostalism appealed strongly to poor people, because it offered a direct encounter with God and a religion of healing, joy, and hope.

Suggestions for Further Reading

Books

Conkin, Paul. *American Originals: Homemade Varieties of Christianity* (University of North Carolina Press, 1997). Historical essays on American religious movements: Restorationists (Christians and Disciples); Unitarians and Universalists; Adventists and Jehovah's Witnesses; Church of Jesus Christ (Mormons); Christian Science; and the Holiness and Pentecostal movements.

Marsden, George. *Fundamentalism and American Culture: The Shaping of Twentieth-Century Evangelicalism 1870–1925* (Oxford University Press, 1980). This study traces the social, historical, and religious currents that produced the fundamentalist movement and places it in the larger context of American religion and culture.

Rauschenbusch, Walter. *A Theology for the Social Gospel* (Westminster John Knox, 1997). First published in 1917, this is the classic statement of the Social Gospel by its foremost American spokesman.

Zink-Sawyer, Beverly. *From Preachers to Suffragists* (Westminster John Knox, 2003). The author traces the careers of three women who were ordained ministers *and* activists in the movement for women's suffrage. This book addresses the history of women in the ministry and social reform.

Websites

The Fundamentals. Online text of the original series of pamphlets for which the Fundamentalist movement was named: www.geocities.com/Athens/Parthenon/6528/fundcont.htm

The Ram's Horn. An international Social Gospel magazine published in Chicago at the turn of the nineteenth to the twentieth century. This site offers period cartoons and graphics on subjects such as immigration, Prohibition, and wealthy businessmen oppressing the poor: ehistory.osu.edu/osu/mmh/Rams_Horn/default.cfm

Discussion Questions

1. What is "religious pluralism," and how has it changed over time?
2. Name several religious movements or strategies that sought to improve conditions among the urban poor. Which of these strategies, if any, are still viable?
3. Drawing upon German liberal theology, Walter Rauschenbusch articulated a theology for the Social Gospel. What were the chief tenets of this theology?
4. Dwight L. Moody was a key figure in American religious history. His legacy flowed in two seemingly opposite directions—what were they?
5. Two new religious movements—the Church of Christ (Scientist) and the Seventh-day Adventists—were founded by women. What is the significance of female leadership for these movements?
6. An eyewitness to the Azusa Street revival marveled that "the color line was washed away by the blood of Jesus." What prompted his observation, and why was this so shocking at the time?

CHAPTER SEVEN

From the "Great War" to the Cold War

The Great War

It often is said that the nineteenth century did not end until the Great War began in Europe. This conflict, later renamed World War I, ended an era of relative peace and optimism and opened the door to suffering on an unimagined scale. Christianity declined in Europe, and in the United States it faced new challenges at almost every turn.

The Great War started in 1914 when the assassination of the Archduke Ferdinand lit the fuse to an explosive network of European alliances. Germany and Austria-Hungary fought against Britain, France, and Russia. The United States stayed out of the war until 1917; but when German submarines sank several American ships, President Woodrow Wilson (who earlier advocated neutrality) asked Congress to declare war.

Except for the historic peace churches (including Quaker, Mennonite, and Brethren), most American Christians were eager to support the war effort. Churches hosted Liberty Loan drives to raise money; they recruited chaplains for the military and volunteers for the Red Cross and similar agencies. A broad swath of American Christians heard their ministers preach patriotic sermons bristling with anti-German rhetoric: Billy Sunday, a celebrity preacher of his day, said, "If you turn hell upside down, you will find 'Made in Germany' stamped on the bottom."[1]

Anti-German propaganda probably hurt more Americans than Germans, since "up to ten million recent European immigrants or their American-born children had strong ties to Germany and Austria-Hungary."[2] Lutherans and Catholics were the largest religious groupings of Americans of German background, and they bore the brunt of the patriotic craze to rid America of everything German. For example, in the Midwest, German Lutherans, having arrived in the U.S. more recently than their co-religionists back east, became targets. Historian Fred Meuser notes that after 1917, hundreds of German Lutheran parochial schools were closed. Worship services were interrupted and meetings of clergy were broken up. "Pastors were sometimes daubed with yellow paint, made to kiss the flag, to pledge allegiance, and to subscribe to war bonds.... German-speaking Lutherans were threatened with dire consequences if they used the forbidden tongue." Such antagonism "hastened the divorce of Lutherans from their former cultural loyalties."[3]

Other groups with German roots, such as the Mennonites, were likewise pressured to abandon their German heritage. Meanwhile, some Americans, unable to distinguish Germans from Scandinavians, harassed Swedish or Norwegian American Lutherans. As American Catholics discovered long before the Great War, ethnic prejudice often has religious dimensions, and on the home front this was a shadow side of the war.

The sunny side was the hope that this war would move history toward the progressive ideals of the late nineteenth century. For example, it was said that America and its allies could clear the path of progress by getting rid of the German military threat; that defeating the Germans would further shape the world along the lines of democracy and Christianity; and, most ambitious of all, that the Great War would "end all wars" and "make the world safe for democracy." With its huge contribution of troops and supplies to the war effort, the U.S. turned the tide of the war and played the role of what Ernest Lee Tuveson has called a "redeemer nation."

When the war ended in 1918, Woodrow Wilson called for a League of Nations to secure world peace on a collective basis. A Presbyterian of the post–Civil War generation, Wilson tended to implement policies shaped by prophetic and progressive views of history. After the war, Wilson said that "America had the infinite privilege of fulfilling her destiny and saving the world,"[4] and now this victory must be translated into a lasting peace by a covenant of the League of Nations. (The covenant language recalls Puritan ideals of sacred and binding agreements between God and nations). The United States Senate, however, refused to approve participation in the League of Nations. At the time, many progressive Christians in America were greatly disappointed with U.S. refusal to join the League.[5] But in the 1920s America turned its attention inward. Thus, in the space of a few years, the U.S. swung from neutrality to war to isolationism.

The Great War did not have nearly the impact on America as it did on Europe. American deaths from combat and disease were about one hundred thousand, and American lands were unscathed by the war "over there." Not so in Europe. The Great War was a cataclysm in which, as a later Irish ballad put it, "a whole generation was butchered and damned." About 6 million European soldiers died in the war; starvation and disease killed some 12.5 million civilians. Huge tracts of land were destroyed by trench warfare. Instead of ending all wars, the Great War gave an opening to the Bolshevik Revolution in Russia and set the stage for the rise of Adolf Hitler. That the Great War soon became known as World War I speaks volumes: it was only the first part of a much larger conflict.

In Europe, wartime nationalism co-opted Christianity so badly that Europe's historic faith, already in decline in the nineteenth century, never fully recovered. And as for the liberal Protestantism of the prewar era, with its values of progress and brotherhood—the carnage of the war made it all seem absurd.

Into this void came "crisis theology" (also called "neo-orthodoxy"). Its primary proponent was Karl Barth (1886–1968). A Reformed pastor born in Switzerland, Barth was trained in liberal theology in Germany. He served as a parish pastor during the Great War, and the suffering he witnessed caused him to reject liberal theology, with its hopeful view of human nature and social progress. In 1922 Barth published his *Commentary on the Romans*, a book said to have fallen "like a bombshell on the playground of liberal theologians." Here Barth saw God as "wholly other" (not a human being writ large). Sin cannot be fixed (not even by education or enlightenment), and evil is real. Human beings cannot save themselves; only God's Word can. That Word comes when God speaks from outside ourselves and intervenes to save us. As the twentieth century unfolded, Barth's theology influenced generations of pastors in the United States, particularly in the mainline Protestant churches.

After the war, many American Christians, chagrined by their binge of religious patriotism, repented in dust and ashes. Historian Garry Bullert documents a "pervasive guilt over the church's championing of World War I." Peace groups, many of them church-related, arose to prevent the churches from ever again supporting war. Overlapping with their efforts was the Outlawry movement, a campaign to make war illegal. The Federal Council of Churches (an ecumenical Protestant group founded in 1908 to address social issues) likewise turned from its former support of the Great War to embrace the new pacifism. Several Protestant journals took strong anti-war stands in the 1920s, and "hundreds of prominent ministers vowed publicly never to support or sanction another war."[6] This reaction against the Great War, however salving it may have been at the time, only made it harder for American Christians to size up the threat posed by Hitler in the 1930s.

Fundamentalist-Modernist Controversy

As we noted in the previous chapter, American Protestantism was already polarizing into conservative and liberal camps before the Great War. This conflict between the so-called liberals (modernists) and the conservatives (fundamentalists) sharpened in the 1920s and continued to shape American Protestantism through the twentieth century. Both sides descended from pre–Civil War evangelicalism, but in responding to modernity, each side went its own way.

Let us look briefly at each position in turn. Fundamentalists charged modernists with denying the authority of the Bible and with revising or rejecting basic beliefs such as the virgin birth and the resurrection of Christ. Modernists, insofar as they questioned the absolute truth claims of Christianity, were undercutting the church's mission of evangelism. The fact that liberal theology was, in large part, "made in Germany" was yet another strike against it in America during and after World War I.

Liberals, for their part, interpreted the Bible developmentally, not as a timeless revelation. Authority belonged to those who could interpret the Bible by the light of modern sciences. Liberals charged fundamentalists with obscurantism, anti-intellectualism, and contempt for progress. They saw fundamentalists as abandoning the church's call to social reform in favor of personal salvation, and as undercutting religious unity in favor of doctrinal orthodoxy.

At stake was the nature of religious authority, and the outcome would determine who was in charge of churchly institutions. The modernist forces and their fundamentalist foes fought for control of seminaries, colleges, and congregations. These conflicts raged through the Presbyterian Church (USA), and among Northern Baptists, though many other denominations also felt the heat.

In the first years of the 1920s, no one knew which side would prevail. Each camp had articulate leaders and strong constituencies. On the liberal side was the Baptist minister Harry Emerson Fosdick (1878–1969), whose 1922 sermon called "Shall the Fundamentalists Win?" became a rallying cry for modernists. On the conservative side was J. Gresham Machen (1881–1937), a professor at Princeton Seminary, whose 1923 book, *Christianity and Liberalism*, argued that liberalism was a different religion altogether from Christianity. When Princeton Seminary became more open to modernists, Machen and other Presbyterian conservatives moved to Philadelphia, where they founded Westminster Theological Seminary.

This battle for control of church institutions took place against the backdrop of larger conflicts. On the global stage, the Russian Revolution ushered in a Communist regime, the sworn enemy of religion and democracy. Alarmed that the world was not "made safe for democracy" after all, Americans sought to root out Communism from labor unions at home. Socialists, suspected radicals, and some immigrants became victims of the "Red Scare" in the 1920s.

While Communism became the new external threat, many people saw the American public school as the internal threat. For good or ill, the relationship between education and religion was changing. Previous generations expected the schools to support Protestant Christianity. But "in the half century since the Civil War, the schools had generally experienced a revolutionary secularization."[7] Early in the twentieth century, many Americans feared that the public schools were abandoning Christianity. The flash point was the teaching of evolution in the public schools. Not only did evolution conflict with a literal interpretation of the creation accounts in Genesis; conservatives argued that if God is not the Creator, then there is no higher authority to whom human beings are morally accountable. Thus, the teaching of evolution in the public schools signaled that the schools were preparing children for life in a godless society.

Alarmed, several southern states passed legislation outlawing the teaching of evolution in the public schools. But John T. Scopes, a science teacher in Dayton, Tennessee, defied the law and openly taught evolution in his classroom. Charges were brought and Scopes' case came to trial in 1925. Defending Scopes was the American Civil Liberties Union, led by the famous lawyer Clarence Darrow. Prosecuting Scopes for the State of Tennessee was William Jennings Bryan, a three-time presidential candidate who had been secretary of state under Woodrow Wilson. The proceedings quickly became a media circus, dubbed the "Monkey Trial" (after the notion that humans evolved from monkeys). John T. Scopes was convicted and fined for breaking Tennessee law. In the larger court of public opinion, however, Scopes won and the fundamentalists lost. William Jennings Bryan's distinguished career of public service did not stop the press from lampooning all conservative Christians as ignorant country bumpkins. Bryan died a broken man five days after the trial.

The Scopes Monkey Trial was a "thumbs down" for the public image of fundamentalism. "The working strength of fundamentalism everywhere depended greatly on the national mood," according to George Marsden. "In the early summer of 1925, fundamentalism was at its peak; by the next year its strength was rapidly sinking."[8] At about the same time, fundamentalists also lost control of the Presbyterian General Assembly.

Fundamentalists now began leaving mainline denominations to create their own churches, Bible schools, publishing houses, and evangelistic ministries. In time an entire network of conservative Christian organizations grew up outside of the mainline denominations. Conservatives who chose to stay in mainline churches were rebuked by those who chose

Clarence Darrow and William Jennings Bryan, 1925, Dayton, Tennessee
Photo © Bettmann/Corbis

to leave. The conservatives were so badly divided that by the 1930s the fundamentalist movement "had been pared back" to those with roots in the "older, interdenominational, pre-millennialist" and "Bible school network," according to historian Joel Carpenter. The surviving fundamentalist movement "would tend its own affairs, nurse its grudges, and prophesy God's impending wrath, yet still hope for a revival."[9]

Liberals predicted that fundamentalism would become extinct like the dinosaurs. But something closer to the reverse was true, for those Protestant groups that had cast their lot with modernism declined steadily throughout the twentieth century. Sidney Ahlstrom has observed that as early as the 1920s several of the "mainstream denominations grew increasingly out of touch with the classic Protestant witness."[10] Thus, to prevail in the older denominations was something short of a triumph.

Unfinished Business of the Progressive Era: Prohibition and Women's Vote

After the Great War, the progressive era and the Social Gospel had some unfinished business to tend to: Prohibition and women's suffrage. We have noted that Prohibition had roots in evangelical reform movements before the Civil War. After decades of campaigning, the Eighteenth Amendment was finally ratified in 1919 and Prohibition went into effect in 1920. For over a decade, it was illegal to manufacture, sell, or transport alcohol in the United States. Prohibition was a victory for progressives and Social Gospel activists battling poverty; it was also a triumph for those who saw alcohol as inherently evil. Prohibition became law through the efforts of a broad coalition of religious and social activists. Thus, Sydney Ahlstrom described Prohibition as "*the* great Protestant crusade of the twentieth century—the last grand concert of the old moral order."[11] In the short term, alcohol consumption went down and Prohibition seemed to be working. But soon organized crime began to thrive on bootlegging and the "speakeasy" culture of illegal bars. The Eighteenth Amendment proved impossible to enforce. It was repealed in 1933.

The drive for Prohibition was closely related to the cause of women's suffrage. Not only did these campaigns overlap in leadership and supporters, but progressive reformers expected *both* Prohibition and women's suffrage to shape American society according to Christian morals.

Like Prohibition, the campaign for the women's rights began in evangelical reforms before the Civil War. But the woman question (as it was then called) had even stronger ties to the anti-slavery movement. In early nineteenth-century America, women who lectured on the abolitionist circuit ran afoul of social taboos against females speaking in public. At every turn, female anti-slavery activists ran into legal and religious, political and social barriers, and these experiences made them all the more determined to work for women's rights. For example, Susan B. Anthony (1820–1906) was an ardent abolitionist of Quaker background who spent the decades after the Civil War in the cause of women's suffrage. Female abolitionists (and a few of their male colleagues) declared that women's position in society resembled that of the slave: women could not vote, had few legal rights, were paid less than men, and were

A suffrage parade in New York City, May 6, 1912
Photo courtesy of the Library of Congress

expected to live under male control. Like blacks, women were told that their place in society was God's will. But religion is a two-edged sword; it can be used to defend the social order, or it can be used to remake it.

The 1848 convention in Seneca Falls, New York, is remembered as the formal beginning of the women's rights movement. Held in a Wesleyan Methodist church, this convention drew ministers and laypeople whose anti-slavery activities led them to seek equal rights for women. Religious issues were closely intertwined with women's rights, as can be seen in Elizabeth Cady Stanton's call to break the male "monopoly of the pulpit."[12] Immediately after the Civil War, women's rights activists hoped to combine female suffrage with voting rights for freed male slaves. But when this effort was rebuffed, the campaign for women's suffrage faced a long, uphill climb.

By the close of the nineteenth century, the women's movement was very diverse. It ranged from local woman's clubs that were largely a-political to national organizations bent on getting the vote for women. Women's groups addressed everything from cultural enrichment to Prohibition to local service projects. Black women's clubs promoted what was then called "racial uplift" through education and mutual support. There was a significant overlap between church membership and activity in women's groups.

But among early feminist leaders, assessments of Christianity varied. Some, like Elizabeth Cady Stanton (1815–1902), saw it as a barrier to women's rights. In 1895 and 1898, Stanton published the *Woman's Bible* to correct what she and others saw as anti-female interpretations of Scripture. This work became a best seller, but the National Woman's Suffrage Association "censured Stanton because it feared that the adverse publicity associated with the book would detract from" their cause.[13]

Moving toward the other side of the spectrum were those who saw Christianity as a possible support for the cause of women's rights. For example, Ida Wells-Barnett (1862–1931) was an African American journalist who promoted women's right to vote. She also led an international campaign against lynching, for which she sought the support of churches and Christian organizations such as the YMCA.[14] Other examples of women who saw Christianity as at least potentially friendly to women's rights include some of the first women to be ordained in the United States. Historian Beverly Zink-Sawyer has chronicled the life's work of three female pastors for whom ministry and advocacy for women's suffrage were closely related. These clergywomen combined "belief in the equality of women and belief in traditional Christian doctrine." They demonstrated that Christianity and women's rights "could be held together and employed for social change."[15] For example, Anna Howard Shaw (1847–1919) was ordained in the Methodist Church and later served as president of the National American Woman's Suffrage Association from 1904 to 1915. She saw her work for women's vote, like her work as a minister, as a divine calling.

Today the campaign for women's suffrage often is remembered as a secular movement. However, it had important religious dimensions; historian Evelyn Kirkley notes three. First, both pro- and anti-suffrage arguments used religion to argue their case—"if not as the primary argument, at least as an element." Second, many individual suffragists were motivated by religious faith. Third, and most important, "suffragists made the vote a religious crusade, imbuing it with respectability and righteousness."[16] A popular argument at the turn of the nineteenth to

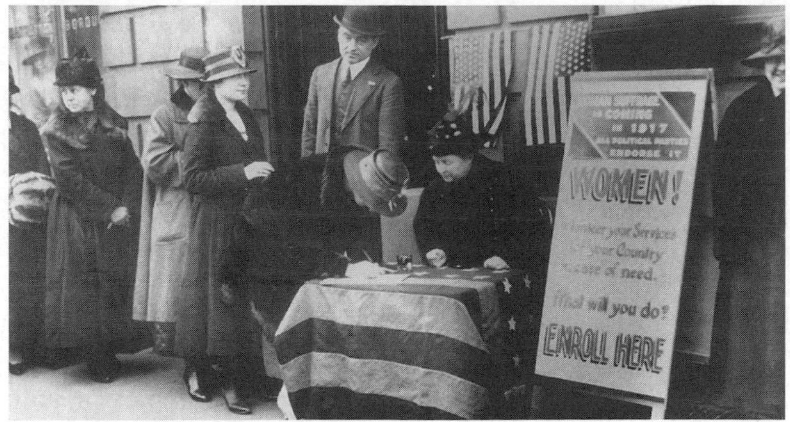

Suffragettes register to work as war volunteers during World War I
Photo courtesy of the National Archives and Records Administration

the twentieth century was that women were naturally more religious and moral than men, and therefore the female vote would elevate the political process and secure the moral improvement of society.[17] The Nineteenth Amendment, securing women's right to vote, was approved by Congress in 1919 and ratified by the states in 1920.

The Roaring Twenties and the Great Depression

The Nineteenth Amendment secured a basic civil right for half of the population. But the progressive era was by that time well past its zenith. Indeed, making money was the national passion between the Great War and the stock market crash of 1929. Some writers, like the advertising executive Bruce Barton (1886–1967), cashed in on Jesus. Barton's book *The Man Nobody Knows* portrayed Jesus as a great salesman whose secrets of success still applied in the modern era. Another religious entrepreneur, Russell Conwell (1843–1925), was a lawyer turned Baptist minister. Conwell wrote perhaps the most famous speech of the era, "Acres of Diamonds," which he delivered countless times. According to Conwell, "We ought to get rich if we can by honorable and Christian methods, and these are the only methods that sweep us quickly toward the goal of riches."[18] Conwell claimed that rich Christians are in a position to help others, as he himself did by founding in Philadelphia in 1888 the college that became Temple University.

But philanthropy could not stabilize American Christianity in the 1920s. We have already noted that the fundamentalist-modernist controversies racked several denominations. Meanwhile, church attendance declined in the 1920s and fewer missionaries were sent overseas. The malaise deepened when the Inter-church World Movement (a grandiose plan for Protestant ecumenism) imploded, leaving partner denominations with major debts. And when Al Smith, a Catholic, ran for president in 1928, many Protestants were alarmed; Smith lost the election to Herbert Hoover, but for the first time a Catholic came close to the presidency.

The 1920s were a time of cultural upheaval. Young women shocked their parents by "bobbing" their hair and wearing short "flapper" skirts. The automobile weakened community control over young adults. Some writers and intellectuals embraced hedonism, perhaps in response to the Great War. And the new science of psychology seemed to explain life apart from religion and to offer new ways to find personal freedom. Some of the changes were ominous: for example, the KKK renewed its terrorism against African Americans and widened its hatred to include Catholics, Jews, and recent immigrants. Gangsters got rich on bootleg liquor, and the Red (Communist) Scare gave people the jitters—but at least the economy was booming.

Then the stock market crash of 1929 derailed the Roaring Twenties and plunged the country into the Great Depression. Companies let workers go and cut back production. Jobs vanished. Farms went bankrupt, banks foreclosed mortgages, and thousands of families were cast adrift. Living standards plummeted, and according to historian J. Bradford DeLong, there was "no effective system of unemployment insurance to cushion job loss." In response to this prolonged crisis, President Franklin Delano Roosevelt brought "social democracy" to America through his New Deal policies. The New Deal laid the foundations for "the post–World War II American welfare state," which was based on "social security and unemployment insurance."[19] But the Depression years were grim; the American economy did not recover fully until World War II.

The Social Gospel, which had been dealt a severe blow by the Great War, made a comeback during the Depression. Many liberal Protestants supported Roosevelt's New Deal, hoping, as historian Mark Toulouse notes, to "socialize capitalism." The flagship publication of liberal Prot-

Dorothy Day, American reformer and journalist
Photo © Bettmann/Corbis

estantism was the *Christian Century*, and it called the nation to reject individualistic capitalism and "engage in a critical assessment of Christ and culture."[20] Some liberal Protestants complained that the New Deal merely tinkered with the old capitalist system instead of radically reforming it, and the Federal Council of Churches revised its social creed in 1932 to call for more radical forms of social planning.

Liberal Protestants were few in number compared to American Catholics. During the Depression, American Catholicism moved toward a greater sense of social responsibility. The immigrant churches were becoming less insular, and Catholics increasingly tried to respond in public ways to the needs of the times.[21]

Of many Catholic responses to the Great Depression, the Catholic Worker Movement stands out. Its guiding spirit was Dorothy Day (1897–1980). As a young adult, Day was a socialist, strongly attracted to Communism. But at age thirty, she dismayed her friends by converting to Catholicism. Deeply compelling to her were those Catholic spiritual traditions that embraced poverty and pacifism. In New York City during the 1930s, Day and her colleague Peter Maurin launched the Catholic Worker Movement. It began with a newspaper, the *Catholic Worker*, which became a forum for Catholic social reform. Day and Maurin then founded a community based on voluntary poverty, which gave food and shelter to the homeless. Several more houses of hospitality opened in the Depression years.

Through the Catholic Worker Movement, young intellectuals discovered voluntary poverty and social compassion. "The mixture of radicalism and Catholicism had an obvious appeal to people who had grown tired of the immigrant church." This was as far Left as you could go and "still be in the Church."[22] Catholic Workers were labor activists who could run soup kitchens and engage in theological debate and social analysis. But the Catholic Worker Movement came under criticism during World War II when Day (who had denounced Nazism in the 1930s) refused to support the war effort because she was a pacifist. The movement endured and trained up a new generation of activists after World War II. The Catholic Worker website recently reported over 185 Catholic Worker communities. All are "committed to nonviolence, voluntary poverty, prayer, and hospitality for the homeless, exiled, hungry, and forsaken. Catholic Workers continue to protest injustice, war, racism, and violence of all forms."[23]

In contrast to Dorothy Day, conservative Christians (both Catholic and Protestant) opposed socialism. Various societies, some of them quasi-religious, sprang up to promote American individualism and democracy and to denounce socialism. Those who believed in dispensationalism saw the Depression not as a failure of capitalism but as part of God's plan to bring about the end of the world. Most evangelicals, however, continued to preach salvation (rather than doomsaying) as God's answer to humanity's problems.

Of the various types of evangelicalism, Pentecostalism grew rapidly and several new expressions of it arose. A famous example is the Foursquare Gospel Church (its name referring to the four squares of salvation, Holy Spirit baptism, divine healing, and Christ's second coming). Its founder was Aimee Semple McPherson (1890–1944), an evangelist

Breadline of the unemployed at the Doyers Street Mission, New York City, 1930
Photo © Snark/Art Resource, NY

and healer. In a time when female religious leaders were rare, McPherson felt empowered by the Holy Spirit and by the words of Joel 2:28: "Your sons and your daughters shall prophesy." After years as a traveling evangelist, McPherson founded the Angelus Temple in Los Angeles. Thousands flocked to hear McPherson preach and to enjoy her flamboyant style of worship. Many claimed to receive miraculous healing of body and spirit. McPherson also opened the Angelus Temple Commissary to offer food, clothing, and short-term help for many who were "down and out." This became a significant relief center in Los Angeles during the Great Depression. McPherson's biographer Edith Blumhofer notes that "the people who had tended to support [McPherson] over the years were the plain folk who in the 1930s were particularly hard hit by the Depression."[24] McPherson became a national celebrity, and she was no stranger to scandal. But in the midst of hard times, she offered hope that miracles can happen.

During the Depression, vast numbers of Americans were tuning in to the new medium of radio, and McPherson was among the first preachers to use it effectively. Probably the most famous radio preacher, however, was Charles Fuller (1887–1969). His radio show, the *Old Fashioned Revival Hour*, was nationally syndicated in 1937, and by the early 1940s Fuller "had the largest audience in national network radio."[25] Evangelicals have always been media savvy, using the latest technologies to reach people with the gospel message. But radio also attracted demagogues with strident political agendas. For example, Father Charles Coughlin (1891–1979) was a priest whose broadcasts were laced with political commentary. During the Great Depression, he had millions of regular listeners. For a time Coughlin supported Franklin Roosevelt, famously urging his listeners to choose between "Roosevelt or ruin." For a while Coughlin promoted the New Deal, but he later drifted toward Nazism. His broadcasts took a sinister turn, and his anti-Jewish harangues convinced his Catholic superiors that it was time to unplug Coughlin. A familiar—and dangerous—voice was silenced.

African American Christianity in the 1920s and '30s

The great migration of black people to the cities continued after World War I, swelling the urban black churches and giving rise to new religious movements. Vincent Synan, a historian of the Pentecostal movement, observes that "since blacks in the South and elsewhere occupied the bottom rung of the social ladder, it was inevitable that large numbers would be drawn to Pentecostalism, representing as it did the religion of the poor."[26] Growing numbers of African American Christians felt blessed and empowered by Pentecostal worship.

Father Divine (c.1880–1965), an African American holiness minister, founded the "best known and most influential of the Holiness Churches"[27] to emerge in the 1930s. Father Divine opened the Peace Mission on Long Island, New York, where people came for worship, healing, and inspiration. He insisted on holy living (abstaining from known sins such as alcohol and tobacco abuse), believed in racial equality, and preached healing through positive thinking. During the Great Depression when so many people suffered from hunger, Father Divine gave lavish feasts for hundreds of poor people. His movement spread as he opened several churches (called "Heavens") in northern cities. Through his inspiring presence and acts of generosity, Father Divine encouraged people of all races to put their faith in him. Some of his followers began to address him as "God" and "Jesus Christ." It was said that Father Divine warned his followers against reading the Bible, lest this detract from his authority. In the 1940s Father Divine became embroiled in a series of financial disputes and his influence waned. He began his ministry in the Holiness tradition, but insofar as he made himself an object of worship instead of God, he departed from Christianity.

In contrast to Father Divine's Heavens, a this-worldly movement arose to confront issues of racism and social justice. Black nationalism celebrated Africanness as the core identity for black people. One can find roots of black nationalism much earlier, but the movement seems to have sharpened when black soldiers returned home from the Great War only to find that despite their military service to their country, racial prejudice was as strong as ever in the United States. Older movements, like progressivism and the Social Gospel, had failed to address racism. The Universal Negro Improvement Association (UNIA) became a new rallying point for black pride and progress. It was founded in 1914 by Marcus Garvey (1887–1940) and grew very strong in the early 1920s. Its main publication, *Negro World*, reached tens of thousands of people with a message of positive racial identity.

The UNIA had much to offer African Americans who were "alienated from a white version of Christianity," according to Albert Raboteau. It "supplied a weekly Sunday service, a baptismal ritual, a hymnal, a creed, a catechism, the image of Jesus Christ as a 'Black Man of Sorrows' and the Virgin Mary as a 'Black Madonna.'"[28] It was one thing to embrace a Christian faith that affirmed blackness. It was another thing to place too much faith in the person of Marcus Garvey. Convicted of financial misconduct, Garvey was sentenced to prison and eventually deported. The movement of black nationalism was of course more enduring than Garvey's personal leadership.

Black nationalist religion took a more strident form in the Nation of Islam or Black Muslims. The Nation of Islam had older roots but coalesced in Detroit in the 1930s. Its rejection of Christianity as the religion of "white devils" and its call for black separatism distinguished the Nation of Islam from traditional forms of Islam (which called for peace and equality among the races). A thorough discussion of Islam and its many forms is beyond the scope of this book. For our purposes, we must note that by the early twentieth century, African Americans were becoming increasingly aware of religions faiths beyond Christianity. Some of these faiths were a direct challenge to Christianity, while others incorporated elements of Christianity. But the black Christian churches remained the spiritual anchor of most African American communities.

World War II and the Cold War

While common folk were grinding their way through the Great Depression, an ominous threat arose in Germany. Preoccupied as they were with surviving the Depression and still recoiling from the Great War, many Americans were slow to recognize the magnitude of evil in Hitler. An exception was the man now widely remembered as America's last public theologian, Reinhold Niebuhr (1892–1971).

Niebuhr was raised in the Evangelical Synod of North America, a small Germanic denomination that combined Lutheran and Reformed heritage. After serving many years as a parish pastor in Detroit, Niebuhr became a professor at Union Theological Seminary in New York. In 1932 he published *Moral Man and Immoral Society.* There he argued that although individuals may at times act nobly, larger groups (such as corporations and nations) can do evil on a grand scale. Social justice, said Niebuhr, may require a confrontation of powers. In the world of the 1930s, Niebuhr thought that hard realism was better than naïve optimism. Thus, he offered an insider critique of liberalism. Niebuhr himself owed much to the liberal theology in which he was trained and with which he identified strongly as a young man. For a time he had also been drawn to socialism. But Niebuhr found that his experience as a pastor and the "heritage of classical Christianity and the reformers" challenged him to develop "Christian realism."[29] The events unfolding in Europe forced him to confront the reality of evil in human history. Niebuhr's Christian realism included faith in God's sovereignty over history and an unflinching view of human sin. This cut against the grain of most of his colleagues in seminaries and colleges. At a time when many were still advocating pacifism, Niebuhr knew that war would be tragically necessary to stop Hitler.

The 1930s saw Hitler's rise in Germany and Japan's advance into China. World events grew more sinister as Hitler began his conquest of Europe in 1936. Still reacting to the conflict that was soon to be renamed World War I, several European leaders sought to appease Hitler. But when the Nazi leader invaded Poland in 1939, war thrust itself upon them. Meanwhile, in the United States, many church leaders clung to fading hopes of neutrality. Niebuhr broke ranks with them all, warning that Nazism, unless confronted by force, would destroy Western civilization. Niebuhr's 1941 article, "Is Neutrality Immoral?" set forth a Christian social ethic in which sinful, fallible people must "exercise moral responsibility in order to attain proximate justice in a complex and tragic world."[30] The United States finally entered the war after Japan bombed Pearl Harbor on December 7, 1941.

On the home front, American churches sent ministers to be trained as chaplains for the military. As in World War I, Christians now supported the Red Cross and other auxiliary service agencies, sent religious literature to servicemen and -women, and offered support to families with members in the military. Amid all this wartime activity, however, the churches did not "repeat the unrestrained capitulation to the war spirit that had left them disgraced after 1918," according to Sidney Ahlstrom. There were several reasons for the change. First, the Great Depression had deeply chastened America. Second, the neo-orthodoxy of Karl Barth and the Christian realism of Reinhold Niebuhr convinced some Christian leaders to see world events more realistically. Finally, the churches did not enjoy the same influence in the culture as they had during the Great War. The years between 1918 and 1941 brought a "distinct decline in the relative moral force of the churches."[31] Even if the churches had wanted to whip up war fever, Pearl Harbor and the Nazi declaration of war against the U.S. made war-fever preaching unnecessary. To be sure, religious services in World War II included national hymns, prayers for victory, and patriotic sermons. But the overall mood differed from that of the First World War. Perhaps Americans sensed the dreadful power of their opponents, or paused to remember that the Great War had failed to end all war.

American churches of all stripes sought to help those who suffered in the war, and this often meant cooperating across denominational lines. Wartime ecumenism took several forms. One form was to have global cooperation among groups stemming from one faith tradition; for example, Lutheran World Relief coordinated Lutheran humanitarianism for German and Scandinavian war refugees. A second type of ecumenism was both global *and* inter-denominational; this was done by the World Council of Churches—which included Anglican, Orthodox, and many Protestant churches from every continent. (The war delayed the official start of WCC until 1948, but even before its formal beginning this group worked to alleviate wartime suffering). A third type of ecumenism bridged the gap between Catholic and Protestant and between Christian and Jew. This was done by the American Council of Voluntary Agencies for Foreign Service, formed in 1943, which coordinated humanitarian efforts of Protestant, Catholic, and Jewish groups from the U.S.

World War II ended in 1945 with the total surrender of Germany and then of Japan. Most American Christians saw this as a clear victory over evil, won at great cost. After the war, the U.S. gave billions of dollars, through the Marshall Plan, to assist European recovery. Historian Ernest Lee Tuveson sees the Marshall Plan as a demonstration of American millennialism (the belief that the U.S. is destined to be a force for good in the world). While it certainly was in the interests of the U.S. to help Western Europe recover from the war, the Marshall Plan also struck a chord with those Americans who believed that "Christian principles, if really triumphant, would redeem the world."[32]

Reinhold Niebuhr, however, warned that those who confront evil are not free of it themselves. The war left Americans with deeply troubling issues. First was the specter of nuclear annihilation, unleashed when the U.S. used nuclear weapons on Japan to end horrific battles in the Pacific. Second was the internment of some 120,000 Japanese Americans, who were forced to live in government camps during the war; their rights as citizens were suspended in the name of national security. Third was that African Americans in the U.S. armed forces continued to face racial discrimination.

Looking inward was sobering, but so was looking outward at the global scene. The magnitude of the Nazi holocaust became widely known only after the war. The Nazis had murdered six million European Jews in death camps, as well as vast numbers of Poles and others. The Holocaust gave new momentum to Zionism, a movement begun in the nineteenth century to establish a Jewish homeland in Palestine. Many American Christians supported the new State of Israel, though a few worried about the consequences of displacing Palestinian Christians and Muslims.

Finally, the wartime alliance with Communist Russia, though necessary to defeat Hitler, left a deep stain on the twentieth century. Stalin killed even more people than Hitler did. A cynical opportunist, Stalin positioned the Soviet Union to fill the vacuum left by the Nazi collapse. With World War II over, Hitler was gone, but Central and Eastern Europe were locked under Communist rule in which Christians, Muslims, and other persons were persecuted for their religious beliefs.

After World War II, the United States and the Soviet Union engaged in a "Cold War" that lasted until the collapse of the Soviet Union in 1991. Over the decades, the Cold War went through many phases. Sometimes it erupted into hot wars in which the United States sent troops to "contain" Communism. Each side amassed an arsenal of nuclear weapons. In the U.S. during the 1950s and early 1960s, some Americans responded to the threat of nuclear war by building bomb shelters. Public schools conducted drills to prepare children for nuclear attack. Senator Joe McCarthy (1908–1957) held congressional hearings to purge from public service those who were "red" (card-carrying Communists) or "pink" (Communist sympathizers). Musicians, teachers, and actors who questioned the reigning political orthodoxy were blacklisted (denied employment).

Like most other aspects of history, the Cold War involved religion. Communism was atheistic, and Christians living under Communism were persecuted as enemies of the state. Behind the "iron curtain" (a Cold-war term for the Soviet border), individuals and organized resistance movements found strength in Christianity. For example, the Russian Orthodox novelist Aleksander Solzhenitsyn (b. 1918) toiled for years, risking his own life, to expose the brutality of Soviet labor camps; and in Poland the Solidarity movement demanded basic rights for workers and found strength and identity in Catholicism.

In the United States, however, the religious face of anti-Communism had less to do with human rights and more to do with doomsaying. Fascination with the end times has a long history in America, but after World War II, apocalyptic scenarios seemed more compelling than ever, thanks especially to two events. First was the atomic bomb. Not long after World War II, the nuclear arms race between the United States and Soviet Russia was under way. Some Christians connected the nuclear threat with specific Bible passages, such as 2 Peter 3:10: "But the day of the Lord will come like a thief, and then the heavens will pass away with a loud noise, and the elements will be dissolved with fire, and the earth and everything that is done on it will be disclosed." For those who saw the Bible as history written in advance, it seemed that nuclear annihilation might be part of God's cosmic plan.

The second event that heightened apocalyptic fervor was the founding of the modern State of Israel. Even before World War I, Christians in the prophecy movement predicted that a Jewish nation in Palestine would arise to set the stage for the return of Christ. So when the modern State of Israel was founded in 1948, "prophecy believers responded with intense emotion, tempered by the gratified awareness that they had known all along that this event would take place."[33] As they saw it, history was moving toward the endgame.

Cashing in on the Cold War, the arms race, and the new State of Israel, a few Christian writers made a fortune on doomsaying. Best known in the 1970s was Hal Lindsey, whose book *The Late Great Planet Earth* convinced thousands of readers that Scripture foretold the Cold War and that the end times were at hand. After the fall of the Soviet Union, a new wave of popular apocalyptic came from Tim LaHaye and Jerry Jenkins, authors of the Left Behind series of novels. These highly successful books took the old nineteenth-century system of dispensationalism and dressed it up with cliff-hanger plots and soap-opera characters. The Left Behind novels sold millions of copies, leaping the barrier between "Christian books" and the broader popular market. LaHaye and Jenkins "helped to make 'rapture,' 'tribulation,' and 'Armageddon' into household words for many Americans."[34] Those who know the proper end-times scenario are assured that no matter how bad things get in this world, the rapture will rescue them just in time. Fortunately for the story of Christianity in America, many Christians, repelled by the sensationalism and fatalism of the Left Behind books, have continued their attempts to serve Christ in this world.

Suggestions for Further Reading

Books

Blumhofer, Edith. *Aimee Semple McPherson: Everybody's Sister* (Eerdmans, 1993). Aimee Semple McPherson was a celebrity preacher in the 1920s and founder of the Foursquare Gospel Church. Her story is important for Pentecostalism in America and for the religious leadership of women.

Boyer, Paul. *When Time Shall Be No More: Prophecy Belief in Modern American Culture* (Belknap, 1994). Boyer traces the origins of prophecy belief in the nineteenth century and shows the enduring appeal of doomsaying in recent times, through the Cold War and beyond.

Carpenter, Joel. *Revive Us Again: The Reawakening of American Fundamentalism* (Oxford University Press, 1997). This book tells the story of how fundamentalism withdrew from older denominations and built an independent movement with its own network of institutions.

Websites

Dorothy Day Library on the Web. Writings and photos of Dorothy Day, radical Catholic social reformer. This is part of the larger Catholic Worker Movement website: www.catholicworker.org/dorothyday/index.cfm

Old Fashioned Revival Hour with Dr. Charles Fuller. Hear the sounds of preaching and hymn singing from famous religious radio broadcasts of the 1930s and '40s: www.biblebelievers.com/OFRH/mp3_archive.html (requires audio capability)

Discussion Questions

1. How did the majority of American Christians respond to the Great War while it was in progress? How did that response change after the war was over? What does this change suggest to you about the relationship of religion and patriotism?

2. What were the key differences between the liberals (modernists) and the conservatives (fundamentalists) in the fundamentalist-modernist controversy? To what extent is religion in American still shaped by this conflict?
3. How did Christianity intersect with women's rights in this period?
4. How did Christians respond to the Great Depression? What conclusions can you draw about faith and social action during this period?
5. How did Reinhold Niebuhr make the case for war against Hitler's Nazi regime?
6. What were some of the religious themes of the Cold War? How and why do some of these themes live on, even though the Cold War is over?

CHAPTER EIGHT

Toward a New Millenium

Civil Rights

In the decades after World War II, the landscape of religion in America was changing. The Catholic Church reinvented itself. A new wave of feminism called for equality for women in all areas of life, including religion. Pentecostalism and non-denominational churches grew at a rapid rate while older Protestant traditions declined. This chapter surveys these and other major developments in American Christianity in the past half-century. We begin with the American civil rights movement—the quest for justice and equality for African Americans.

The civil rights movement drew deeply from the wells of African American Christianity. It was a religious event as well as a political, social, and economic movement. It sought to end racial segregation in the U.S. and to secure equal rights for all Americans. The civil rights movement built on the work of previous generations, but a new phase began in 1954, when the Supreme Court ruled against segregation in the public schools. Then came years of marches, boycotts, and sit-ins—aimed at desegregating public schools and public accommodations across the South. African-Americans Christians, including many clergy, were deeply involved in the movement. To coordinate their efforts, the Southern Christian Leadership Conference (SCLC) was created in 1957 and led by Martin Luther King Jr. High points of the movement include the March on Washington (1963) and the march from Selma to Montgomery (1965), as well as the passing of the Civil Rights Act (1964) and the Voting Rights Act (1965). Racism has not gone away, but the civil rights movement was a spectacular breakthrough in the long quest for racial justice in America.

That breakthrough came at a price. Civil rights activists were beaten and jailed; several were murdered. Children died when white racists burned or bombed African American churches. The KKK and other hate groups violently opposed the civil rights movement; they would go to any lengths to maintain segregation. Most segregationists, however, valued respectability and so defended segregation without resorting to violence. There were a host of passive observers who would not lift a finger for either side. And there were some southern whites who publicly supported civil rights. Southern Baptists and Presbyterians voted in favor of desegregation in the 1950s and '60s;[1] the evangelist Billy Graham integrated the seating in his revivals—even in southern cities—as far back as 1954. As for northern whites, one could find a similar spectrum of attitudes, ranging from the KKK at one extreme, to the inert majority in the middle, all the way out to those people of faith who traveled south to join in marches, freedom rides, and sit-ins.

Even though African American churches were the spiritual base for the movement, not all black Christians agreed with the strategies of civil rights. Urging caution were the "gradualists," who sought incremental improvements and avoided conflict. The gradualists looked toward a heavenly reward more than toward social reform. Martin Luther King Jr. warned against the "tranquilizing drug of gradualism" and insisted that "justice too long delayed is justice denied."[2] The goal of the civil rights movement was racial integration, and its method was to confront segregation using techniques of nonviolent resistance. However, some African Americans called for black separatism (rather than integration). Some black militants were wiling to use violence. And as we have seen, a growing Nation of Islam (black Muslims) promoted black pride but rejected Christianity. Given the diversity of black America, the achievement of the civil rights movement in building a coalition powerful enough to topple segregation is all the more remarkable.

Of many leaders in this movement, the best known is Rev. Martin Luther King Jr. (1929–1968). Nonviolence, redemptive suffering, and justice were the guiding principles of King's life and of the movement

Martin Luther King Jr. gives his "I have a dream" speech
Photo © Bettmann/Corbis

he led. Raised in Atlanta, Georgia, King was the son and grandson of Baptist clergy. He studied for the ministry and pursued graduate work in systematic theology at Boston University. King was impressed by the Christian realism of Reinhold Niebuhr, particularly the insight that "coercion is tragically necessary to achieve justice."[3] In 1954 King became pastor of a Baptist church in Montgomery, Alabama (he later served as pastor of Ebenezer Baptist Church in Atlanta). The Montgomery Bus Boycott began when Rosa Parks (1913–2005) refused to move to the back of the bus where blacks were required to sit. Rosa Parks' noncompliance with segregation, and her arrest, sparked a massive boycott of public transportation in Montgomery. The boycott forced the city to change its policies of segregation on the busses. King became a leader in this effort, the purpose of which is summed up in his speech at the 1963 March on Washington, D.C. Speaking from the Lincoln Memorial, King challenged America to "live up to the true meaning of its creed—that all men are created equal." King was awarded the Nobel Peace Prize in 1964.

The climax of this phase of the civil rights movement was the 1965 march from Selma to Montgomery, on behalf of voting rights for blacks. The first attempt at the march was violently turned back by police; that night James Reeb, a white Unitarian minister who had joined in the demonstrations, was killed by white supremacists. Public outrage at the murder focused national attention on the march, which finally was carried out under protection of a court order. At the end of the march, King assured his audience that the day of racial justice would not be long in coming. Quoting the "Battle Hymn of the Republic" (and with it, the nation's unfinished business of racial justice), King declared, "Mine eyes have seen the glory of the coming of the Lord... his truth is marching on."

King had received many death threats over the years, and April 1968 was no exception. Nevertheless, he traveled to Memphis, Tennessee, to support striking garbage workers. In his last public speech, King said that he, like Moses, had looked over into the promised land [of racial equality] but might not live to get there. On April 4, 1968, as he stood on the balcony of his motel, he was shot by an assassin. King's birthday became a national holiday in 1986.

The civil rights movement could not have happened without black churches. And yet, as the research of historian David Chappell demonstrates, "the most important element"[4] missing from the public perception of the civil rights movement is religion. African American churches were not merely staging areas for nonviolent activism—they were centers of inspiration where Christian preaching, praying, and singing moved people to risk their lives to follow God's call to freedom and justice. Chappell shows that black Christianity had the prophetic courage to confront evil and the power to inspire the masses. It used the resources of southern revivalism to strengthen people for nonviolent confrontation. Like the Great Awakenings in American Christian history, the civil rights movement changed individuals and changed society.

A Revival of Religion

American religion prospered in the 1950s. New churches sprang up in the suburbs while older churches added education wings for Sunday schools bulging from the baby boom. An even more significant development for American Christianity after World War II was the mainstreaming of Pentecostalism. This has been called the "charismatic movement" or, alternatively, "second-wave Pentecostalism." Pentecostals, once despised as holy rollers, began to penetrate Catholic and mainline Protestant churches. One group working to spread the charismatic movement into mainline churches was the Full Gospel Businessmen; this interdenominational group introduced healing and speaking in tongues into churches where such manifestations had been unknown. Another movement contributing more generally to spiritual renewal was *Cursillo* (Spanish for "short course" in Christianity). Although *Cursillo* events today are not known for an emphasis on speaking in tongues, "many of the first leaders of the [Catholic] charismatic movement were influenced by the intense emotional experience of a *Cursillo* retreat."[5] This movement began in Spain among Catholics; the first *Cursillo* event in the United States was held in 1957 in Waco, Texas, in Spanish. Since then, *Cursillo* has spread far and wide, using weekend retreats as venues for spiritual awakening. Except for a few sensational news stories, the charismatic movement took place largely behind the scenes.

The most public form of Christianity after World War II was revivalism, that old-time religion of repentance and salvation. Its greatest apostle was Billy Graham (1918–). Through his large stadium revivals and mass media broadcasting, Graham reached more people than any other preacher in Christian history. No matter how large the crowd, Graham somehow made each individual feel personally addressed. Graham's voice rang with the authority of scripture as he denounced sin, warned of judgment, and proclaimed Christ as the only way to God. Graham closed every message with an invitation for people to come forward and make a public commitment to Christ. Radio and television audiences were directed to bow their heads, admit they were sinners, and ask Jesus into their lives.

Over a ministry spanning several decades, Billy Graham was able to change with the times and yet maintain a very consistent message. For example, during the Cold War years, his sermons bristled with anti-Communist rhetoric, but later in life he called for nuclear disarmament and preached to huge crowds in Moscow and Kiev. Graham came from a fundamentalist background, yet his ecumenical stature grew until by

Billy Graham preaching at the Greenville, South Carolina, Crusade, 1966
Photo courtesy of the Billy Graham Evangelistic Association

the late twentieth century, a very broad swath of American Christians identified with him personally and volunteered to work at his revivals. When scandals over sex and money discredited other famous preachers, Graham's personal integrity remained intact. Through it all, his gospel of salvation never wavered.

Billy Graham became the unofficial chaplain to the White House. Beginning with Eisenhower, a long succession of American presidents invited Graham to Washington to serve as a spiritual counselor and to lead prayer meetings for high-ranking leaders. Of course, Graham's presence in the White House did not mean that every president believed in evangelical Christianity. Take, for example, Eisenhower's oft-quoted remark: "Our government makes no sense unless it is founded on a deeply felt religious faith—and I don't care what it is."[6] If American presidents used Graham for political advantage—as Richard M. Nixon seems to have done—then Graham was willing to take that risk.

Billy Graham preached to prepare sinners for heaven, but another brand of religion looked for success here on earth. Norman Vincent Peale (1898–1993) proclaimed the power of positive thinking. A minister of the Reformed Church in America, Peale mixed religion and psychology; the result was a gospel of self-improvement. His book *The Power of Positive Thinking* (1952) promised success and peace of mind to those who think positively. Peale's message lacked any sense of tragedy, injustice, or sin; we have only to improve ourselves and all will be well!

Positive thinking fit well into the 1950s—the Depression was over, the war had been won, and people longed to pursue their own dreams. Positive thinking also drew from earlier forms of what Sidney Ahlstrom has called "harmonial religion." In this view, a person's oneness with the cosmos brings spiritual and physical health, and even economic well-being.[7] Ralph Waldo Emerson, the poet of nature and self-reliance, as well as Mary Baker Eddy, the founder of the Church of Christ (Scientist) are nineteenth-century thinkers belonging in this stream. Norman Vincent Peale was neither the first preacher of harmonial religion nor the last. His legacy lived on in Robert Schuller (b. 1926), promoter of "possibility thinking." Schuller's life was success incarnate, for he began his ministry in a rented drive-in theater in Southern California and ended up in the majestic Crystal Cathedral, completed in 1980. The religion of self-esteem and success continues to have new prophets and a wealth of followers in America.

Fame was not "for Protestants only" in the 1950s. Archbishop Fulton Sheen (1895–1979) was a religious leader of national renown. Unlike Norman Vincent Peale (who saw nothing wrong with America that could not be fixed by positive thinking), Sheen saw a need for social reform. Like Billy Graham, he took seriously the classic Christian doctrines of sin and salvation and was an ardent foe of Communism.

Sheen showed himself to be a brilliant communicator at Catholic University, where he taught theology for many years. Sheen's teaching went far beyond the classroom to reach a very broad audience. His books, especially *Peace of Soul* (1949) and *Life of Christ* (1958), were best sellers. From 1930 to 1952, he preached and lectured for the *Catholic Hour* radio broadcasts. Sheen was quick to embrace the new medium of television. His weekly television show, *Life Is Worth Living*, drew about thirty million viewers a week, running from 1951 to 1957 and earning an Emmy award.[8]

In addition to being a pioneer in religious uses of media, Sheen was a bridge builder between Protestants and Catholics. He helped to dispel anti-Catholic prejudice by making Catholic teachings better known. Americans who had no prior contact with Catholicism saw Sheen as a Catholic bishop who was "warm, friendly and intelligent."[9] Sheen delivered the basics of Christian theology with conviction graced by Irish wit. No wonder Billy Graham called him "one of the greatest preachers of our century."[10]

We have noted several preachers who reached the masses in the 1950s. Theological seminaries, in contrast, reached a more specialized audience: future theologians and pastors. Two seminaries in particular illustrate two contrasting sectors of postwar Protestantism. The first is Union Seminary in New York City. Union was in its glory days in the 1950s. The brilliant German theologian Paul Tillich (1886–1965) began teaching at Union in 1933, after his criticism of Hitler caused him to be expelled from his professorship in Frankfurt. A Christian existentialist, Tillich used insights from classical theology and modern psychology to probe the "ultimate concern" of human existence. His three-volume *Systematic Theology* (1951–65) stands as one of the great works of theology in the twentieth century. Tillich came to Union in large part through the efforts of Reinhold Niebuhr, who also taught at Union. We have already described Niebuhr's "Christian realism" in relation to World War II and civil rights. Niebuhr and Tillich helped to put Union Seminary in New York in the vanguard of postwar theological education for mainline Protestants.

The second school is Fuller Theological Seminary in Pasadena, California, founded in 1947. Not only was Fuller on the other side of the country from New York's Union; it was on the other end of the theological spectrum. Union served a mainline and liberal constituency, while Fuller began with students and faculty who came from a fundamentalist background. The founders of Fuller wanted to remain theologically conservative while breaking away from the in-fighting, anti-intellectualism, and indifference to social issues that marred fundamentalism. Fuller sought to train leaders who would engage with

American culture instead of separating from it. Historian George Marsden describes the struggle that took place in the early years as Fuller tried to chart a new course. Battles over biblical inerrancy raged, as did power struggles between competing visions of the new conservatism.[11] Over time, a broader evangelicalism developed. Fuller now draws students from almost every denomination and from nondenominational churches (present-day fundamentalists regard Fuller as too liberal).

By the close of the twentieth century, Fuller Seminary enjoyed wide recognition for academic excellence and innovative programs. But Union Seminary in New York fell on hard times and had to sell some of its property. The West Coast school was thriving, and the East Coast school was struggling to survive. Although the stories of these seminaries are more complex than can be described here, their opposite trajectories over the course of half a century illustrate a larger trend in the recent history of Christianity in America: mainline decline and evangelical growth.

Even before the founding of Fuller Seminary, a new evangelicalism was being born. The National Association of Evangelicals (NAE) was founded in 1943, providing a network for cooperation in evangelism, education, and humanitarianism. The NAE also launched the National Religious Broadcasters. Pentecostal Christians, traditionally shunned by fundamentalists, were included in the NAE.

Of several leaders who helped conservatives and moderates break away from fundamentalism, Billy Graham is the best known. When Graham accepted mainline support for his revivals in the 1950s, fundamentalists denounced him. But Graham knew that evangelism requires a big tent, not a phone booth. Another key leader was Carl Henry (1913–2003), whose 1957 book, *The Uneasy Conscience of Fundamentalism*, called conservative evangelicals to social responsibility. A third major player in the new movement was Harold Ockenga (1905–1985), a pastor, scholar, and journalist who helped establish the NAE, Fuller Seminary, and *Christianity Today*, the popular magazine of the new evangelicalism (founded in 1956).

Thanks to these and many other leaders, a new evangelical (post-fundamentalist) network began to flourish. It included publishing ventures, colleges and seminaries, evangelistic and humanitarian aid ministries, and Christian popular music. This movement is "trans-denominational...built around networks of para-church agencies."[12] According to one estimate, near the close of the twentieth century, about twenty million Americans identified themselves as evangelicals; this includes a host of mainline Protestants and Catholics who describe themselves as "born again." Evangelicals come in an astonishing variety, but their core conviction is that Christianity begins with a spiritual transformation—conversion to Christ changes lives.

Catholicism in the 1960s

In 1960 John F. Kennedy became the first Catholic president of the United States. In the course of the campaign, Kennedy had to address the fears—still common in America—that a Catholic president would serve the interests of Rome rather than of the United States. He had to convince the public that a Catholic president would respect the separation of church and state. Even though anti-Catholic bias was still "out there," Kennedy's election showed that the nation was moving toward a broader religious pluralism. Indeed, Americans of many backgrounds identified with Kennedy and the image of youth and courage conveyed by his administration. The assassination of Kennedy in 1963 plunged the nation into mourning, blurring old religious antagonisms.

Even greater changes for Catholics were wrought by the Second Vatican Council (also known as Vatican II). Pope John XXIII convened this council in Rome in 1962 for the purpose of *aggiornamento* or "updating" of the Church. More than two thousand Catholic bishops and theologians attended the council; persons from several non-Catholic traditions came as observers. Religious pluralism, the role of the laity, and the need for accessible worship were among the issues addressed by Vatican II. The Council produced formal statements that set new directions for Catholic mission and identity. Almost a century earlier, the First Vatican council had reacted to modern challenges by asserting papal infallibility, and condemning modernity. But Vatican II, to use a phrase popular at the time, "opened the windows" of the church to modernity.

Among the most important documents produced by Vatican II was its Declaration on Religious Freedom. Its principal author was the American Jesuit theologian John Courtney Murray (1904–1967). Murray invested much of his life exploring the question of what it meant to be Catholic in a pluralistic society. He strove "to relate the American, democratic, pluralistic public sphere with traditional Catholicism."[13] As historian Catherine Wolfteich observes, Murray affirmed religious liberty and the separation of church and state. He did not, however, want faith to be banished from public life. In the words of the Declaration on Religious Freedom, "the Church . . . is not identified with any political community nor bound by ties to any political system. . . . The political community and the Church are autonomous and independent of each other in their own fields."[14] Murray showed that Catholicism and democracy are compatible and that the Catholic Church can flourish in a pluralistic, democratic society.

Murray worked at the theoretical level, but Vatican II also changed life for the faithful in very tangible, practical ways—especially in matters of worship. Common languages such as English or Spanish replaced Latin in worship. Altars were pulled out from the wall so that the priest faced toward the people instead of away from them. The ministry of lay people was affirmed as never before. The numbers of Catholic-Protestant marriages increased. And Catholics could now eat meat on Friday—a change seemingly trivial to outsiders and yet very significant. The old rule (no meat on Friday) reminded Catholics of Christ's sacrifice and vividly distinguished them from Protestants. But Vatican II made this mark of Catholic identity optional. These and other changes affected Catholics in different ways. Now that the "updating" had begun, there was no telling where it would end. The question "What will they change next?" expressed dismay for some and hope for others.

Life changed for the religious as well as for the laity. Some orders allowed their members to live outside the cloister or to wear street clothes instead of habits. Many religious left their orders during the 1960s and '70s to marry or to pursue secular callings. The numbers of new recruits (young adults seeking religious vocations) dropped sharply: "In the pre-Vatican era, young Catholic males were about ten times more likely to enter the priesthood" than in 1990.[15] Although other factors probably contributed to this decline in religious vocations, one cannot overlook Vatican II. Sociologists Roger Finke and Rodney Stark have suggested that after Vatican II fewer young people saw the religious life as a good bargain.[16] If one can please God just as much by raising a family and pursuing a secular career as by living in a cloister, then fewer people will feel motivated to pursue a religious vocation.

One Catholic historian describes the significance of Vatican II in terms of authority and dissent. The pre–Vatican II church was used to "authoritarianism and papal absolutism," but after Vatican II "Catholics acquired the authority to dissent."[17] No issue sparked more dissent among American Catholics than the church's ban on birth control. Among the general populace, the birth control pill contributed to a sexual revolution of the 1960s by separating sexual intercourse from procreation. Officially, Catholics were forbidden to use artificial means of birth control, but in practice American Catholics increasingly decided for themselves. Many hoped that in the wake of Vatican II, the official policy would be updated; they were encouraged when a papal commission assigned to study the issue recommended a change in policy. These hopes were dashed when Pope Paul VI, in his 1968 encyclical *Humanae Vitae*, forbade the use of birth control. Many American Catholics were dismayed by what seemed like a return to an old-style, pre–Vatican II authoritarianism. The use of birth control was already growing among Catholics before 1968, and it rose steadily thereafter, until "close to 90 percent of Catholic laity rejected the church's teaching on birth control."[18] Clergy who publicly disagreed with the pope's decision faced reprisals, and some eventually left the priesthood. The controversy over birth control meant that dissent from, disagreement with, and even disobedience of the pope increased among American Catholics.

Vietnam, Drug Culture, and Jesus People

In the cultural upheaval that was the 1960s, no issue was more volatile than the war in Vietnam. This was a hot war within the Cold War, in which the U.S. sought to contain Communism. If South Vietnam became Communist (so ran the argument), the other countries in Southeast Asia would fall like dominoes.

From its murky beginnings under presidents Eisenhower and Kennedy, the war escalated under Johnson and was finally abandoned under Nixon. As the war unfolded, American soldiers were dying in a conflict that began to seem unwinnable, while civilians were being killed by bombs from above and atrocities on the ground. Television news brought the war into every home. As one historian put it, "The war rent the fabric of trust that traditionally clothed American polity."[19] World War II united Americans; Vietnam divided them.

Like all wars, this one had religious dimensions. Especially during the early years of the conflict, many Christians thought that supporting the war was their duty to God and country. With World War II only two decades in the past, some Americans saw the war in Vietnam as another stage in the conflict with evil, with the future of the free world turning on whether America could succeed in containing Communism. The most famous American Christian of that era, Billy Graham, visited the troops in Vietnam and seems to have supported American involvement; if he had any misgivings, he did not make them public at the time.[20]

But public support for the war was eroding, especially because of the draft. The prospect of being forced into military service provoked a moral crisis for many young men. A few won "conscientious objector" status on religious grounds, but most young men who were drafted had to decide whether to comply with, resist, or evade the draft. One strategy was to seek educational deferment from the draft, and studying for the ministry was one way to get a deferment. A professor who taught at a mainline seminary during the Vietnam era recalled that "hundreds of men swarmed to the seminary during the war, then left in droves once peace came."[21]

Religious protest increased as the war in Vietnam dragged on. Opponents not only came from the historic peace churches (which categorically oppose war) but also represented Catholics and Protestants who came to see this *particular* conflict as morally wrong. Their stance reflected moral objections to civilian casualties in Vietnam, together with doubts about whether the U.S. had "just cause" for the war in the first place. Martin Luther King Jr. and other religious leaders began to make public their opposition to the war. When some of King's colleagues urged him to limit his efforts to racial justice, King responded, "I have fought against segregation . . . for too long now, to segregate my moral life" by remaining silent on Vietnam.[22]

Christians who opposed the war employed a wide range of tactics to make themselves heard. The most flamboyant protestors were Catholic priests, the brothers Philip and Daniel Berrigan. The Berrigan brothers poured pints of human blood over files of draft board records. They burned draft records with napalm (a chemical used as a weapon in Vietnam) and made sure that journalists would be present with cameras. Another type of anti-war effort was conducted by "Clergy and Laity Concerned about Viet Nam," an ecumenical group that sought to influence public opinion through education. Yet another approach was tried by some local churches that offered their sanctuaries as "safe havens" to draft resisters and protestors; but as historian Patrick Allitt notes, police did not hesitate to make arrests on church property.[23] Finally, campus ministries at colleges and universities across the nation supported anti-war protests. All of these religious protests swelled the tide of anti-war activism engulfing the country.

American troops withdrew in 1973, and South Vietnam collapsed to Communism in 1975. But long after the war was over, "the antiwar protests that Vietnam precipitated made peace activism a primary component of the religious left's identity."[24] The 1980s saw religious protests against nuclear proliferation and religious objections to U.S. involvement in Central and South America; these activities continued the trajectory of Vietnam-era protest. No American war has enjoyed the unanimous support of Christians, but Vietnam made it much more difficult to equate United States policy with God's will. In 1975 Robert McAffee Brown (1920–2001), a professor of religion and ethics at the Pacific School of Religion, wrote about the religious implications of Vietnam. Moral constraint, said Brown, had eroded to the point where the unthinkable became doable. "'We'—not just 'they'—shot civilians, tortured prisoners, bombed hospitals, napalmed children and gave medals to those who did so." This, said Brown, was a tribute to "human depravity."[25] Many American soldiers in Vietnam used illegal drugs to escape from this depravity, only to find themselves plunging deeper into it.

Back in the States, a new drug culture arose as more young adults began to "tune in, turn on, drop out." Drug use was recreational for many, but for some it was also a protest against the war and "the establishment" (which included organized religion). Some youth and young adults wondered why they should go to church if marijuana, LSD, or cocaine could take them higher. Indeed, drug use became quasi-sacramental at music festivals and anti-war protests. Peace was the buzzword, but the violent side of the drug culture soon revealed itself in addiction, drug-related crime, and death by overdose. A few desperate addicts literally "came to Jesus" as their last resort. These converts preached to drugged-out hippies, promising that Jesus could set them free from bad trips and give them a spiritual high. So the Jesus People movement was born. Conversions, beach baptisms, and house churches became the stuff of countercultural Christianity.

The Jesus People movement, though short-lived, contributed to at least two important developments in American Christianity. The first such development, described by sociologist Donald Miller, is the "new paradigm church." Calvary Chapel and Hope Chapel, as well as the Vineyard, exemplify the new paradigm. Evangelical to the core, these churches prize conversion and the transformed life. They innovate freely in worship but are traditional in belief and lifestyle. Instead of requiring formal seminary education for clergy, they mentor their own leaders and "grow congregations" through local start-ups. Donald Miller reports that the first new paradigm church began in the 1960s in Costa Mesa, California, when Chuck Smith, a pastor with roots in Pentecostalism, took an interest in the Jesus People. Smith invited some homeless converts to live with his family. Soon Smith and his congregation were evangelizing and sheltering hippies. Knowing how suspicious the new converts were of "the establishment" (including the church), Smith offered worship that spoke directly to their experience through Bible teaching and music written by Jesus People.

This leads to a second contribution of the Jesus People: new forms of Christian music. Expressing their own religious experiences was more important for the Jesus People than connecting to churchly traditions through hymns and liturgies. Beginning in the 1960s, some churches began to experiment with rock and roll, blues, folk, and jazz music in worship. Folk masses and rock bands drew people who could not relate to the church of their parents. In time, Catholic parishes offered mass in a variety of musical styles, while mainline churches had "alternative" and "contemporary" worship services.

Conflicts over music and worship styles sometimes sparked "worship wars" with partisans on each side contending for "traditional" versus "contemporary" worship. Donald Miller astutely observes that each major change in religious culture involves new music, and "the very songs that create revolutions" will later "represent the established cultural traditions to be overthrown."[26] What was "contemporary" in the 1960s was passé by the 1980s: praise bands replaced the Christian protest and folk music.

Overlapping with the new worship music was the rise of an entirely new recording industry. Among the now-classic examples of this Christian music was singer Amy Grant's version of "Thy Word Is a Lamp unto My Feet." Contemporary Christian music is now a big business in its own right, and the work of Christian recording artists has become increasingly sophisticated. Some artists are able to blur the boundaries from "Christian" to "secular" markets. By the year 2000, Christian music included everything from Bach to Bono.

Women Clergy

It commonly is believed that women were not ordained until the 1960s or '70s. But in 1853 Antoinette Brown became the first woman to be ordained, in a Congregationalist church in upstate New York. In the decades that followed, very few women were ordained. Churches depended on women as fundraisers, teachers, and social reformers but almost never allowed women to be pastors. Even if women were permitted to earn a degree in theology, denominations were highly unlikely to approve them for ordination and congregations were just as unlikely to call them as pastors. Thus, by 1900 only a tiny fraction of Protestant clergy were women. By the close of the twentieth century, the proportion of women among the clergy reached about 10 percent.[27]

Women's leadership in the church (which should not be measured only by ordination) intersects with the feminist movement in the United States. After women gained the vote in 1920, the next watershed was World War II; some women served in the military, while most contributed to the war effort by holding down factory and other jobs previously considered "man's work." When the war was over, homemaking again became the cultural ideal for women, although many women continued working outside the home. In the 1960s a new phase of feminism began. One contributing factor was the birth control pill, which made it easier for women to manage childbearing and careers. In her landmark book *The Feminine Mystique* (1963), Betty Friedan argued that women who decided between home and career made a mistaken choice. If men did not have to make this choice, why should women? By the 1970s Gloria Steinem and other feminists were pushing for "equal pay for equal work." Women began to enter law school, medical school, and theological seminaries in ever greater numbers.

Not until this wave of modern feminism swept through society did mainline churches begin to accept women as pastors on a regular basis. But despite recent gains, "patterns of institutional discrimination continue to limit the ministries of women."[28] In the 1980s and early '90s, female pastors still were paid less than men, occupied positions that men did not want, or served under male senior pastors. Especially those women pastors who were mothers had to reshape the boundaries of ministry, since they had no "pastor's wife" at home to care for the children and run the household.

While women were entering the ministry in greater numbers, feminist theology was finding a voice in colleges and seminaries. As framed by feminist theologian Rosemary Radford Ruether, feminist theology begins with the conviction that all of Christian theology is shaped by male bias, which has barred women from ordained ministry, kept them out of higher theological education, and sealed women's experience off from theology. Feminist theology therefore tries to discover sources that "support the full personhood of women." Reuther describes a broad spectrum of feminist theology. At one end are those who view Christianity as hopelessly patriarchal and who therefore seek divine inspiration elsewhere. Toward the middle of the spectrum are mediating approaches that seek to "discover, within the Christian tradition, an alternative feminist reading of Christian origins."[29] An important goal here is to retrieve women's contributions that have been lost, neglected, or censored from the Christian past. Then at the conservative end of the spectrum, Reuther notes the "biblical feminists," who do not see Christianity as being defined by sexism. They may use theories of complimentarity to show that the sexes are created to support and supplement each other, neither one being superior to the other. Male domination is an aspect of sin in the world but not a fatal flaw in Christianity itself. Feminist theologies, in all their variety, continue to challenge and change the teaching of religion in many colleges and seminaries.

Cultural Change and Political Action

In the last decades of the twentieth century, homosexuality was gaining broader public acceptance. Homosexual advocacy groups arose to demand full acceptance in every aspect of American life, including religion. In 1974 the American Psychiatric Association removed homosexuality from its list of mental illnesses. Christian churches responded to these developments in different ways. Maintaining the church's traditional stand, that sexual activity is only legitimate within marriage between one man and one woman, were the Hispanic, evangelical, and Pentecostal churches. African American churches were strongly traditionalist on marriage and sexual ethics, with some notable dissenting voices. The official stance of the Roman Catholic Church remained firmly traditionalist, despite the existence of dissent.

Thus, it was the mainline Protestant churches that felt the most pressure to revise their teaching and practice with regard to homosexuality. Considerable energy and money were expended by denominations on studies and task forces addressing issues related to homosexuality. Some of the specific changes contemplated or enacted by mainline groups include (1) affirming homosexual orientation and sexual activity in committed partnerships; (2) allowing clergy to conduct blessings or wedding services for same-sex couples; (3) allowing practicing homosexuals in committed relationships to become (or continue as) ordained pastors. Such proposals had vigorous advocates and sparked equally vigorous opposition in several mainline denominations.

Beneath all the debates about homosexuality was the deeper issue of authority—who or what has authority in the church? Should it be the Scriptures, or theology, or church hierarchy, or cultural norms, or even the process of deliberation itself? As of this writing, several mainline denominations continue to struggle with issues related to homosexuality, with no clear end in sight. The churches' response to homosexuality was perhaps the most contested item in a larger cluster of issues, turned loose in the 1960s and collectively known as the "culture wars."

Joining battle in the culture wars were Protestant fundamentalists, who reentered the political arena in the 1970s after decades of relative isolation. Major catalysts for fundamentalist activism were Supreme Court rulings banning prayer from public schools (1962 and 1963) and legalizing abortion (1973). Other developments were the feminist campaign for an Equal Rights Amendment (which did not pass) and the gay rights movement.

To address such issues, fundamentalists invoked the Puritan vision of America as a moral beacon to the world. Like-minded Catholics, Jews, and Protestants—dubbed collectively "the Religious Right"—formed coalitions to address issues such as legalized abortion. Leading the charge was Jerry Falwell, a Baptist minister who founded the Moral Majority in 1979. The Moral Majority worked to elect politicians who would promote conservative domestic policies. In matters of foreign policy, some groups lobbied for strong U.S. support for the State of Israel, which they saw as having a divinely ordained role in history.[30] Another political arm of the Religious Right was the Christian Coalition, which described itself as "America's Leading Organization Defending Our Godly Heritage."[31] Voter education (including the use of "score cards") helped the Christian Coalition to support the election bids of selected candidates to national, state, and local offices. The Christian Coalition was founded in 1989 by Pat Robertson, a southern Baptist minister and religious broadcaster.

When it comes to religion and politics, mainline folk are often tempted to lump evangelicals, conservatives, and fundamentalists into a one-size-fits-all category. This tendency can be traced all the way back to the fundamentalist-modernist debates of the 1920s. However, the religious landscape had changed considerably by the post-Vietnam era. Take, for example, President Jimmy Carter, who was both a Democrat and a "born-again" Baptist. Carter did not have backing of the Religious Right for his reelection bid in 1980. The Moral Majority instead supported Ronald Reagan, a man not known to be particularly devout. Reagan "failed to deliver" on his promises to conservative religious supporters[32] when it came to appointing conservative Christians to high office or to supporting anti-abortion measures, according to historian William Martin. What seemed like a triumph for the Religious Right in the 1980 and 1984 presidential elections may have been more of a triumph for the "Great Communicator," Ronald Reagan.

The Religious Right has received lavish media attention and has served as a negative rallying point for mainline and liberal Protestants—a "we're not them" approach to religious identity. Sociologist of religion Robert Wuthnow suggests that "liberalism needs to become a counterculture to secularism, instead of a reaction to fundamentalism."[33]

In the author's experience, members of mainline churches tend to relegate evangelical activism to a cluster of right-wing causes. Nevertheless, evangelical activism has moved far beyond the stereotypes and has been moving for decades. Take, for example, the 1973 Chicago Declaration of Evangelical Social Concern. Historian Joel Carpenter notes that this document signaled a "radical shift in modern evangelicalism," which kindled a "renewed passion for social justice."[34] A key participant in the Chicago event was John Perkins (1930–). An African American evangelical, Perkins created ministries in rural Mississippi that worked for spiritual conversion *and* social justice—all in the context of community. Then there is Habitat for Humanity, which builds homes with and for poor people around the world. Habitat was founded in 1976 by evangelicals Linda and Millard Fuller. As of this writing, some nine hundred thousand people around the world are living in Habitat homes.[35] Habitat is a broadly ecumenical organization, welcoming participation from people of any faith or of no faith. Mainliners have a high rate of participation in Habitat for Humanity, but they may be unaware of its strong evangelical roots.

Evangelical authors with a prophetic message should also be noted. Among these are Ron Sider (*Rich Christians in an Age of Hunger*, 1977) and Jim Wallis (editor of *Sojourners Magazine*), both of whom have long track records in addressing issues of racism, poverty, war, and social injustice.[36] And in terms of the general population, a Princeton University survey, conducted at the turn of the twentieth to the twenty-first century, indicates that fewer than half of those who call themselves evangelicals identify with the Religious Right.[37]

For some time now, evangelical activism has not been confined to the right wing. But in the last part of the twentieth century, the mainline was still the sector of American Christianity with the highest rate of participation in community services.[38] According to a recent study conducted by the Lilly Foundation, the top priority for mainline public ministry is to "tend the most vulnerable of society's members,"[39] often in the local community. Such compassion is practiced by congregations, neighborhood ecumenical groups, and denominational networks such as Lutheran Social Services.[40] LSS works with adoption and foster care for children, care for the elderly, disaster response, social services for the poor, and refugee resettlement.

In the last decades of the twentieth century, mainline churches made their chief contribution to public life through social ministries. According to sociologist Nancy Ammerman, mainline congregations are part of a "vast network of care through which social services are delivered and public engagement takes place." Mainline churches often provide meeting space to groups such as Alcoholics Anonymous or host blood drives for the Red Cross. Many community organizations would find it hard to survive if these churches did not supply meeting space, money, and volunteers. As Ammerman puts it, mainline churches create informal coalitions, which "allow religious values and religious caring to pass freely between mainline churches and public life."[41]

Protestant Reconfiguration

Despite these vital contributions to society, mainline denominations have declined in membership for the past several decades. Combined mainline membership dropped from twenty-nine million in 1960 to twenty-two million by the year 2000.[42] By the end of the twentieth century, surveys conducted by sociologist of religion Christian Smith showed that those who self-identify as "mainline" Christians very seldom tell others about the Christian faith and hardly ever invite people to church.[43] Nor can mainline churches assume that the next generation will carry on their traditions, since they often have difficulty retaining their youth and young adults. In their study of mainline decline, sociologists Johnson, Hoge, and Luidens found that "the single biggest predictor of church participation . . . [is] *belief*—orthodox Christian belief, and especially the teaching that a person can be saved only through Jesus Christ."[44]

If one looks only at mainline membership, the overall story of Christianity in America since the 1960s is one of decline. On the other side of the ledger, however, is the dramatic growth of evangelical—especially Pentecostal—churches. Taken together, mainline decline and evangelical growth point to a reconfiguration of American Protestantism.

Ever since the publication of *Why Conservative Churches Are Growing* (Dean Kelly, 1972), sociologists of religion have sought to explain the rise of evangelical churches and the decline of mainline ones. One explanation was offered by Roger Finke and Rodney Stark in their 1992 volume, *The Churching of America 1776–1990: Winners and Losers in Our Religious Economy*. Here the authors use a market typology to explain the growth and decline of religious groups. In this view, religious "firms" exist in a competitive religious economy. Each firm has a product, a sales force, and a market that it serves. "Translated into more churchly language, the relative success of religious bodies (especially when confronted with an unregulated economy) will depend upon their polity, their clergy, their religious doctrines, and their evangelization techniques."[45] Finke and Stark show how "upstart sects" (religious entrepreneurs like the Methodists and the Baptists in frontier America) grew from having small market shares to being the largest Protestant denominations in America. And the Catholics, though cultural outsiders, built an extremely successful network of parishes and schools.

However, if upstart groups prosper, they often trade their religious zeal for cultural respectability. As this transition unfolds, people who seek vivid religious experience, and who want their religion to stand out from the culture, will gravitate toward new and more intense religious firms. Thus, as Finke and Stark put it, "the mainline bodies are always headed for the sideline."[46]

Every rule has exceptions, and as Finke and Stark show in a subsequent study, some mainline churches are growing. Those most likely to grow have young pastors committed to traditional theology, Scripture, and evangelism.[47] Pastors who fit this description are often connected with renewal movements, which encourage evangelicals to stay within the denomination instead of leaving for greener pastures.

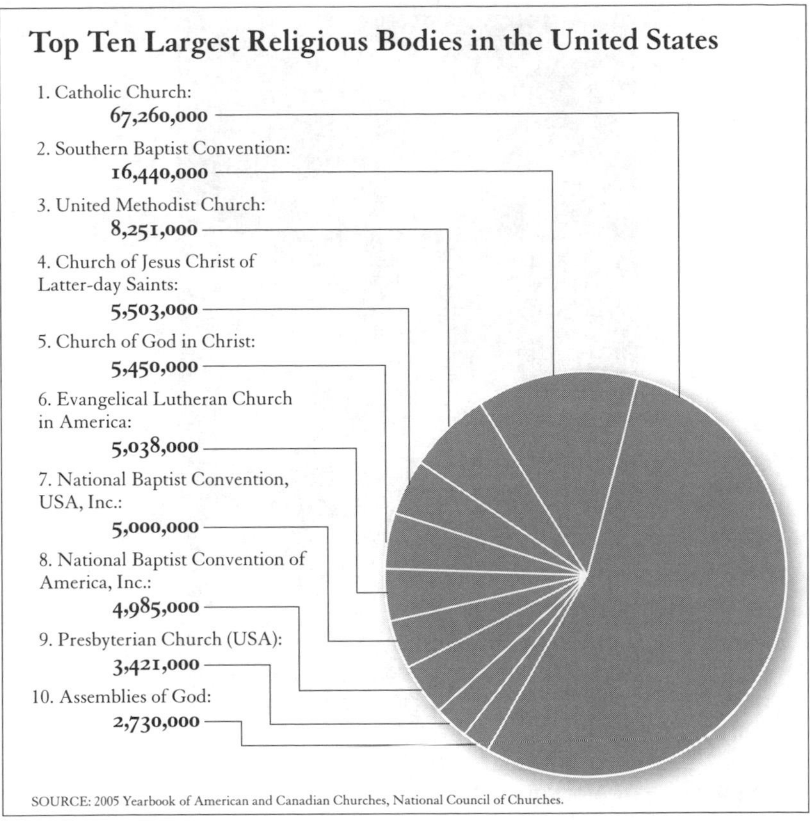

A trailblazer for mainline Protestant renewal movements was Charles Keysor (1925–1985). A journalist who converted to Christianity as an adult, Keysor went to seminary and became a Methodist pastor. He was dismayed at the gap he saw between historic Methodism (in which evangelism was primary and flowed into social concern) and United Methodism in the 1960s (in which evangelism was displaced by social and political agendas). Keysor published an article expressing his lament. Other Methodists rallied to his standard. In 1966 Keysor founded *Good News: A Forum for Scriptural Christianity within the United Methodist Church* as a voice for evangelicals in the United Methodist Church. *Good News* began as a magazine but soon offered Sunday school curriculum, held national gatherings, sent missionaries, and created networks for pastors. By the close of the twentieth century, every mainline denomination had renewal groups, as did the Catholic Church.

Crucifix, 1971. Jose Mondragon.
Photo © Smithsonian American Art Museum, Washington, D.C., Hemphill/Art Resource, NY

In the recent history of Christianity in the U.S., it may be that the greatest change of all has been (and continues to be) wrought by Hispanic immigration. Hispanics are moving beyond their traditional population centers and establishing communities throughout the United States. By the year 2000, Hispanic population in the U.S. reached 35.3 million people, making them the largest minority group in the U.S. If current growth rates continue, one in every four Americans will be Hispanic by the year 2050.[48]

Hispanics traditionally have identified with Catholicism; as of this writing, 39 percent of the Catholics in the United States were Hispanic.[49] Earlier, we noted several ways in which Hispanic Catholicism is distinctive. How Hispanic forms of Catholicism will relate to thus-far dominant forms of Catholicism in the U.S. will be important for Christianity in America.

After Catholicism, Pentecostalism attracts the largest number of Hispanics in the United States. A growing number of Hispanics in the U.S. are joining Pentecostal and other Protestant churches; according to recent census data, about 22 percent of Hispanics in the U.S. are Protestant, up from 18 percent in the late 1980s.[50] It seems likely that the Hispanic population will shape, and be shaped by, American Christianity. It almost seems as though the story has come full circle, since the first Christian communities in America were planted by Spanish Catholics.

Many American Christians have been slow to grasp the fact that the United States is not the center of the Christian world. Although Christianity is more robust in America than in Europe, it is Africa and parts of Asia and South America that now experience dramatic Christian growth through conversion. As Phillip Jenkins explains, these new centers of Christianity appeal strongly to miracles and the supernatural, make absolute truth claims, and often place much authority in their religious hierarchy.[51] In other words, this new global Christianity is dramatically "other" than the culturally approved forms of Christianity in the West.

Before most Americans were aware of this new global Christianity, we were forced to come to terms with a radicalized form of Islam. On September 11, 2001, terrorists invoking the name of God hijacked four jet planes full of passengers. Two planes were crashed into New York City's World Trade Center. A third plane hit the Pentagon in Washington, D.C., while a fourth plane, (presumably headed for the White House or Capitol building in Washington) crashed in a Pennsylvania field. Some 2,800 people died that day, both American citizens and foreign nationals.

Across the United States, churches overflowed with people praying, lamenting, and singing hymns. Ecumenical and interfaith worship services gathered people who normally do not worship together while candlelight vigils illumined the night. At the attack sites (and in countless other places) makeshift shrines were decorated with crosses, flags, candles, and pictures of the victims. Ever practical, American Christians rolled up their sleeves and opened their wallets to help the victims and their families. Churches in New York City and Washington offered food, shelter, and medical care for rescue workers. Predictably, doomsayers pronounced the events of September 11 as God's judgment on a decadent and godless America and warned that the rapture was at hand. Much more widely shared, however, was the outpouring of civil religion: faith in God and country brought Democrats and Republicans together in Washington, D.C., to pray and sing hymns—including of course the "Battle Hymn of the Republic."

In a long-term response, many American Christians recognized their need to learn more about Islam in its various forms. Congregations all over the country made Islam the subject of adult education and, where possible, interfaith dialog.

The long-term effects of 9/11 are still unfolding. But that day and its aftermath revealed that the United States, though in many ways a secular nation, is still deeply religious at its core. Religious diversity is on the rise but Christianity still is far and away the dominant faith, still a force to be reckoned with in American society.

This book has explored how Christianity has shaped and been shaped by American life. Recall the Puritans, who believed that God chose them and sent them on an "errand in the wilderness." Their errand was to complete the Reformation of church and society. More than two centuries later, Abraham Lincoln was more circumspect; he referred to Americans as "God's almost chosen people." Lincoln's comment suggests that no nation can assume special favor from God. History is full of ambiguity, as Lincoln knew so well. But it is clear from the historical record that Christians have sought to awaken, reform, and renew American life and continue to do so today.

Suggestions for Further Reading

Books

Badillo, David. *Latinos and the New Immigrant Church* (Johns Hopkins University Press, 2006). This history of Latino Catholicism in the U.S. examines the story of Mexican, Puerto Rican, and Cuban American Christians in urban environments.

Chappell, David. *A Stone of Hope: Prophetic Religion and the Death of Jim Crow* (University of North Carolina Press, 2004). A fresh look at the religious dimensions of the civil rights movement, this book explores the role of black prophetic and revival religion in civil rights.

Cox, Harvey. *Fire from Heaven: The Rise of Pentecostal Spirituality and the Reshaping of Religion in the Twenty-first Century* (DaCapo, 1995). As a sympathetic outsider to the movement, Cox chronicles the history of Pentecostalism and gives reasons for its global appeal.

Websites

"A Call to Conscience: The Landmark Speeches of Martin Luther King, Jr." Made available by Stanford University: www.stanford.edu/group/King/publications/speeches/contents.htm

The "Time 100 Profile" of Billy Graham by Harold Bloom. Brief biography and assessment of Graham's significance for Christianity in America: www.time.com/time/time100/heroes/profile/graham01.html

Discussion Questions

1. What was the role of the black churches in the civil rights movement? What happens to our understanding of this movement when religion is "airbrushed" out of it?
2. The revival of religion in the 1950s has sometimes been described as "a mile wide and an inch deep." Based on your reading, respond to this assessment.
3. What were the goals of the "new evangelicalism" that arose in the late 1940s and early 1950s? What specific forms did this movement take?
4. What were the most significant events for American Catholicism in the 1960s? How did these events affect the lives of American Catholics?
5. What role(s) did religion play in American attitudes about the Vietnam War?
6. Several contemporary issues are noted toward the end of this chapter. Select one issue that you find especially significant. What theological concerns are involved? What do you hope will happen with regard to this issue?

NOTES

Chapter One: Colonial Beginnings

1. Sam Gill, "Native American Religions," in *Encyclopedia of the American Religious Experience*, ed. Charles Lippy and Peter Williams (New York: Scribner's, 1988), 1:137 (hereafter *EARE*).

2. Edwin Gaustad and Philip Barlow, *New Historical Atlas of Religion in America* (Oxford: Oxford University Press, 2001), 30.

3. Ibid., 49.

4. Stephen Neill, *A History of Christian Missions* (London: Penguin, 1990), 143.

5. Mark Noll, *A History of Christianity in the United States and Canada* (Grand Rapids: Eerdmans, 1992), 15, 16.

6. David Weber, "The Spanish-Mexican Rim," in *The Oxford History of the American West*, ed. Clyde Milner, Carol O'Connor, and Martha Sandweiss (New York: Oxford University Press, 1994), 55–57.

7. David Holmes, "The Anglican Tradition and the Episcopal Church," in *EARE*, 1:391, 393.

8. Sidney Ahlstrom, *A Religious History of the American People* (New Haven: Yale University Press, 1972), 105.

9. Ibid., 192, 193.

10. Abdel Ross Wentz, *A Basic History of Lutheranism in North America* (Philadelphia: Muhlenberg, 1955), 21.

11. For a fuller treatment of this early period of slavery and the Africans who became free, see Ira Berlin, *Generations of Captivity* (Cambridge, Mass.: Belknap, 2003), 23–49. Berlin defines slavery as labor exacted by irresistible force (2). He also distinguishes between "slave societies" (in which the economy and social relationships were built on slavery) and "societies with slaves" (in which slavery was present but not foundational to the culture and economy) (8, 9).

12. Ahlstrom, *Religious History,* 191.

13. David Gelernter, "Americanism—and Its Enemies," *Commentary*, January 2005, 41–48.

14. In a more formal theological sense, most Puritans subscribed to the five-point Calvinism laid down by the Synod of Dort (Netherlands) in 1618–19. The five points are (1) total depravity of human beings; (2) unconditional election (God determines who is saved); (3) limited atonement (salvation is limited to those whom God chooses); (4) irresistible grace; and (5) perseverance of the saints. The Puritans were also theologically committed to the Westminster Standards of 1648.

15. Harry Stout, "Salem Witch Trial," in *Dictionary of Christianity in America*, ed. Daniel Reid (Downers Grove: InterVarsity, 1990), 1041. See also Ahlstrom, *History*, 161.

16. Patricia Bonomi, "Middle Colonies," in *The Reader's Companion to America History*, ed. Eric Foner and John Garraty (Boston: Houghton Mifflin, 1991), 727.

17. Berlin, *Generations of Captivity*, 34.

18. Gaustad and Barlow, *New Historical Atlas*, 52.

19. Amandus Johnson, ed. *The Instruction for Johan Printz, Governor of New Sweden* (Port Washington: Friedman, 1969), 94–96, cited in Robert Fisher, "Lutherans in American Life: A Bicentennial Reflection," *The Lutheran*, January 1, 1975, 7.

20. Gaustad and Barlow, *New Historical Atlas*, 38.

21. Ian Hazlett, "Demanding Faith," in *Christian History*, May 1995, 25.

Chapter Two: Awakening, Enlightenment, and Revolution

1. Sidney Ahlstrom, *A Religious History of the American People* (New Haven: Yale University Press, 1972), 217–18.

2. Henry Melchior Muhlenberg, *Notebook of a Colonial Clergyman*, 2d ed., ed. and trans. Theodore Tappert and John Doberstein (Minneapolis: Fortress Press, 1998), 46.

3. George Marsden, *Jonathan Edwards: A Life* (New Haven: Yale University Press, 2003), 407.

4. Early reports of revival came from Congregationalist minister Solomon Stoddard (1643–1729), Dutch Reformed preacher Theodore Freylinghuysen (1691–1747), and Presbyterian minister Gilbert Tennant (1703–1764).

5. See Harry Stout, *The Divine Dramatist: George Whitefield and the Rise of Modern Evangelicalism* (Grand Rapids: Eerdmans, 1991).

6. L. B. Weeks, "Samuel Davies," in *Dictionary of Christianity in America*, ed. Daniel Reid (Downers Grove: InterVarsity, 1990), 342.

7. Mark Noll, *A History of Christianity in the United States and Canada* (Grand Rapids: Eerdmans, 1992), 106–7.

8. *Boston Evening Post*, July 5, 1742, cited in Edwin Gaustad, *The Great Awakening in New England* (Gloucester: Peter Smith, 1965), 39. The information on Davenport relies on Gaustad, 37–41.

9. Holmes, "The Anglican Tradition and the Episcopal Church," in *Encyclopedia of the American Religious Experience*, ed. Charles Lippy and Peter Williams (New York: Scribner's, 1988), 1:394.

10. Noll, *History of Christianity*, 98. Besides pro- or anti-revival splits, the other permutations in this four-way fracture involved how to respond to Enlightenment views of God and humanity and whether to remain an "established" church or renounce any official ties with the civil order.

11. Anne Pinn and Anthony Pinn, *Fortress Introduction to Black Church History* (Minneapolis: Fortress Press, 2002), 8.

12. Catherine Brekus, *Strangers and Pilgrims: Female Preaching in America, 1740–1845* (Chapel Hill: University of North Carolina Press, 1998), 45, 74–80.

13. Gordon Wood, *The Radicalism of the American Revolution* (New York: Random House, 1991), 23, 145.

14. Henry May, *The Enlightenment in America* (New York: Oxford University Press, 1976).

15. Benjamin Franklin, "Letter to Ezra Stiles," in *Franklin: Writings* (Library of America, 1987), 1179.

16. See the discussion of Common Sense Realism in Mark Noll, *America's God: From Jonathan Edwards to Abraham Lincoln* (New York: Oxford University Press, 2002), 91–113.

17. Paul Johnson, *A History of the American People* (New York: HarperCollins, 1998), 116–17.

18. Noll, *America's God*, 54. For a detailed analysis of this issue, see Noll's chap. 4: "Republicanism and Religion: The American Exception."

19. Alexis de Tocqueville, *Democracy in America* (New York: Harper & Row, 1988), 293.

20. Holmes, "Anglican Tradition," in *EARE*, 1:394.

21. See Nathan Hatch, *The Sacred Cause of Liberty: Republican Thought*

and the Millennium in Revolutionary New England (New Haven: Yale University Press, 1977).

22. Charles Royster, "Battling Irreligion in the Ranks," in *Christian History: The American Revolution* 50 (1996): 32–34.

23. Holmes, "Anglican Tradition," in *EARE*, 1:394. See also "Selfish, Ungrateful Rebels" in *Christian History: The American Revolution* 50 (1996): 40.

24. In a similar vein, Article VI of the U.S. Constitution (1787) states, *"No religious test shall ever be required as a qualification to any office of public trust under the United States."*

25. John Locke, *A Letter Concerning Toleration* (Buffalo: Prometheus, 1990) 65; see also 22.

26. William Lee Miller, *The First Liberty: Religion and the American Republic* (New York: Paragon House, 1988), 215. For religious groups that supported the Virginia Bill, see 38–41.

27. Isaac Backus, "1774 Address to the Massachusetts Legislature," in *A Documentary History of Religion in America to the Civil War*, ed. Edwin Gaustad (Grand Rapids: Eerdmans, 1993), 256.

28. Thomas Jefferson used the phrase "wall of separation between church and state" in a letter to Baptists in Danbury, Conn., in 1801; see Miller, *First Liberty*, 56.

29. Johnson, *History of the American People*, 209. My paragraph relies on Johnson's work. Note that the Bill of Rights first had to be passed by Congress (1789) and then ratified on a state-by-state basis (completed in 1791). This accounts for the two different dates associated with the Bill of Rights.

30. Wood, *Radicalism of the American Revolution*, 218. For the broader discussion, see 213–25.

31. Phillis Wheatley, "Letter to Samson Occom, 1774," in Gaustad, *Documentary History*, 253.

Chapter Three: Christianity in the New Republic

1. Paul Johnson, *A History of the American People* (New York: HarperCollins, 1998), 294.

2. Edwin Gaustad and Philip Barlow, *New Historical Atlas of Religion in America* (Oxford: Oxford University Press, 2001), 114; for map see 116–17.

3. The account of the Cherokee relies on Mark Noll, *A History of Christianity in the United States and Canada* (Grand Rapids: Eerdmans, 1992), 187–88; see also www.studyworld.com/indian_removal_act_of_1830.htm.

4. Elliot West, "American Frontier," in *The Oxford History of American West*, ed. Clyde Milner, Carol O'Connor, and Martha Sandweiss (New York: Oxford University Press, 1994), 136.

5. Peter Cartwright, *Autobiography of Peter Cartwright* (Nashville: Abingdon, 1956), 30.

6. Mark Noll, *America's God: From Jonathan Edwards to Abraham Lincoln* (New York: Oxford University Press, 2002), 9 and passim.

7. Charles Finney, *Lectures on Revivals of Religion* (Cambridge: Belknap, 1960), 403.

8. Keith Hardman, *Charles Grandison Finney* (Grand Rapids: Baker, 1990) 184–86; 203–5; 255–57. See also Charles Hambrick-Stowe, *Charles Grandison Finney and the Spirit of American Evangelicalism* (Grand Rapids: Eerdmans, 1996).

9. Hardman, *Finney*, 253.

10. Finney's condemnation of slavery stemmed from his view that human beings are "free moral agents" accountable to God for their actions. Slavery distorts human nature by making slaves the mere extension of their master's will instead of free moral agents. To rob a person of "moral agency" was the worst sort of crime—a crime that must stop lest the nation suffer God's well-deserved wrath, according to Finney.

11. Nathan Hatch, *The Democratization of American Christianity* (New Haven: Yale University Press, 1989), 83.

12. Noll, *America's God*, 341.

13. Jay Dolan, *Catholic Revivalism, the American Experience: 1830–1900* (Notre Dame: University of Notre Dame Press, 1978), 16. See also Roger Finke and Rodney Stark, *The Churching of America, 1776–1990: Winners and Losers in Our Religious Economy* (New Brunswick: Rutgers University Press, 1992), 109–44.

14. Hatch, *Democratization*, 9, 10.

15. Catherine Brekus, *Strangers and Pilgrims: Female Preaching in America, 1740–1845* (Chapel Hill: University of North Carolina Press, 1998), 135.

16. Ibid., 281.

17. Ibid., 309, 318, 319.

18. C. E. White, "Phoebe Palmer," in *Dictionary of Christianity in America*, ed. Daniel Reid (Downers Grove: InterVarsity, 1990), 860–61.

19. Brooks Holifield, *Theology in America: Christian Thought from the Age of the Puritans to the Civil War* (New Haven: Yale University Press, 2003), 281.

20. The largest segment of Mormons is known officially as the Church of Jesus Christ of the Latter-day Saints (LDS), with headquarters in Salt Lake City, Utah; the next largest group is the Community of Christ (formerly the Reorganized Church of Jesus Christ of the Latter-day Saints) headquartered in Independence, Missouri, and moving closer to mainstream Protestantism. In the West there are splinter groups that still practice polygamy, though the LDS long ago renounced polygamy and the Community of Christ never endorsed it.

21. Paul Conkin, *American Originals: Homemade Varieties of Christianity* (Chapel Hill: University of North Carolina Press, 1997), 162–225; and Richard Ostling and Joan Ostling, *Mormon America: The Power and the Promise* (San Francisco: HarperSanFrancisco, 1999), 1–55.

22. Holmes, "The Anglican Tradition and the Episcopal Church," in *Encyclopedia of the American Religious Experience*, ed. Charles Lippy and Peter Williams (New York: Scribner's, 1988), 398. Holmes' essay is the basis for this paragraph.

23. Noll, *America's God*, 319.

24. William Ellery Channing, "A Discourse at the Ordination of the Rev. Frederick A. Farley," in *American Sermons: The Pilgrims to Martin Luther King Jr.* (New York: Library of America 1999), 551–52.

25. William Hutchinson, *Religious Pluralism in America: The Contentious History of a Founding Ideal* (New Haven: Yale University Press, 2003), 118–19.

26. Ralph Waldo Emerson, "An Address …" in *Ralph Waldo Emerson: Essays and Lectures* (New York: Library of America, 1983), 79.

27. Gaustad and Barlow, *New Historical Atlas*, 91.

28. Ibid., fig. C.15.

29. Ibid., 131.

30. Mark Noll, introduction to *The Princeton Theology, 1812–1921* (Grand Rapids: Baker, 1983), 30; see also 25–34.

31. Gaustad and Barlow, *New Historical Atlas*, fig. C.19 and C.20.

32. Jay Dolan, *The American Catholic Experience* (New York: Doubleday, 1985), 159.

33. Ibid.

34. Alexis de Tocqueville, *Democracy in America*, trans. George Lawrence (New York: Harper & Row, 1988), 288; for a broader discussion, see 287–90.

35. Sidney Ahlstrom, *A Religious History of the American People* (New Haven: Yale University Press, 1972), 563.

36. Dolan, *American Catholic Experience*, 323.

37. Abdel Ross Wentz, *A Basic History of Lutheranism in North America* (Philadelphia: Muhlenberg, 1955), 73, 74.

38. Ibid.

Chapter Four: Slavery and Civil War

1. Albert Raboteau, *Canaan Land: A Religious History of African Americans* (New York: Oxford University Press, 2001), 56.

2. Eugene Genovese, *Roll, Jordan, Roll: The World the Slaves Made* (New York: Vintage, 1976), 249.

3. Ibid., 240.

4. Raboteau, *Canaan Land*, 48, 52.

5. Schaff, *Slavery in the Bible*, cited in Mark Noll, *America's God: From Jonathan Edwards to Abraham Lincoln* (New York: Oxford University Press, 2002), 418–19.

6. Eric Foner, *A Short History of Reconstruction* (New York: Harper & Row, 1990), 59.

7. Genovese, *Roll, Jordan, Roll*, 5–6.

8. Raboteau, *Canaan Land*, 46.

9. Noll, *America's God*, 405.

10. Eric Foner, "Slave Rebellions," in *The Reader's Companion to American History*, ed. Eric Foner and John Garraty (Boston: Houghton Mifflin, 1991), 995–97.

11. Anne Pinn and Anthony Pinn, *Fortress Introduction to Black Church History* (Minneapolis: Fortress Press, 2002), 8.

12. Genovese, *Roll Jordan Roll*, 162.

13. Pinn and Pinn, *Fortress Introduction*, 72; Raboteau, *Canaan Land*, 22; see also the website "Africans in America Resource Book," available at www.pbs.org/wgbh/aia/part2/2p28.html.

14. Raboteau, *Canaan Land*, 23.

15. Pinn and Pinn, *Fortress Introduction*, 32.

16. Richard Allen, "The Life Experience and Gospel Labors," in *A Documentary History of Religion in America to the Civil War*, ed. Edwin Gaustad (Grand Rapids: Eerdmans, 1993), 301–2.

17. Frederick Douglass, "What to the Slave Is the Fourth of July?" in *The American Intellectual Tradition*, ed. David Hollinger and Charles Capper (New York: Oxford University Press, 1999), 1:455.

18. Noll, *America's God*, 387.

19. C. C. Goen, *Broken Churches, Broken Nation: Denominational Schisms and the Coming of the Civil War* (Macon: Mercer University Press, 1985), 4.

20. Oswald Villard, "John Brown's Last Prophecy" (Public Broadcasting Service, cited in Oswald Garrison Villard, *John Brown: A Biography*, available at www.pbs.org/wgbh/amex/brown/filmmore/reference/primary/index.html.

21. Ernest Lee Tuveson, *Redeemer Nation: The Idea of America's Millennial Role* (Chicago: University of Chicago Press, 1968), 201.

22. Gardiner Shattuck Jr. "Revivals in the Camp," *Christian History* 33 (1992): 28.

23. Steven Woodworth, *While God Is Marching On: The Religious World of Civil War Soldiers* (Lawrence: University Press of Kansas, 2001), 253.

24. Gardiner Shattuck Jr., *A Shield and Hiding Place: The Religious Life of the Civil War Armies* (Macon: Mercer University Press, 1987), 24.

25. James Moorehead, "Preaching the Holy War," *Christian History* 33 (1992): 38–41.

26. Mary Chestnut, *A Diary from Dixie*, ed. Isabella Martin and Myrta Avary (New York: Gramercy, 1997), 334.

27. Alan Guelzo, *Abraham Lincoln: Redeemer President* (Grand Rapids: Eerdmans, 1999), 327.

28. Richard Wolf, introduction to William Clebsch, *Christian Interpretations of the Civil War* (Philadelphia: Fortress Press, 1969), vii; see also 7–8, 12, 14.

29. Eugene Genovese, *A Consuming Fire: The Fall of the Confederacy in the Mind of the White Christian South* (Athens: University of Georgia Press, 1998), 105.

30. Sidney Ahlstrom, *A Religious History of the American People* (New Haven: Yale University Press, 1972), 692.

31. Sally McMillen, *To Raise Up the South: Sunday Schools in Black and White Churches, 1865–1915* (Baton Rouge: Louisiana State University Press, 2001), 1–2.

32. Foner, *History of Reconstruction*, 40–41.

33. Ibid., 184

34. Chester Quarles, *The Ku Klux Klan and Related American Racialist and Anti-Semitic Organizations* (Jefferson: McFarland, 1999), 40; see also 38, 48. Quarles notes that other religious aspects of the Klan (anti-Semitism, anti-Catholicism, and the burning of crosses) developed after the Reconstruction era.

Chapter Five: Moving People

1. The melting pot ideal has been traced back to Hector St. John de Crevecoeur. In his 1782 *Letters from an American Farmer*, Crevecoeur said of America that "here individuals of all nations are melted into a new race of men." Quoted in William Hutchison, *Religious Pluralism in America: The Contentious History of a Founding Ideal* (New Haven: Yale University Press, 2003), 12. For "melting pot" as a metaphor for inclusion, see William Hutchison, *The Modernist Impulse in American Protestantism* (Cambridge: Harvard University Press, 1976), 114, 134–35.

2. John Corrigan and Winthrop Hudson, *Religion in America*, 7th ed. (Upper Saddle River: Pearson Prentice Hall, 2004), 275.

3. Abdel Ross Wentz, *A Basic History of Lutheranism in North America* (Philadelphia: Muhlenberg, 1955), 242.

4. Jon Gjerde, *The Minds of the West: Ethnocultural Evolution in the Rural Middle West, 1830–1917* (Chapel Hill: University of North Carolina Press, 1997), 10.

5. Ibid., 15.

6. "Education, Protestant Theological," in *Dictionary of Christianity in America*, ed. Daniel Reid (Downers Grove: InterVarsity, 1990), 379.

7. Albert Raboteau, *Canaan Land: A Religious History of African Americans* (New York: Oxford University Press, 2001), 82, 84.

8. Edwin Gaustad and Philip Barlow, *New Historical Atlas of Religion in America* (Oxford: Oxford University Press, 2001), 70, fig. 2.11.

9. John O'Sullivan, "Annexation," *United States Magazine and Democratic Review* 17 (1845): 5–10.

10. The story of John Dyer is drawn from Ferenc Morton Szasz, "Preparing a Way in the Wilderness." Information on Sheldon Jackson is drawn from Randy Bishop, "Out Yonder, on the Edge of Things." Both articles are in *Christian History* 66 (2000): 12, 30–34.

11. Ferenc Szasz and Margaret Szasz, "Religion and Spirituality," in *The Oxford History of American West*, ed. Clyde Milner, Carol O'Connor, and Martha Sandweiss (New York: Oxford University Press, 1994), 369–79.

12. Jay Dolan, *The American Catholic Experience* (New York: Doubleday, 1985), 50; see also 176–78.

13. Stephen Neill, *A History of Christian Missions* (New York: Penguin, 1990), 420.

14. Jeffrey M. Burns, "The Mexican American Catholic Community in California, 1850–1980," in *Religion and Society in the American West*, ed. Carl Guarneri and David Alvarez (Lanham: University Press of America, 1987), 258, 260.

15. Szasz and Szasz, "Religion and Spirituality," 378.

16. Richard Ostling and Joan Ostling, *Mormon America: The Power and the Promise* (San Francisco: HarperSanFrancisco, 1999), 46.

17. Jan Shipps, "The Latter-day Saints," in *EARE*, ed. Charles Lippy and Peter Williams (New York: Scribner, 1988), 1:661.

18. Ostling and Ostling, *Mormon America*, 54.

19. See Joseph Smith, *The Doctrine and Covenants of the Church of Jesus Christ of Latter-day Saints*, #132. (Salt Lake City: Church of Jesus Christ of the Latter-day Saints).

20. Shipps, "Latter-day Saints," in *EARE*, 1:661.

21. Ostling and Ostling, *Mormon America*, 76.

22. Jon Krakauer, *Under the Banner of Heaven* (New York: Doubleday, 2003).

23. Henry Warner Bowden, "North American Indian Missions," in *EARE*, 3:1681.

24. Charles Phillips, "December 29, 1890" [the Battle of Wounded Knee], *American History*, December 2005, 16.

25. Matthew Glass, "Ghost Dance" in *Encyclopedia of American Religious History*, Steven Prothero, Edward Queen, and Gardiner Shattuck,

eds. (New York: Facts on File, 1996), 1:256–58.

26. Clyde Milner, "National Initiatives," in *Oxford History of the American West*, 174.

27. Bowden, "Indian Missions," in *EARE*, 3:1680.

28. Andrew Walls, *The Missionary Movement in Christian History: Studies in the Transmission of Faith* (Maryknoll: Orbis, 1996), 226.

29. Ibid., 229.

30. Ibid., 239.

31. Raboteau, *Canaan Lands*, 73, 76.

32. Anne M. Boylan, *Sunday School: The Formation of an American Institution* (New Haven: Yale University Press, 1988), 33.

33. Ibid., 147, 149.

34. John Westerhoff, *McGuffey and His Readers* (Nashville: Abingdon, 1978), 19.

35. James Fraser, *Between Church and State: Religion and Public Education in America* (New York: St. Martin's, 1999), 60.

36. Dolan, *American Catholic Experience*, 270.

37. Nancy Woloch, "Education," in *The Reader's Companion to American History*, ed. Eric Foner and John Garraty (Boston: Houghton Mifflin, 1991), 322.

38. George Marsden, *The Soul of the American University: From Protestant Establishment to Established Non-belief* (New York: Oxford University Press, 1994), 156; see also 100, 157, 240.

39. Ibid., 287, 366. See also James Burtchaell, *The Dying of the Light: The Disengagement of Colleges and Universities from Their Christian Churches* (Grand Rapids: Eerdmans, 1998).

40. "The Catholic University of America: History of the University" (Washington, D.C.: Catholic University of America) available at http://development.cua.edu/1887society.cfm.

41. W. E. B. DuBois, *The Souls of Black Folk* (London: Archibald Constable, 1905), 41–59.

Chapter Six: Responses to Modernity

1. The World Parliament is now active as the Council for a Parliament of the World's Religions. The organization's website is available at www.cpwr.org.

2. William Hutchison, *Religious Pluralism in America: The Contentious History of a Founding Ideal* (New Haven: Yale University Press, 2003), 132.

3. Richard Seager, *The World's Parliament of Religions: The East/West Encounter, Chicago, 1893* (Bloomington: Indiana University Press, 1995), 44, 45. My description of the World Parliament relies on 43–58.

4. Robert Crunden, "Progressivism," in *The Reader's Companion to American History*, ed. Eric Foner and John Garraty (Boston: Houghton Mifflin, 1991), 868–71.

5. Jay Dolan, *The American Catholic Experience* (New York: Doubleday, 1985), 332; see also 333–35.

6. Rima Lunin Schultz, "Urban Experience in Chicago: Hull House and Its Neighborhoods," available at www.uic.edu/jaddams/hull/urban-exp/introduction/introduction.htm.

7. "A Brief History of the YMCA Movement," available at www.ymca.net/about/cont/history.htm.

8. *1000 Events That Changed America* (Skokie: Rand-McNally, 2006), 27.

9. Ruth Bordin, *Frances Willard: A Biography by Ruth Bordin* (Chapel Hill: University of North Carolina Press, 1986).

10. William Hutchison, *The Modernist Impulse in American Protestantism* (Cambridge: Harvard University Press, 1976), 165 n. 36.

11. Ibid., 165.

12. Walter Rauschenbusch, *Christianity and the Social Crisis* (Louisville: Westminster John Knox, 1991), 143.

13. James Livingston, *Modern Christian Thought from the Enlightenment to Vatican II* (New York: Macmillan, 1971), 254–60.

14. David Maas, "The Life and Times of D. L. Moody," *Christian History* 25, no. 1 (1990): 7.

15. Andrew Walls, *The Missionary Movement in Christian History: Studies in the Transmission of Faith* (Maryknoll: Orbis, 1996), 230.

16. George M. Marsden, *Fundamentalism and American Culture: The Shaping of Twentieth-Century Evangelicalism, 1870–1925* (New York: Oxford University Press, 1980), 33.

17. Ibid. For the original source of this quote, see Moody's sermon, "The Second Coming of Christ," in *The Best of D. L. Moody*, ed. Wilbur Smith (Chicago: Moody, 1971), 193–95.

18. Paul Boyer, *When Time Shall Be No More: Prophecy Belief in Modern American Culture* (Cambridge: Belknap, 1992), 92.

19. Marsden, *Fundamentalism and American Culture*, 117.

20. See B. J. Longfield, "Briggs, Charles Augustus," in *Dictionary of Christianity in America*, ed. Daniel Reid (Downers Grove: InterVarsity, 1990), 188.

21. Jay P. Dolan, *In Search of American Catholicism: A History of Religion and Culture in Tension* (New York: Oxford University Press, 2002), 117.

22. Ibid., 108, 115.

23. See Paul Conkin, *American Originals: Homemade Varieties of Christianity* (Chapel Hill: University of North Carolina Press, 1997), the source for this phrase.

24. Ibid., 134–45.

25. Ibid., 136.

26. "Facts and Figures" (Silver Spring: Seventh-day Adventist Church official website); available from www.adventist.org/world_church/facts_and_figures/index.html.en

27. Stephen R. Prothero, "Christian Science," in *Encyclopedia of American Religious History*, Steven Prothero, Edward Queen, and Gardiner Shattuck, eds. (New York: Facts on File, 1996), 1:120. See also articles on Mary Baker Eddy, New Thought, and Phineas Quimby.

28. Harvey Cox, *Fire from Heaven: The Rise of Pentecostal Spirituality and the Reshaping of Religion in the Twenty-first Century* (Cambridge: DaCapo, 2001), 58.

29. Vinson Synan, "The Ten Most Influential Christians of the Twentieth Century: William Seymour," in *Christian History* 65, no. 1: 17–19. See also Synan, *The Holiness-Pentecostal Tradition: Charismatic Movements in the Twentieth Century* (Grand Rapids: Eerdmans, 1997).

30. Conkin, *American Originals*, 300.

31. Synan, "Ten Most Influential Christians," 19.

32. Conkin, *American Originals*, 310.

Chapter Seven: From the "Great War" to the Cold War

1. Cited by R. D. Linder, "World War I," in *Dictionary of Christianity in America*, ed. Daniel Reid (Downers Grove: InterVarsity, 1990), 1278 (hereafter *DCA*).

2. David Kennedy, "World War I," in *The Reader's Companion to American History*, ed. Eric Foner and John Garraty (Boston: Houghton Mifflin, 1991), 1171 (hereafter *RCAH*).

3. Fred W. Meuser, "Facing the Twentieth Century, 1900–1930," in *Lutherans in North America*, ed. E. Clifford Nelson et al., rev. ed. (Philadelphia: Fortress Press, 1980), 396–98.

4. Cited in Ernest Lee Tuveson, *Redeemer Nation: The Idea of America's Millennial Role* (Chicago: University of Chicago Press, 1968), 212.

5. Although the League of Nations was promoted by President Wilson, the U.S. Congress voted not to join the institution.

6. Gary Bullert, "Reinhold Niebuhr and the *Christian Century*: World War II and the Eclipse of the Social Gospel," *Journal of Church and State* 44 (Spring 2002): 272–74; see also Sidney Ahlstrom, *A Religious History of the American People* (New Haven: Yale University Press, 1972), 884, 930.

7. George M. Marsden, *Fundamentalism and American Culture: The Shaping of Twentieth-Century Evangelicalism, 1870–1925* (New York: Oxford University Press, 1980), 160.

8. Ibid., 184.

9. Joel Carpenter, *Revive Us Again: The Reawakening of American Fundamentalism* (New York: Oxford University Press, 1997), 8.

10. Sidney Ahlstrom, *A Religious History of the American People* (New Haven: Yale University Press, 1972), 899.

11. Ibid., 901.

12. Beverly Zink-Sawyer, *From Preachers to Suffragists: Women's Rights and Religious Conviction in the Lives of Three Nineteenth-Century American Clergywomen* (Louisville: Westminster John Knox, 2003), 6.

13. K. E. Guenther, "The Woman's Bible," in *DCA*, 1267.

14. Darlene Clark Hine, "Ida B. Wells-Barnett," in *RCAH*, ed. Eric Foner and John Garraty (Boston: Houghton Mifflin, 1991), 1144.

15. Zink-Sawyer, *Preachers to Suffragists*, 22.

16. Evelyn Kirkley, "This Work Is God's Cause," cited in Zink-Sawyer, *Preachers to Suffragists*, 13.

17. Early arguments for women's suffrage appealed to Enlightenment and democratic ideals: women, by virtue of common humanity, have natural, inalienable right to vote. But in the late nineteenth century, the sentimental view (that women were naturally more virtuous and more religious than men) gave moderates and conservatives a rationale for sup-

porting woman's suffrage. For a discussion of the changing rhetoric of women's suffrage, see Zink-Sawyer, 177–180.

18. Joseph Carter, "Temple's Founder, Russell W. Conwell," Temple University website, available from www.temple.edu/about/temples_founder.html

19. J. Bradford De Long, "Depressions," in *RCAH*, 280.

20. Mark Toulouse, "Socializing Capitalism: The *Century* during the Great Depression," *Christian Century*, April 12, 2001, 418.

21. Jay Dolan, *The American Catholic Experience* (New York: Doubleday, 1985), 408.

22. Ibid., 410–11.

23. Catholic Worker Movement home page; available from www.catholicworker.org/index.cfm

24. Edith Blumhofer, *Aimee Semple McPherson: Everybody's Sister* (Grand Rapids: Eerdmans, 1993), 329.

25. Carpenter, *Revive Us Again*, 139.

26. Vinson Synan, *The Holiness-Pentecostal Tradition: Charismatic Movements in the Twentieth Century* (Grand Rapids: Eerdmans, 1997), 169.

27. Nathan Aaseng, *African American Religious Leaders* (New York: Facts on File, 2003), 68–70.

28. Albert Raboteau, *Canaan Land: A Religious History of African Americans* (New York: Oxford University Press, 2001), 85.

29. James Livingston. *Modern Christian Thought from the Enlightenment to Vatican II* (New York: Macmillan, 1971), 447–88.

30. Gary Bullert, "Reinhold Niebuhr and the *Christian Century*: World War II and the Eclipse of the Social Gospel," *Journal of Church and State* 44 (Spring 2002): 283.

31. Ahlstrom, *History*, 949–50.

32. Tuveson, *Redeemer Nation*, 214.

33. Paul Boyer, *When Time Shall Be No More: Prophecy Belief in Modern American Culture* (Cambridge: Belknap, 1992), 187; see also 183–86.

34. Craig Koester, *Revelation and the End of All Things* (Grand Rapids: Eerdmans, 2001), 19.

Chapter Eight: Toward a New Millennium

1. David Chappell, *A Stone of Hope: Prophetic Religion and the Death of Jim Crow* (Chapel Hill: University of North Carolina Press, 2004), 5.

2. Martin Luther King Jr., "Speeches of Martin Luther King Jr." (MPI Video, 1988), videocassette.

3. Chappell, *Stone of Hope*, 53. See also 49–54.

4. Ibid., 193. This paragraph is indebted to insights from Chappell's book.

5. Jay Dolan, *In Search of American Catholicism: A History of Religion and Culture in Tension* (New York: Oxford University Press, 2002), 431.

6. Sidney Ahlstrom, *A Religious History of the American People* (New Haven: Yale University Press, 1972), 954 n. 5.

7. Ibid., 1019.

8. K. R. Fields, "Fulton Sheen," in *Dictionary of Christianity in America*, ed. Daniel Reid (Downers Grove: InterVarsity, 1990), 1081.

9. Kathleen Riley, "Fulton Sheen," in *Concise Encyclopedia of Preaching*, ed. William Willimon and Richard Lischer (Louisville: Westminster John Knox, 1995), 439–40.

10. Jay Dolan, *The American Catholic Experience* (New York: Doubleday, 1985), 393.

11. See George M. Marsden, *Reforming Fundamentalism: Fuller Seminary and the New Evangelicalism* (Grand Rapids: Eerdmans, 1987).

12. Christian Smith, *American Evangelicalism: Embattled and Thriving* (Chicago: University of Chicago Press, 1998), 13 n. 5. Smith's first chapter, "Resurrecting an Engaged Orthodoxy," provides a brief history of the rise of modern evangelicalism.

13. Claire Wolfteich, *American Catholics through the Twentieth Century: Spirituality, Lay Experience and Public Life* (New York: Crossroad, 2001), 56.

14. Ibid., 56.

15. Roger Finke and Rodney Stark, *Acts of Faith: Explaining the Human Side of Religion* (Berkeley: University of California Press, 2000), 258.

16. Ibid., 266.

17. Dolan, *American Catholic Experience*, 426.

18. Dolan, *In Search of American Catholicism*, 435.

19. David Anderson, "Viet Nam War," in *The Reader's Companion to American History*, ed. Eric Foner and John Garraty (Boston: Houghton Mifflin, 1991), 1121.

20. Marshall Frady, *Billy Graham: A Parable of American Righteousness* (Boston: Little, Brown, 1979), 416–17.

21. Roy Harrisville Jr., "Luther Seminary History," in *Thanksgiving and Hope* (Northfield: Northfield Printing, 1998), 52.

22. Martin Luther King Jr., "Speeches of Martin Luther King Jr." (MPI Video, 1988), videocassette.

23. Patrick Allitt, *Religion in America Since 1945: A History* (New York: Columbia University Press, 2003), 100–107.

24. Edwin Gaustad and Leigh Schmidt, *The Religious History of America* (San Francisco: HarperSanFrancisco, 2002), 399.

25. Robert McAffee Brown, "On 'Forgetting Viet Nam,'" *Christianity and Crisis* 35 (June 1975): 154.

26. Donald Miller, *Reinventing American Protestantism: Christianity in the New Millennium* (Berkeley: University of California Press, 1998), 82. My description of the New Paradigm churches is based on Miller's book.

27. Barbara Zikmund, Adair Lummis, and Patricia Mei Yin Chang, *Clergy Women: An Uphill Calling* (Louisville: Westminster John Knox, 1998), 6.

28. These claims refer to the research of Zikmund, Lummis, and Chang, in *Clergy Women: An Uphill Calling.*

29. Rosemary Radford Ruether, "Feminist Theology," in the *Westminster Dictionary of Christian Theology*, ed. Alan Richardson and John Bowden (Philadelphia: Westminster, 1983), 210–12.

30. George Marsden, *Understanding Fundamentalism and Evangelicalism* (Grand Rapids: Eerdmans, 1991), 77.

31. "Christian Coalition of America," available from www.cc.org/mission.cfm.

32. William Martin, "How Ronald Reagan Wowed Evangelicals," *Christianity Today*, August 2004, 49.

33. Robert Wuthnow, *Christianity in the Twenty-first Century* (New York: Oxford University Press, 1993), 134.

34. Joel Carpenter, "Compassionate Evangelicalism," *Christianity Today*, December 2003: 40–42.

35. Official website for Habitat for Humanity International, available at www.habitat.org/how/tour/1.html. For the evangelical roots of Habitat, see Michael Maudlin, "God's Contractor: How Habitat for Humanity's Millard Fuller Persuaded Corporate America to Do Kingdom Work," *Christianity Today*, 14 June 1999, 45–47.

36. Recent titles by prophetic evangelicals include Ron Sider, *The Scandal of the Evangelical Conscience: Why Are Christians Living Just Like the Rest of the World?* (Grand Rapids: Baker, 2005); Jim Wallis, *God's Politics: Why the Right Gets It Wrong and the Left Doesn't Get It* (San Francisco: HarperSan-

Francisco, 2005); Tony Campolo and Michael Battle, *The Church Enslaved: A Spirituality of Racial Reconciliation* (Minneapolis: Fortress Press, 2005).

37. Carpenter, "Compassionate Evangelicalism," 41. The full quote reads: "In a Princeton University survey conducted three years ago, 45 percent of evangelicals said they were political moderates, and 19 percent self-identified as liberals."

38. Mainline denominations include American Baptist Churches in the USA, the Christian Church (Disciples of Christ), the Episcopal Church USA, the Evangelical Lutheran Church in America, the Presbyterian Church (USA), the Reformed Church in America, the United Church of Christ, and the United Methodist Church.

39. Nancy Ammerman, "Connecting Mainline Protestant Churches with Public Life," in *The Quiet Hand of God: Faith-Based Activism and the Public Role of Mainline Protestantism*, ed. Robert Wuthnow and John Evans (Berkeley: University of California Press, 2002), 140.

40. "Lutheran Social Services: About Us," available at www.lsss.org/aboutus.htm.

41. Ammerman, "Connecting," 154.

42. *Presbyterian Layman*, May–June 2001, 3. For a table of statistics on mainline membership decline and evangelical and Catholic growth from 1940–85, see Finke and Stark, *Churching of America*, 248.

43. For research supporting these claims, see Smith, *Evangelicalism*, 23, 40, 128.

44. Benton Johnson, Dean Hoge, and Donald Luidens, "Mainline Churches: The Real Reason for Decline," *First Things*, 1993, 15.

45. Finke and Stark, *Churching of America*, 17.

46. Ibid., 275.

47. Finke and Stark, *Acts of Faith*, 266, 268.

48. Joshua Bonilla, "Executive Summary: A Demographic Profile of Hispanics in the U.S." (Population Resource Center, Washington, D.C.), available at www.prcdc.org/summaries/hispanics/hispanics.html.

49. David Van Biema, "Jose Gomez, the Humble High Priest," *Time*, August 22, 2005, 50.

50. Unsigned editorial, *Christian Century*, May 23–30, 2005, 12.

51. Philip Jenkins, *The Next Christendom: The Coming of Global Christianity* (New York: Oxford University Press, 2002).

GLOSSARY

Abolitionists: nineteenth-century activists who worked to abolish slavery. The American Anti-slavery Society, founded in 1833, was a major abolitionist group.

Adventism: from the word *advent*, meaning "coming." Adventists make the literal return of Christ central to their belief system.

African American churches: black congregations, both slave and free, existed even before the American Revolution. The first black denomination was the African Methodist Episcopal Church, organized in 1816.

Apocalyptic: pertaining to the end of the world; relating current events to the biblical book of Revelation and other scriptures. Select events in history (such as the founding of the modern State of Israel) are interpreted by some Christians as having apocalyptic significance.

Baptism: the rite of entry into the Christian faith. The meanings, modes, and methods of baptism have been much debated.

Baptists: a variegated tradition of Protestants emphasizing "believer's baptism" and baptism by total immersion in water. There are a variety of Baptist denominations and independent congregations, exhibiting a range of religious and social concerns.

Benevolence: active good will. A public virtue through which the good of society is placed ahead of private gain. A popular ideal from the late eighteenth to the mid-nineteenth century, benevolence was thought to be essential for the success of the new American republic.

Benevolent societies: organizations dedicated to the moral and religious reform of society in the late eighteenth to mid-nineteenth centuries. Most benevolent societies were explicitly Christian, and many were trans-denominational.

Black nationalism: an ideology that makes Africanness the core identity for black people. Some black nationalist movements have related to Christianity and some have not.
Calvinism: a theology or system of doctrines in the tradition of John Calvin (1509–1564), the reformer of Geneva. New England Puritans and Dutch Reformed were staunchly Calvinist.
Charismatic movement: the penetration of Pentecostal practices into Catholicism and Protestant denominations in the mid- to late twentieth century.
Christendom: the medieval ideal of one civilization united by one faith.
Christian realism: a theological and ethical response to the crisis posed by Nazi Germany, developed by Reinhold Niebuhr (1892–1971).
Church of England (Anglican) and its worldwide communion: The Church of England is defined by its threefold ministry of bishops, priests, and deacons, believed to exist in unbroken succession from the apostles of New Testament times. After the American Revolution, the term "Episcopal" was used in the United States rather than "Anglican."
Circuit riders: traveling preachers in frontier America who covered routes assigned by their superiors. Methodists were especially known for their system of itinerant ministry (in contrast to an incumbent or settled ministry).
Civil rights movement: beginning in the 1950s, an extended campaign to end racial segregation in the U.S. and to secure equal rights for all Americans. The civil rights movement drew deeply from African American Christianity.
Cold War: political and military standoff between the Soviet Union and the West from about 1946 to 1991. Religious dimensions included persecution of Christians, Muslims, and others under Communism and, among some sectors of Christianity in the U.S., doomsaying about the end of the world.
Common Sense Realism: also called the Scottish philosophy. A philosophy that harmonized religion and science, faith and reason by appealing to common sense and "self-evident truths"; it shaped American higher education through much of the nineteenth century.
Confessionalism: movements to secure the theological integrity of Christian traditions by appealing to confessional documents such as

the Augsburg Confession (Lutheran) or the Westminster Confession (Presbyterian).

Conversion: also called "new birth." Watershed experience in which a person becomes Christian. Some Christians hold that a conversion experience is necessary for salvation.

Crisis theology: also called neo-orthodoxy. Swiss theologian Karl Barth (1886–1968) developed this response to the horrors of World War I and the failure of liberal optimism. Barth saw God as "wholly other" and human beings as completely sinful.

Culture wars: a collective term for conflicts over a series of moral issues (such as abortion and changing views on sexuality) in the late twentieth century.

Denominations: large networks of congregations and supporting agencies (colleges, publishing houses, etc). Each denomination has a distinctive heritage, yet most acknowledge each other's validity.

Disestablishment: a policy for relating religion to the civil order in the newly independent United States. The First Amendment to the U.S. Constitution provided for religion to function on a voluntary basis, without federal support or interference. There would be no officially "established" religion.

Dispensationalism: a system of biblical interpretation that claims to match biblical prophecy with events in modern history, making it possible to know the timetable for Christ's return. John Nelson Darby (1800–1883) invented the system eventually popularized in American Christianity.

Dissenters: Religious groups that did not belong to the established or official church. In colonial times, Congregationalists, Baptists, Presbyterians, Quakers, and others were "dissenters" from the Church of England.

Ecumenism, ecumenical movement: the attempt to achieve or express unity, or practice cooperation, among the various Christian traditions.

Encyclical: a general letter sent by the pope to all Roman Catholic bishops (and through them to the whole church) on matters of faith and life.

Enlightenment: a cluster of movements to promote reason and progress, ushering in the modern era in eighteenth-century Europe and America.

Episcopal: having to do with the office of bishop; or, a church defined by its threefold office of bishop, priest, and deacon.

Established church: a church approved of and supported by the government; the official church of a particular nation, state, territory or colony. Established churches had various policies with regard to tolerating or not tolerating dissent.
Evangelicalism: a trans-denominational movement in which the Christian life begins with spiritual transformation (conversion).
Feminist theology: begins with the conviction that all of Christian theology is shaped by male bias; offers a range of critiques and alternatives.
Freedom of conscience: The individual is accountable to God alone in matters of faith, and not to any external authority, civil or religious. Or, freedom of conscience is a basic human right, with or without reference to God.
Fundamentalism: a protest against modernity—especially evolution, liberal theology, and text-critical methods of biblical study.
Ghost Dance: a religious movement among several Native American tribes of the western plains in the late nineteenth century. It sought a return to life as it was before the arrival of whites.
Great Awakening: a series of revivals in colonial America in which conversion was the defining experience. Itinerant preaching, popular religious excitement, and a relative disregard for religious convention were hallmarks of this era.
Heresy: a religious opinion or teaching contrary to orthodox Christianity.
Holiness movements: nineteenth-century Protestant quest for complete freedom from sin. Holiness groups include the Church of the Nazarene, the Salvation Army, and the Wesleyan Methodist Church.
Idolatry: making an idol (object of worship) out of something that should not be worshiped.
Inerrancy: a particular view of biblical authority that insists on the literal truth of the Bible in all things.
Itinerant minister: one who travels widely to preach the gospel rather than serving a settled congregation or parish in one specific place.
Justification: the teaching that people are sinful but through faith in Christ they may be freely justified (made right with God); center of Lutheran theology.
Liberal theology: a movement to adapt Christianity to modernity using the new social sciences. Nineteenth-century German universities were a seedbed for liberal theology.

Lutheranism: the first of several movements in the Protestant Reformation. In Europe this movement was called *evangelisch* (evangelical), but in America it became known as "Lutheran" in honor of its theological mentor, Martin Luther (1483–1546).

Mainline denominations: a somewhat contested term referring to Protestant groups that enjoy cultural respectability. There is an implied contrast between the "mainline" and other groups that find themselves in greater tension with society.

Manifest destiny: the belief that God willed the United States to possess the land from the Atlantic to the Pacific.

Methodism: a renewal movement within the Church of England founded by John Wesley (1703–1791). Methodists became a separate denomination and were for a time the largest Protestant group in the U.S.

Millennium: the thousand-year reign of Christ with the saints (see Revelation 20:1–6). Core concerns relating to the millennium are the meaning of history and the ways in which Christians participate in God's purposes.

Mission societies: voluntary groups that send and support missionaries. Mission societies could be congregational, denominational, or ecumenical. Many were run by women.

Modernist: a term used almost interchangeably with "liberal" in the late nineteenth and early twentieth centuries. Modernists questioned absolute truth claims and sought to adapt Christianity to changing times.

Moral agency: the capacity of human beings to make rational, moral choices, including the choice to believe in God. Moral agency displaced older theologies in which human beings were thought to be morally incapable of doing good apart from God's help.

Moravians: Protestants with pre-Reformation roots, originating in central Europe. Active in global mission, Moravians were known for fervent, mystical piety.

Mormonism: a religious movement based on the visions of Joseph Smith (1805–1844) as recorded in the *Book of Mormon* and other writings. The largest Mormon group is the Church of Jesus Christ of the Latter-day Saints.

Nativism: a nineteenth-century American movement to discourage immigration and to keep jobs, schools, and political power away from newcomers. Nativism was anti-Catholic.

Ordination: a rite or ceremony in which a person officially becomes clergy. Practices vary from one church tradition to another.

Pacifist: one who categorically opposes all warfare and violence. Some pacifists base their views on religion. Note that opposition to a *particular* war does not make a person a thoroughgoing pacifist.

Parish: the local Roman Catholic community (though some Protestants also use the term "parish"). More than a church building, the parish is a network of the faithful who have created schools, businesses, and charities, with the church as the focal point.

Paternalism: a sense of obligation between a superior (master) and an inferior (slave). Paternalism and racism were twin pillars of American slavery.

Pentecostalism: a form of Christianity that emphasizes direct personal experience of the Holy Spirit. Conversion must be followed by the "baptism of the Holy Spirit," in which the believer receives supernatural gifts such as "speaking in tongues," an ecstatic language of praise.

Pietism: a movement within Lutheranism, beginning in the late 1600s, to renew heartfelt faith, active Christian love, and evangelism. Many Lutherans who came to the United States were Pietists.

Pluralism: a term meaning that religious diversity is accepted as the norm.

Polity: a mode of church organization based on differing definitions of the church. For example, the church is the congregation (Congregational polity); the church is a fellowship of congregations in a region (Presbyterian polity); the church is the bishop, presiding over congregations in a given region (Episcopal polity). Several hybrids or combinations of these polities exist. There are also "state" or national churches and international churches, such as the Anglican Communion, which has an Episcopal polity. In the Roman Catholic Church, the pope is the head of all the bishops in a global church.

Polygamy: the practice of having more than one wife; also called "plural marriage." Joseph Smith introduced polygamy into the Mormon community. The Church of Jesus Christ of the Latter-day Saints banned polygamy in 1890, but some splinter groups still practice it.

Positive thinking: a gospel of self-improvement popularized by Norman Vincent Peale (1898–1993).

Predestination: God decides who is saved and who is not, apart from any human choice or merit.

Presbyterianism: a Reformed tradition distinguished by its polity in which the church is a presbytery (synod or region) of member congregations.

Prohibition: a movement to ban the manufacture, sale, and consumption of alcohol.

Providence: God's will is accomplished in nature and history; all events directly or indirectly fulfill God's purposes.

Puritanism: a movement to "purify" the Church of England by purging away vestiges of Roman Catholicism. This movement began in England and was transplanted to the New England colonies, where it had a formative influence on American religion and culture.

Quakers: also called the Society of Friends. A radical Protestant sect founded by George Fox (1624–1691). Quakers rejected hierarchy, sacraments, and liturgy and refused military service. They were active in founding the colony of Pennsylvania.

Rapture: the belief that Christians will be miraculously taken up to heaven before a great outbreak of evil and suffering at the end of the world. See also dispensationalism.

Rationalist clergy: ministers influenced by the Enlightenment who sought to adjust Christian teaching to Enlightenment agendas.

Reconstruction: the period from 1865 to 1876 in which the South was to be brought back into the Union without slavery; the policies instituted by the federal government to reform southern labor and protect the citizenship and rights of former slaves.

Reformed tradition: a cluster of Protestant movements whose chief theological mentor was John Calvin (1509–1564), the reformer of Geneva.

Religious Right: a coalition of individuals and groups (such as the Moral Majority, founded in 1979) that promoted a conservative social agenda and became active in politics.

Renewal movements: Beginning in the late 1960s, these groups sought to reverse the decline in mainline denominations by recommitting to evangelism, Bible study, and traditional theology.

Restorationism: a nineteenth-century movement to restore the church to its New Testament purity. The Disciples of Christ and the Christian Church are among the groups that began in the Restorationist movement.

Revival: a religious event that aims to convert people to Christianity through intense prayer and preaching.

Sanctification: living a sinless life by the power of God's love; also called "holiness" or "perfection."

Segregation: the division of society along racial lines, in the North as well as the South. Segregation, also called "Jim Crow," denied black people equal access to education, housing, employment, transportation, and voting.

Slave trade: the capture and sale of Africans, conducted internationally. After 1808 it was illegal to bring new slave laborers from Africa into the United States. Demands for slave labor were then met by "natural increase" and by the internal slave trade, which typically flowed from older, eastern states such as Virginia to newer slave states in the South and West.

Slavery: a condition of servitude in which persons were property. The owner had complete control over the time, labor, and body of the slave and of any children born to the slave. American slavery lasted from 1619 to 1865.

Social Gospel: a late nineteenth- and early twentieth-century movement to reform society along the lines of Christian principles.

Southwestern Catholicism: a distinctive regional form of Catholicism, blending Spanish and Mexican Catholicism with Native American culture.

Sunday schools: an educational experiment begun in late eighteenth-century England to help urban youth escape from poverty. In America, Sunday schools have had various goals, including social reform, literacy, evangelism, and Christian nurture.

Territorialism: a strategy for dealing with the religious differences after the Reformation. It applied the concept of "Christendom" to smaller units such as nations and territories.

Theocracy: literally, the rule of God. A society governed by religious beliefs, in which the civil order supports the church.

Theology: literally, the study of God. A formal religious teaching; a doctrine or system of doctrines; the exposition of religious beliefs.

Toleration: a limited form of religious pluralism in which an "established" or official church allowed one or more dissenting churches to exist, provided they met certain conditions. Toleration could be given or taken away; it was a privilege, not a right.

Transubstantiation: the Roman Catholic teaching that in the sacrament of Holy Communion, the bread and wine become the body of Christ, even while the physical appearance of these elements remains unchanged.

Underground Railroad: a network of people, escape routes, and hiding places by means of which runaway slaves made their way to the northern states and Canada.

Unitarianism: an offshoot of New England Congregationalism, revised according to Enlightenment rationalism. The Unitarians rejected the doctrines of the Trinity, original sin, and predestination.

Vatican II: the Second Vatican Council, convened in Rome in 1962 for the purpose of updating the church.

Vatican: the headquarters of the Roman Catholic Church in Rome.

Women's suffrage: the movement to secure for women the right to vote. Many Christian activists were involved in this effort, achieved in 1920.

BIBLIOGRAPHY

Aaseng, Nathan. *African American Religious Leaders.* New York: Facts on File, 2003.

Ahlstrom, Sidney. *A Religious History of the American People*. New Haven: Yale University Press, 1972.

Allitt, Patrick. *Religion in America Since 1945: A History.* New York: Columbia University Press, 2003.

Ammerman, Nancy. "Connecting Mainline Protestant Churches with Public Life." Pages 129–58 in *The Quiet Hand of God: Faith-Based Activism and the Public Role of Mainline Protestantism*. Edited by Robert Wuthnow and John Evans. Berkeley: University of California Press, 2002.

Berlin, Ira. *Generations of Captivity*. Cambridge, Mass.: Belknap, 2003.

Bishop, Randy. "Out Yonder, on the Edge of Things." *Christian History*, May 2000, 30–34.

Blumhofer, Edith. *Aimee Semple McPherson: Everybody's Sister*. Grand Rapids: Eerdmans, 1993.

Bordin, Ruth. *Frances Willard: A Biography.* Chapel Hill: University of North Carolina Press, 1986.

Boyer, Paul. *When Time Shall Be No More: Prophecy Belief in Modern American Culture*. Cambridge, Mass.: Belknap, 1992.

Boylan, Anne. *Sunday School: The Formation of an American Institution.* New Haven: Yale University Press, 1988.

Brekus, Catherine. *Strangers and Pilgrims: Female Preaching in America 1740–1845.* Chapel Hill: University of North Carolina Press, 1998.

Brown, Robert McAffee. "On 'Forgetting Viet Nam.'" *Christianity and Crisis* 35 (1975): 154.

Bullert, Gary. "Reinhold Niebuhr and the *Christian Century*: World War II and the Eclipse of the Social Gospel." *Journal of Church and State* 44 (Spring 2002): 271–90.

Carpenter, Joel. *Revive Us Again: The Reawakening of American Fundamentalism.* New York: Oxford University Press, 1997.

________. "Compassionate Evangelicalism." *Christianity Today*, December 2003, 40–42.

Cartwright, Peter. *Autobiography of Peter Cartwright.* Nashville: Abingdon, 1956.

Channing, William Ellery. "A Discourse at the Ordination of the Rev. Frederick A. Farley." In *American Sermons: The Pilgrims to Martin Luther King, Jr.* Edited by Michael Warner. New York: Library of America, 1999.

Chappell, David. *A Stone of Hope: Prophetic Religion and the Death of Jim Crow.* Chapel Hill: University of North Carolina Press, 2004.

Chestnut, Mary. *A Diary from Dixie.* Edited by Isabella Martin and Myrta Avary. New York: Gramercy, 1997.

Clebsch, William. *Christian Interpretations of the Civil War.* Philadelphia: Fortress Press, 1969.

Conkin, Paul. *American Originals: Homemade Varieties of Christianity.* Chapel Hill: University of North Carolina Press, 1997.

Corrigan, John, and Winthrop Hudson. *Religion in America.* 7th ed. Upper Saddle River: Pearson Prentice Hall, 2004.

Cox, Harvey. *Fire from Heaven: The Rise of Pentecostal Spirituality and the Reshaping of Religion in the Twenty-first Century.* Cambridge, Mass.: DaCapo, 2001.

Dolan, Jay. *The American Catholic Experience.* New York: Doubleday, 1985.

________. *Catholic Revivalism, the American Experience: 1830–1900.* Notre Dame, Ind.: University of Notre Dame Press, 1978.

________. *In Search of American Catholicism: A History of Religion and Culture in Tension.* New York: Oxford University Press, 2002.

Douglass, Frederick. "What to the Slave Is the Fourth of July?" In *The American Intellectual Tradition*. Vol. 1. Edited by David Hollinger and Charles Capper. New York: Oxford University Press, 1999.

DuBois, W. E. B. *The Souls of Black Folk.* London: Archibald Constable & Co., 1905.

Emerson, Ralph Waldo. "An Address …" In *Ralph Waldo Emerson: Essays and Lectures.* New York: Library of America, 1983.

Finke, Roger, and Rodney Stark. *Acts of Faith: Explaining the Human Side of Religion*. Berkeley: University of California Press, 2000.

________. *The Churching of America, 1776–1990: Winners and Losers in Our Religious Economy.* New Brunswick: Rutgers University Press, 1992.

Finney, Charles. *Lectures on Revivals of Religion.* Cambridge, Mass.: Belknap, 1960.

Fisher, Robert. "Lutherans in American Life: A Bicentennial Reflection." *The Lutheran*, January 1, 1975, 7.

Foner, Eric. *A Short History of Reconstruction.* New York: Harper & Row, 1990.

Foner, Eric, and John Garraty, eds. *The Reader's Companion to American History*. Boston: Houghton Mifflin, 1991.

Frady, Marshall. *Billy Graham: A Parable of American Righteousness.* Boston: Little, Brown & Co., 1979.

Franklin, Benjamin. "Letter to Ezra Stiles." In *Franklin: Writings.* New York: Library of America, 1987.

Fraser, James. *Between Church and State: Religion and Public Education in America.* New York: St. Martin's, 1999.

Gaustad, Edwin. *The Great Awakening in New England*. Gloucester, Mass.: Peter Smith, 1965.

________, ed. *A Documentary History of Religion in America to the Civil War*. Grand Rapids: Eerdmans, 1993.

Gaustad, Edwin, and Philip Barlow. *New Historical Atlas of Religion in America.* New York: Oxford University Press, 2001.

Gaustad, Edwin, and Leigh Schmidt. *The Religious History of America.* San Francisco: HarperSanFrancisco, 2002.

Gelernter, David. "Americanism—and Its Enemies." *Commentary*, January 2005, 41–48.

Genovese, Eugene. *A Consuming Fire: The Fall of the Confederacy in the Mind of the White Christian South.* Athens, Ga.: University of Georgia Press, 1998.

________. *Roll, Jordan, Roll: The World the Slaves Made.* New York: Vintage, 1976.

Gjerde, Jon. *The Minds of the West: Ethnocultural Evolution in the Rural Middle West, 1830–1917.* Chapel Hill: University of North Carolina Press, 1997.

Goen, C. C. *Broken Churches, Broken Nation: Denominational Schisms and the Coming of the Civil War.* Macon, Ga.: Mercer University Press, 1985.

Guarneri, Carl, and David Alvarez, eds. *Religion and Society in the American West.* Lanham, Md.: University Press of America, 1987.

Guelzo, Alan. *Abraham Lincoln: Redeemer President.* Grand Rapids: Eerdmans, 1999.

Hambrick-Stowe, Charles. *Charles Grandison Finney and the Spirit of American Evangelicalism*. Grand Rapids: Eerdmans, 1996.

Hardman, Keith. *Charles Grandison Finney.* Grand Rapids: Baker, 1990.

Harrisville, Roy Jr. "Luther Seminary History." In *Thanksgiving and Hope*. Northfield, Minn.: Northfield Printing, 1998.

Hatch, Nathan. *The Democratization of American Christianity*. New Haven: Yale University Press, 1989.

________. *The Sacred Cause of Liberty: Republican Thought and the Millennium in Revolutionary New England*. New Haven: Yale University Press, 1977.

Hazlett, Ian. "Demanding Faith." *Christian History*, May 1995, 24–25.

Holifield, Brooks. *Theology in America: Christian Thought from the Age of the Puritans to the Civil War*. New Haven: Yale University Press, 2003.

Hutchison, William. *The Modernist Impulse in American Protestantism*. Cambridge: Harvard University Press, 1976.

________. *Religious Pluralism in America: The Contentious History of a Founding Ideal*. New Haven: Yale University Press, 2003.

Jenkins, Philip. *The Next Christendom: The Coming of Global Christianity*. New York: Oxford University Press, 2002.

Johnson, Benton, Dean Hoge, and Donald Luidens. "Mainline Churches: The Real Reason for Decline." *First Things*, March 1993, 13–18.

Johnson, Paul. *A History of the American People*. New York: HarperCollins, 1998.

King, Martin Luther, Jr. "Speeches of Martin Luther King, Jr." MPI Video, 1988. Videocassette.

Koester, Craig. *Revelation and the End of All Things*. Grand Rapids: Eerdmans, 2001.

Krakauer, Jon. *Under the Banner of Heaven*. New York: Doubleday, 2003.

Lindley, Susan Hill. *You Have Stept Out of Your Place: A History of Women and Religion in America*. Louisville: Westminster John Knox, 1996.

Lippy, Charles, and Peter Williams, eds. *Encyclopedia of the American Religious Experience*. 3 vols. New York: Charles Scribner's Sons, 1988.

Livingston, James. *Modern Christian Thought from the Enlightenment to Vatican II*. New York: Macmillan, 1971.

Locke, John. *A Letter Concerning Toleration*. Buffalo: Prometheus, 1990.

Maas, David. "The Life and Times of D. L. Moody." *Christian History*, February 1990, 5–11.

Marsden, George M. *Jonathan Edwards: A Life*. New Haven: Yale University Press, 2003.

________. *The Soul of the American University: From Protestant Establishment to Established Non-belief*. New York: Oxford University Press, 1994.

———. *Understanding Fundamentalism and Evangelicalism.* Grand Rapids: Eerdmans, 1991.

———. *Reforming Fundamentalism: Fuller Seminary and the New Evangelicalism.* Grand Rapids: Eerdmans, 1987.

———. *Fundamentalism and American Culture: The Shaping of Twentieth-Century Evangelicalism, 1870–1925.* New York: Oxford University Press, 1980.

Martin, William. "How Ronald Reagan Wowed Evangelicals." *Christianity Today*, August 2004, 48–49.

May, Henry. *The Enlightenment in America.* New York: Oxford University Press, 1976.

McMillen, Sally. *To Raise Up the South: Sunday Schools in Black and White Churches, 1865–1915.* Baton Rouge: Louisiana State University Press, 2001.

Miller, Donald. *Reinventing American Protestantism: Christianity in the New Millennium.* Berkeley: University of California Press, 1998.

Miller, William Lee. *The First Liberty: Religion and the American Republic.* New York: Paragon, 1988.

Milner, Clyde II, Carol O'Connor, and Martha Sandweiss, eds. *The Oxford History of the American West.* New York: Oxford University Press, 1994.

Moorehead, James. "Preaching the Holy War." *Christian History* 33 (February 1992): 38–41.

Muhlenberg, Henry Melchior. *Notebook of a Colonial Clergyman.* Edited and translated by Theodore Tappert and John Doberstein. Minneapolis: Fortress Press, 1998.

Neill, Stephen. *A History of Christian Missions.* New York: Penguin, 1990.

Nelson, E. Clifford, et al., eds. *Lutherans in North America.* Rev. ed. Philadelphia: Fortress Press, 1980.

Noll, Mark. *America's God: From Jonathan Edwards to Abraham Lincoln.* New York: Oxford University Press, 2002.

———. *A History of Christianity in the United States and Canada.* Grand Rapids: Eerdmans, 1992.

———, ed. *The Princeton Theology, 1812–1921.* Grand Rapids: Baker, 1983.

Ostling, Richard, and Joan Ostling. *Mormon America: The Power and the Promise.* San Francisco: HarperSanFrancisco, 1999.

O'Sullivan, John. "Annexation." *United States Magazine and Democratic Review* 17 (1845): 5–10.

Phillips, Charles. "December 29, 1890" [the Battle of Wounded Knee]. *American History*, December 2005, 14–20, 68.

Pinn, Anne, and Anthony Pinn. *Fortress Introduction to Black Church History*. Minneapolis: Fortress Press, 2002.

Prothero, Steven, Edward Queen, and Gardiner Shattuck Jr. *The Encyclopedia of American Religious History*. 2 vols. New York: Facts on File, 1996.

Quarles, Chester. *The Ku Klux Klan and Related American Racialist and Anti-Semitic Organizations.* Jefferson, N.C.: McFarland, 1999.

Raboteau, Albert. *Canaan Land: A Religious History of African Americans.* New York: Oxford University Press, 2001.

Rauschenbusch, Walter. *Christianity and the Social Crisis.* Louisville: Westminster John Knox, 1991.

Reid, Daniel, ed. *Dictionary of Christianity in America.* Downers Grove, Ill.: InterVarsity, 1990.

Richardson, Alan, and John Bowden, eds. *Westminster Dictionary of Christian Theology*. Philadelphia: Westminster, 1983.

Riley, Kathleen. "Fulton Sheen." In *Concise Encyclopedia of Preaching*. Edited by William Willimon and Richard Lischer. Louisville: Westminster John Knox, 1995.

Royster, Charles. "Battling Irreligion in the Ranks." *Christian History*, May 1996, 32–34.

Ruether, Rosemary Radford. "Feminist Theology." In *Westminster Dictionary of Christian Theology,* eds. Alan Richardson and John Bowden. Philadelphia: Westminster, 1983.

Seager, Richard. *The World's Parliament of Religions: The East/West Encounter, Chicago, 1893*. Bloomington: Indiana University Press, 1995.

Shattuck, Gardiner, Jr. "Revivals in the Camp." *Christian History*, February 1992, 28–31.

_________. *A Shield and Hiding Place: The Religious Life of the Civil War Armies.* Macon, Ga.: Mercer University Press, 1987.

Smith, Christian. *Evangelicalism: Embattled and Thriving.* Chicago: University of Chicago Press, 1998.

Stout, Harry. *The Divine Dramatist: George Whitefield and the Rise of Modern Evangelicalism*. Grand Rapids: Eerdmans, 1991.

_________. *Upon the Altar of the Nation: A Moral History of the Civil War.* New York: Penguin, 2006.

Synan, Vinson. *The Holiness-Pentecostal Tradition: Charismatic Movements in the Twentieth Century.* Grand Rapids: Eerdmans, 1997.

________. "The Ten Most Influential Christians of the Twentieth Century: William Seymour." *Christian History*, February 2000, 17–19.

Szasz, Ferenc. "Preparing a Way in the Wilderness." *Christian History*, May 2000, 10–16.

Tocqueville, Alexis de. *Democracy in America*. Translated by George Lawrence. New York: Harper & Row, 1988.

Toulouse, Mark. "Socializing Capitalism: The *Century* during the Great Depression." *Christian Century*, April 12, 2001, 415–18.

Tuveson, Ernest Lee. *Redeemer Nation: The Idea of America's Millennial Role*. Chicago: University of Chicago Press, 1968.

Van Biema, David. "Jose Gomez, the Humble High Priest." *Time*, August 22, 2005, 50.

Villard, Oswald. *John Brown: A Biography*. New York: Doubleday, 1910.

Wacker, Grant. *Heaven Below: Early Pentecostals and American Culture*. Cambridge, Mass.: Harvard University Press, 2001.

Walls, Andrew. *The Missionary Movement in Christian History: Studies in the Transmission of Faith*. Maryknoll: Orbis, 1996.

Wentz, Abdel Ross. *A Basic History of Lutheranism in North America*. Philadelphia: Muhlenberg, 1955.

Westerhoff, John. *McGuffey and His Readers*. Nashville: Abingdon, 1978.

Wolfteich, Claire. *American Catholics through the Twentieth Century: Spirituality, Lay Experience and Public Life*. New York: Crossroad, 2001.

Wood, Gordon. *The Radicalism of the American Revolution*. New York: Random House, 1991.

Woodworth, Steven. *While God Is Marching On: The Religious World of Civil War Soldiers*. Lawrence, Kans.: University Press of Kansas, 2001.

Wuthnow, Robert. *Christianity in the Twenty-first Century*. New York: Oxford University Press, 1993.

Zikmund, Barbara, Adair Lummis, and Patricia Mei Yin Chang. *Clergy Women: An Uphill Calling*. Louisville: Westminster John Knox, 1998.

Zink-Sawyer, Beverly. *From Preachers to Suffragists: Women's Rights and Religious Conviction in the Lives of Three Nineteenth-Century American Clergywomen*. Louisville: Westminster John Knox, 2003.

INDEX